EVIDENCE-BASED INVESTIGATIVE INTERVIEWING

For as long as we have been researching human memory, psychologists have been investigating how people remember and forget. This research is regularly drawn upon in our legal systems. Historically, we have relied upon eyewitness memory to help judge responsibility and adjudicate truth, but memory is malleable, prone to error, and susceptible to bias. Even confident eyewitnesses make mistakes, and even accurate witnesses sometimes find their testimony subjected to harsh scrutiny.

Emerging from this environment, the Cognitive Interview (CI) became a means of assisting cooperative witnesses with recalling more information without sacrificing accuracy. First used by police interviewing adult witnesses, it is now used with many populations in many contexts, including public health, accident reconstruction, and the interrogation of terror suspects. *Evidence-Based Investigative Interviewing* reviews the application of cognitive research to investigative interviewing, revealing how principles of cognition, memory, and social dynamics may increase the accuracy of eyewitness testimony. It provides evidence-based applications for investigators beyond the forensic domain in areas such as eyewitness identification, detecting deception, and interviewing children.

Drawing together the work of thirty-three authors across both the academic and practice communities, this comprehensive collection is essential reading for researchers in psychology, forensics, and disciplines such as epidemiology and gerontology.

Jason J. Dickinson, Ph.D., is a Professor of Psychology and the Director of the Robert D. McCormick Center for Child Advocacy and Policy at Montclair State University.

Nadja Schreiber Compo, Ph.D., is an Associate Professor of Psychology at Florida International University.

Rolando N. Carol, Ph.D., is an Associate Professor of Psychology at Auburn University at Montgomery.

Bennett L. Schwartz, Ph.D., is a Professor of Psychology at Florida International University.

Michelle R. McCauley, Ph.D., is a Professor of Psychology at Middlebury College.

EVIDENCE-BASED INVESTIGATIVE INTERVIEWING

Applying Cognitive Principles

Edited by Jason J. Dickinson,
Nadja Schreiber Compo, Rolando N. Carol,
Bennett L. Schwartz, Michelle R. McCauley

Routledge
Taylor & Francis Group

NEW YORK AND LONDON

First published 2019
by Routledge
52 Vanderbilt Avenue, New York, NY 10017

and by Routledge
2 Park Square, Milton Park, Abingdon, Oxon, OX14 4RN

Routledge is an imprint of the Taylor & Francis Group, an informa business

Library of Congress Cataloging-in-Publication Data
A catalog record for this title has been requested

ISBN: 978-1-138-06468-3 (hbk)
ISBN: 978-1-138-06469-0 (pbk)
ISBN: 978-1-315-16027-6 (ebk)

Typeset in Bembo
by Newgen Publishing UK

CONTENTS

ILLUSTRATIONS

Figures

Tables

CONTRIBUTORS

Pedro B. Albuquerque is Associate Professor in the Department of Basic Psychology of the School of Psychology of the University of Minho. He has published more than 50 papers on the topic of human memory both in basic (e.g., variables that influence the production of false memories based on the DRM paradigm) and applied fields. Recently he was involved in research about one new technique that can be used on the Cognitive Interview: Category Clustering Recall. In his curriculum, there are also several postdoctoral and doctoral supervisions, all funded by the Foundation for Science and Technology, the Portuguese agency that supports scientific research.

Mohammed M. Ali is completing his Ph.D. through the Centre for Investigative Interviewing at Griffith University, Australia. His research explores how best to modify existing interview protocols used by investigators with adult complainants of sexual assault. Mohammed has strong research interests in interviewing witnesses about sexual and violent offences, cross-cultural interviewing of witnesses and suspects, and intelligence interviewing.

Christopher Altman is a User Experience (UX) Researcher at BenefitFocus, a platform that allows organizations and individuals to shop for, enroll in, manage and exchange benefits. Before his tenure at BenefitFocus, Christopher received his BS in Psychology from the University of Pittsburgh, Greensburg (2012) and his MS degree in Social and Cognitive Psychology from Ball State University (2014). Christopher then received his Ph.D. in Legal Psychology from Florida International University (2018). During his graduate career, Christopher's research focused on investigative interviewing and eyewitness identifications. For his dissertation he examined how elevated levels of alcohol affect eyewitness memory.

His work has been presented at various research conferences across the country and published in peer-reviewed journals.

Susan E. Brandon is Research Psychologist at the Defense Intelligence Agency (DIA). Prior to this, she served for eight years as the Research Program Manager for the High-Value Detainee Interrogation Group (HIG). She was Chief for Research of the Behavioral Science Research Program at DIA (2006–2010), a Program Officer at the National Institutes of Health and Assistant Director at the Office of Science and Technology Policy (OSTP) (2003–2006), and Visiting Scientist at the American Psychological Association (2001–2003). Before those posts, she spent 15 years as a faculty member in the Behavioral Neuroscience Division of the Department of Psychology at Yale University.

Sonja P. Brubacher is a Researcher in Developmental Psychology and Trainer with the Centre for Investigative Interviewing, based at the Griffith Criminology Institute, Griffith University, Australia. She received her Ph.D. in Canada (2011) and then spent two years as a Canada Banting Postdoctoral Fellow at Central Michigan University, USA. Her research focuses on understanding the cognitive foundations underlying children's memory development, and the socio-motivational factors that influence whether and how memories are reported. She has over 35 peer-reviewed publications and 5 book chapters in the areas of children's memory for repeated events, interview protocol development, and interview preparatory phases (ground rules and narrative practice).

Ray Bull is Professor of Criminal Investigation (part-time) at the University of Derby. In 2014 he became President of the European Association of Psychology and Law (until 2017). In 2010 Ray was 'Elected by acclaim' an Honorary Fellow of the British Psychological Society (this honor is restricted to a maximum of 40 living psychologists). In 2009 Ray received from the International Investigative Interviewing Research Group the Senior Academic Award for his 'significant life-time contribution to the field of investigative interviewing'. In 2008 Ray received from the European Association of Psychology and Law the Award for Life-time Contribution to Psychology and Law. He has authored/co-authored over 200 research publications and has advised a large number of police forces in a great variety of countries, as well as testifying as an expert witness in many court cases.

Colin Clarke is a Researcher at Kingston University, London. He has over 30 years' experience of interviewing and investigation within the military and a large UK police force. During his police career he conducted research into the interviewing of children and the impact of police training to enhance interviewing skills, at local and national levels. He was a founding member of the Association of Chief Police Officers Investigative Interviewing Steering Group for England and Wales. Colin was awarded his Ph.D. for research into the effectiveness of the PEACE training program for investigative interviewing development, which led to the implementation of a tiered approach to investigative interviewing in England and Wales, and has subsequently been adopted in other countries. He has numerous publications in this field.

Coral Dando is a Professor of Psychology at the University of Westminster, London, and a registered Forensic Psychologist. Her primary research interests are centered on applying contemporary theories of long-term memory to understand cognition in goal directed interview settings with witnesses and victims, and suspected offenders. Coral's Ph.D. (awarded in 2008) concerned understanding how the Cognitive Interview was applied by police officers in the UK, and then modifying elements of the procedure to countenance its application by frontline officers, including developing the Sketch Reinstatement of Context Technique. Prior to completing her Ph.D. Coral was a British police officer, completing 12 years' service with the Metropolitan Police, London. Coral has published over 35 peer-reviewed scientific journal articles and book chapters on the Cognitive Interview, detecting deception, and investigative decision-making, and her research has attracted over £2 million of national and international funding.

Jason J. Dickinson is a Professor of Psychology and Director of the Robert D. McCormick Center for Child Advocacy and Policy at Montclair State University. His research on children's eyewitness testimony (understanding how children remember, misremember, forget, and tell about events they've experienced) uses psychological theory and research to generate evidence-based recommendations for questioning children in forensic contexts. He regularly consults with the child protection and law enforcement communities to bring research findings to the forefront of investigative efforts where children and other witnesses are involved.

Becky Earhart is a Postdoctoral Fellow at the Griffith Criminology Institute at Griffith University, Brisbane, Australia. She received her Ph.D. in Developmental Psychology at Wilfrid Laurier University in Canada in 2016. She is a researcher and industry trainer with the Centre for Investigative Interviewing, where she conducts research on children's memory, children's eyewitness testimony, and interviewing strategies that facilitate complete and accurate recall of experienced events. Her work has been supported by the Social Sciences and Humanities Research Council of Canada. In her role at the Centre for Investigative Interviewing, Dr. Earhart has been involved in curriculum development for courses targeting forensic interviewers and legal professionals who interview children and vulnerable people. She facilitates training with practitioners across North America.

Jacqueline R. Evans is an Assistant Professor at Florida International University. She received her Ph.D. from Florida International University's Legal Psychology program in 2008. Her dissertation was conducted under the mentorship of Dr. Ronald P. Fisher and investigated metacognition in the context of eyewitness interviews. She then went on to work as an Intelligence Community Postdoctoral Research Fellow at the University of Texas at El Paso. Her research focuses on investigative interviewing in its many forms, to include interviewing cooperative witnesses, interrogating uncooperative suspects, gathering intelligence from sources, and the ability (or lack thereof) to assess interviewee credibility.

Ronald P. Fisher is Professor of Psychology at Florida International University. Ron served as the editor-in-chief of the *Journal of Applied Research in Memory and Cognition* in addition to serving on the editorial boards of several other journals. Ron co-developed the Cognitive Interview technique (with Ed Geiselman) to enhance witness recall. He has conducted many training workshops on the Cognitive Interview with investigative agencies such as the FBI and the National Transportation Safety Board. Ron has also worked with several federal investigative and law enforcement agencies both in the USA and abroad, including NASA, the US Army and Navy, British and Australian Police, and the Israeli Air Force. Ron served on the Planning and Technical Working Groups of the US Department of Justice to develop national guidelines on collecting eyewitness evidence. His current research also examines alternative methods to detect deception and interpreting inconsistent witness testimony.

Fiona Gabbert is Professor of Applied Psychology, and Director of the Forensic Psychology Unit at Goldsmiths University of London. She holds an MSc in Social Psychology and a Ph.D. in Applied Psychology from the University of Aberdeen. Fiona is interested in the strengths and weaknesses of human memory. She has an international reputation for her research in the fields of suggestibility of memory and investigative interviewing for work focusing on improving the usability, credibility, and reliability of evidence from victims and witnesses. Her work has had an international impact on police operational procedure and policy including the introduction of new evidence-based investigative interview tools and training resources to the field, such as the Self-Administered Interview and the Structured Interview Protocol. Fiona chairs the Scientific Committee of the International Investigative Interviewing Research Group (iIIRG).

R. Edward Geiselman is the Co-Developer of the Cognitive Interview technique. He has been a Professor of Psychology at the University of California, Los Angeles, for 34 years. He earned his Bachelor's degree from Purdue University in 1972 where he studied engineering and psychology. Subsequently, he earned both Masters and Ph.D. degrees from Ohio University in experimental psychology. Since joining the faculty at UCLA, he has published over 100 research papers in social-science and police-science journals. He is the author of five books including *The Psychology of Murder, Intersections of Psychology, Psychiatry, and Law*

(Volumes 1, 2, & 3), *Eyewitness Expert Testimony*, and *Memory Enhancing Techniques for Investigative Interviewing: The Cognitive Interview.* Professor Geiselman has conducted training and offered other consulting services for numerous investigative agencies including the FBI, Homeland Security, US Secret Service, US State Department, Los Angeles Police Department, Los Angeles Sheriff's Department, Singapore Police Force, Health and Human Services, NTSB, Los Angeles Metropolitan Transit Authority, US Marine Corps, Walter-Reed Army Hospital, Black Hat, Force Science Institute, and Hong Kong's Independent Commission Against Corruption. He also conducts investigative interviews for local police departments in ongoing cold-case investigations. Dr. Geiselman was awarded the Mary-Ellen McCormick award by the LASD in 2013 for his career contributions to the investigation of child abuse cases.

Andy Griffiths is a Research Fellow at the University of Portsmouth, UK, Associate Tutor at the College of Policing, and international Consultant. He is both a former Senior Investigating Officer (SIO) and head of major crime for a UK police force, having completed 30 years' service specializing in interviewing and investigation, and during which he led numerous major crime investigations. Throughout his police career he also contributed to UK national policy and training on investigative interviewing, as a member of the national council advising all police forces. He was awarded his Ph.D. for research on the effectiveness of training on real life major crime suspect and witness interviews and has numerous publications in this field. He has contributed to miscarriage of justice investigations in the USA, New Zealand, and the UK on a *pro bono* basis, and lectured in many different countries.

Angelica V. Hagsand earned her Ph.D. in psychology in 2014 at the Department of Psychology, University of Gothenburg, Sweden. From 2015–2018 she was a postdoc researcher in Sweden as well as at the Department of Psychology, Florida International University, USA. Dr. Hagsand's research interest lies within the interdisciplinary research area of applied cognitive psychology, legal psychology, and addiction psychology. Her research concerns the effects of alcohol on cognitive functions such as memory, especially in an eyewitness context. Dr. Hagsand has published several scientific papers on this topic in high impact peer-reviewed journals, and has presented her work at many international conferences. She has also raised funding from the Swedish Research Council as well as numerous smaller grants. Beyond this, Dr. Hagsand has been invited as a speaker for practitioners (e.g., social workers, politicians, and judges) and held several popular science presentations for the public in Sweden.

Lorraine Hope is Professor of Applied Cognitive Psychology at the University of Portsmouth and a core member affiliated with the Information Elicitation programme of the UK National Centre for Research and Evidence on Security

Threats (CREST). She is also the Strategic Lead for the International Investigative Interviewing Research Group (iIIRG). Over the past 15 years, her research has resulted in the development of innovative tools and techniques for eliciting information and intelligence across a range of investigative contexts. She regularly delivers tools, research, evaluation and training for investigative interviewing and information elicitation in international policing, intelligence and security sectors, including for international and multinational agencies. She has published widely on memory and information elicitation topics and speaks regularly at academic and practitioner conferences.

Drew A. Leins is an Experimental Psychologist and Senior Scientist at Aptima, Inc. He is interested in studying social cognition, judgment, and decision making in a variety of domains, most often focusing on law enforcement and military operations. In a recent line of research for the US Army, he explored the effects of different decision contexts, including ambiguity, task familiarity, and time pressure, on soldiers' use of decision-making strategies when assessing threats in an operational environment. In another line of research, sponsored largely by the High-Value Detainee Interrogation Group (HIG) and the Combating Terrorism Technical Support Office (CTTSO), he has been developing a comprehensive model of judgment and decision making in investigative interviewing. Drew holds graduate degrees in psychology from Northeastern University and Florida International University, where he was mentored by Dr. Ronald P. Fisher. Drew would like to thank Ron for his wisdom, kindness, patience, and support. He considers Ron a mentor, colleague, and friend for life.

Nicole E. Lytle is an Assistant Professor of Social Work and Child Advocacy at Montclair State University. She received her Ph.D. in experimental psychology from the University of Toledo. Nicole's research interests are in forensic developmental psychology and include examining interviewing techniques used with child witnesses.

Michelle R. McCauley is Professor of Psychology at Middlebury College in Vermont. She received her Ph.D. in 1995 from Florida International University's Legal Psychology program. While at FIU, she was fortunate to be a member of Dr. Ronald P. Fisher's lab team where she began her career adapting the CI to facilitate children's recall. Michelle has continued to examine the value of the CI with children, and she has broadened her research to include assessment of rapport and motivation in the interview setting. Additionally, she oversees the Conservation Psychology major at Middlebury College where she and her students test methods (e.g., providing visual feedback of electricity or manipulating the frame of information) to nudge environmental behavior (e.g., energy use, policy support). Michelle is extremely grateful to Ronald P. Fisher for his generous mentoring and friendship.

Becky Milne is a Professor of Forensic Psychology at the Institute of Criminal Justice Studies at the University of Portsmouth. She is also the Director of the Centre of Forensic Interviewing, which is an internationally recognized center of excellence for investigative interviewing that brings together research, teaching, and innovation activities. Becky is a member of the National Police Chiefs Council (NPCC, UK), Investigative Interviewing Strategic Steering Group and was part of a writing team who developed the 2007 version of the Achieving Best Evidence document, National guidelines for interviewing vulnerable groups. She is a CREST researcher and is currently developing National Guidance for Witness Interviewing Strategies for Critical Incidents (WISCI). She was given the Tom Williamson award for her outstanding achievements in the field of investigative interviewing by NPCC in April 2009.

Alexandra E. Mosser received her Ph.D. in legal psychology from the Florida International University Legal Psychology program in 2017. During her graduate training she studied the Cognitive Interview under Dr. Ronald P. Fisher and has published empirical articles, book chapters, and essays on eyewitness memory and interviewing in psychology and law enforcement outlets. Her dissertation, conducted under Dr. Jacqueline Evans, investigated the use of the Cognitive Interview during questioning for infectious disease contact tracing. After graduation, she served as an Oak Ridge Institute for Science and Engineering postdoctoral visiting scientist at the Federal Bureau of Investigation.

Galit Nahari is a Senior Lecturer and the Head of the MA research track in the Department of Criminology at Bar-Ilan University. She is the Editor of *Legal and Criminological Psychology*. Her main research interests are legal and investigative decision-making, applied memory, detection of deception and witnesses' credibility assessments. As part of it, she develops interrogation and lie-detection methods (a prime example is the Verifiability Approach), examines their validity and suitability in different contexts, and their vulnerability to judgmental biases. A major part of her research further focuses on the cognitive processes underlying credibility and veracity assessments, as well as on individual differences which impact these assessments. She works closely with practitioners in development of interview methodology

Rui Paulo is a Lecturer in Psychology at Bath Spa University. His research is focused on human memory and investigative interviewing, namely developing new procedures to enhance witnesses' memory and obtaining more information from crime witnesses and victims, as well as evaluating which of the recalled information is more likely to be accurate. His work resulted in several publications in peer-reviewed journals and books and several presentations at international conferences.

Debra A. Poole is a Professor of Psychology at Central Michigan University. After receiving her BA in psychology from the University of Connecticut, she completed a Ph.D. in developmental psychology from the University of Iowa and started a program of research on the interface between cognitive development and social policy. Her research has explored the impact of repeated questioning and misinformation from parents on children's event reports, how children respond to different question forms, their ability to report the sources of knowledge, and the risks and benefits of interview props. She is the author of *Interviewing Children: The Science of Conversation in Forensic Contexts* (2016).

Martine Powell is a Professor of Psychology at Griffith University, and Founding Director of the Centre for Investigative Interviewing. Martine's area of expertise is investigative interviewing, in particular interviewing of children and vulnerable witnesses, and in cases of sexual offences and child abuse. Martine has extensive experience conducting research in this area, and has designed, implemented, and evaluated interviewer training programs for a diverse range of professional groups, both nationally and internationally. Martine's research is best described as practice-based, conducted in collaboration with industry partners to inform decisions about how to improve investigative and evidential interviewing.

Angela C. Santee received her BA in psychology from Middlebury College in 2013. As an undergraduate, she worked closely with Dr. Michelle R. McCauley to complete an honors thesis focused on rapport development and children's autobiographical recall performance. Since graduating, she has worked at the University of Rochester as a Research Coordinator for Dr. Catherine Glenn and Dr. Kimberly Van Orden on a series of projects examining risk factors for suicidal thoughts and behaviors across the lifespan. In the fall of 2018, she began her first year in the doctoral program at the University of Rochester under mentorship of Dr. Lisa Starr. Her research will investigate the complex interplay of risk factors for internalizing disorders, with a particular emphasis on understanding the reciprocal influences of interpersonal functioning and internalizing symptoms among youth.

Nadja Schreiber Compo is an Associate Professor at Florida International University and the Co-Director of the Legal Psychology Doctoral Program. Her research focuses on investigative interviewing and witness memory, and she is interested in both potentially detrimental and beneficial interviewing techniques and their underlying cognitive and social mechanisms to improve quality and quantity of witness and victim recall. She has been an invited speaker on numerous occasions including the International Association of Forensic Toxicologists, the International Association of Chiefs of Police, the Miami-Dade Forensic Services Bureau, the Dade-County and Allegheny County Public Defender's Office, the Texas Criminal Defense Attorneys Association, the University of Gothenburg in

Sweden, and Wofford College. She has published numerous peer-reviewed articles, and has (co-) authored over 70 presentations at national and international conferences. She has worked with several law enforcement agencies on research and investigative interviewing training. Her lab's research has been funded by NIJ, NSF, and the Swedish Research Council.

Aldert Vrij is Professor of Applied Social Psychology, University of Portsmouth (UK). His main research interest is deception, resulting in more than 500 publications, which have been widely cited (more than 16,000 citations and H-index 63). He received grants from British research councils, trusts and foundations, insurers, Federal Bureau of Investigation, High-Value Detainee Interrogation Group, and American, British, Dutch, and Singapore governments, totaling more than $7,500,000. He works closely with practitioners (police, security services, and insurers) in terms of conducting research and disseminating its findings. His 2008 book *Detecting Lies and Deceit: Pitfalls and Opportunities is* a comprehensive overview of research into (non)verbal and physiological deception and lie detection. He is the contact person of the European consortium of Psychological Research on Deception Detection (EPRODD) www.eprodd.eu. In 2016 he received the International Investigative Interviewing Research Group (iiiRG) Lifetime Achievement Award in recognition of his significant contribution to investigative interviewing.

Simon Wells is Co-Director of Acacia 17, based in the UK. He serves in the Ministry of Defence and as the Research to Practice Fellow for the Centre for Research and Evidence in Security and Threat (CREST). He previously served with London's Metropolitan Police, retiring as a Detective Chief Inspector after 30 years' service. Accredited as an offender profiler, he has profiled over 1000 cases, working throughout the world supporting investigations and operations. He was Course Director of the UK National Hostage Crisis Negotiation Course and head of Operations for Crisis Negotiation in London. Between 2008 and 2013 he was seconded to the UK's Ministry of Defence to support the counter terrorism effort within the UK, Iraq, Afghanistan and other theatres of operation. Most recently, he has been supporting the High-Value Detainee Interrogation Group (HIG) interrogation training.

Nina J. Westera began her career as an officer in the New Zealand Police, where she implemented evidence-based policy and practice for the interviewing of witnesses and suspects. She then took up a Research Fellowship at the Griffith Criminology Institute in Australia, continuing her research into investigative interviewing, eyewitness testimony, and the criminal investigation and prosecution of sexual and violent offences. During this time, she also educated and advised police officers, lawyers, judges, and other criminal justice sector professionals – both nationally and internationally – about best practice techniques for interviewing witnesses. With profound sadness we report that Nina passed away in 2017.

Rachel Zajac is an Associate Professor of Psychology at the University of Otago, New Zealand, where she also trained as a Clinical Psychologist. She studies the psychological factors involved in the investigation of crime, focusing primarily on eyewitness evidence, courtroom questioning, social influences on memory and decision-making, and bias in clinical and forensic settings. Rachel is regularly called on to advise police, lawyers, judges, and healthcare professionals on methods to interview children and adults about events in their past.

Laura A. Zimmerman is a Senior Researcher at the Federal Law Enforcement Training Centers (FLETC). Her research focuses on high-stakes decision making, primarily in law enforcement and military domains. She is currently conducting research to characterize de-escalation and escalation behaviors during police/civilian interactions. She is also working to ensure all FLETC training curriculum is evidence-based. In a previous program of research, sponsored by the High-Value Detainee Interrogation Group (HIG), she tested evidence-based interrogation techniques and characterized interrogator decision making during interrogations. She has also conducted research on high-stakes decision-making during large-scale multi-agency emergencies, threat detection on vehicle and foot patrol, and issues surrounding the transition of military veterans to law enforcement careers. Throughout her career, Laura's research has involved the use of the Cognitive Interview, often with invaluable guidance from Dr. Ronald P. Fisher. Laura holds a Ph.D. in experimental psychology from University of Texas at El Paso.

FOREWORD

Human memory is not perfect. We neglect to encode some information, forget other information, and occasionally fail to retrieve information we did encode. Nonetheless, much in our world depends on our ability to remember. In daily life, remembering can be as simple as where we left our car keys to as complex as recalling exactly what was said in a critical business meeting. But the consequences can also be far more complicated. Societies have historically relied on eyewitness memory to help judge responsibility and adjudicate truth. However, memory is malleable, prone to error, and susceptible to bias. Consequently, even confident eyewitnesses make mistakes, and even accurate witnesses sometimes find their testimony subjected to harsh scrutiny. The Cognitive Interview (CI) emerged from this environment as a means of assisting cooperative witnesses with recalling more information without sacrificing accuracy. From this seminal beginning, the CI has used empirical assessment, data, and design flexibility, to grow into a powerful tool for investigators tasked with helping people recall their experiences.

Ever since Ebbinghaus pioneered the study of human learning and memory, psychological scientists have been investigating how people remember and forget. Ronald P. Fisher and Edward Geiselman followed in Ebbinghaus's tradition by constructing the CI from experimental research that was guided by strong theoretical principles. Moreover, the development and success of the CI represents an ideal scenario for how good scientists carry out the research process: establish a solid theoretical foundation, apply the findings to real-world problems, encourage others to embrace and adopt evidence-based recommendations (psychologists and non-psychologists alike), and encourage future scientists to replicate, scrutinize, expand, and improve upon the findings. These are the primary reasons why the CI has emerged as such an effective investigative tool and likely explains its extraordinary staying power in both the academic and applied realms. Since its inception, the number of scholarly works inspired by the CI has increased dramatically. Throughout the first decade after Fisher and Geiselman's initial publication on the CI (i.e., between 1984 and 1993), a quick search of Google Scholar returns 181 articles and abstracts discussing the CI protocol. Between 1994 and 2003, there were 1120 new articles and abstracts published on the topic, and then between 2004 and 2013 an additional 4030 CI-related articles and abstracts made it to print. Just in the last four-and-a-half years (i.e., from January 2014 through May 2018) there have been 3570 new articles and abstracts on the CI.

The CI began as a collaborative effort between Ronald P. Fisher and Ed Geiselman, who were colleagues and close friends. Work on the CI embodied a spirit of collaboration from the start, and this legacy continues as evidenced by the ever-increasing number of collaborative studies and experiments it has inspired. One would be hard pressed to find single-author publications investigating or evaluating the CI, and multinational research teams are common. The collaborative spirit of the CI can clearly be seen in this volume: Thirty-four authors from both the academic and practice communities, representing four continents, contributed thirteen chapters that focus on a vast spectrum of interviewing contexts.

Although the CI began as an application of cognitive theory to the interviewing of cooperative witnesses, its focus and emphasis has expanded in the ensuing years. Fisher and Geiselman point out that its application is, can be, and should be, much broader. In this volume, in additional to discussing how the CI can be used to facilitate eyewitness testimony in traditional investigative contexts, a number of chapters discuss different applications of the CI (e.g., epidemiological interviews, deception detection), revealing the ways the CI continues to develop as our understanding of memory and social processes expands.

We hope this edited volume will prove useful to the academic community for designing applied experiments and helpful for introducing students to the field of investigative interviewing (particularly for students enrolled in cognitive and legal psychology courses). However, this volume is not just for academics. Many of this book's authors are professional investigators for the police and the military, and many have first-hand experience applying principles of the CI in the field. As readers will come to see, the application of this technique is rapidly expanding to other investigative contexts, which in turn is ushering in a new era of research on the CI.

When editing this book we had specific goals that we aimed to achieve. First, we wanted a book that would allow those unfamiliar with the CI to learn about this technique directly from the experts, including the creators of the CI themselves (Fisher and Geiselman). Second, we wanted to update readers on the latest findings and future directions of research on investigative interviewing. Third, we wanted this book to reflect the current fascinating and diverse landscape of experts, fields, and projects inspired by the CI. We hope readers will find these chapters valuable, and that perhaps some may decide to join the field as collaborators in researching and applying the CI to improving eyewitness testimony.

1

EXPANDING THE COGNITIVE INTERVIEW TO NON-CRIMINAL INVESTIGATIONS

Ronald P. Fisher and R. Edward Geiselman

Introduction

Information is the lifeblood of many investigations, whether about crime, accidents, public health, national security, or a host of others. Some of that information may result from analysis of physical records (e.g., instruments, a patient's medical chart, skid marks, explosive devices, the plane's black box), and some will come from interviewing people who have first-hand knowledge of the event (e.g., pilots, soldiers, physicians, victims, bystander witnesses, informants). The present chapter focuses on eliciting information from human sources.

On the surface, it might seem that if interviewers are knowledgeable about the event to be investigated, i.e., they know what kind of information to elicit (e.g., the robber's appearance, the train's speed, which terrorists attended a meeting) it should be relatively easy to extract that information – assuming, of course, that the interviewee is motivated to provide the requested information (see Brandon & Wells, this volume, Leins & Zimmerman, this volume for interview techniques with uncooperative respondents). Thus, for instance, if a police investigator needs to find out the criminal's ethnicity, the police officer/interviewer can simply ask: Was he White, Black, Hispanic, or Asian? And, in fact, that is how many investigative interviewers proceed. That is, investigators think in terms of content (the information to be gathered) and then ask specific questions targeting each to-be-gathered fact, e.g., how fast was the car going? (Fisher, Geiselman, Raymond, Jurkevich, & Warhaftig, 1987). Although this method of interviewing (asking specific questions) is common among police – and others – it is not an effective method to gather information from human sources. Geiselman and Fisher therefore set out to devise an alternative method of interviewing, one that revolved around witnesses' mental processes (rather than around the facts to be gathered) to elicit more information from human sources. The resulting procedure, called the Cognitive Interview (CI), was born out of this need, to devise an interview process based on the witness's and the interviewer's psychological processes.

The original version of the CI was developed specifically for criminal investigation. That the CI took this direction was mainly happenstance. It emanated from a brief conversation we had in Ed Geiselman's office about what profession could best profit from applying psychological researchers' knowledge about memory-enhancing techniques. Ed's immediate thought was that police could benefit most from enhancing witness memory, because solving crimes depends mainly on witness evidence – despite the more exotic, but uncommon, solutions often found on television shows. And so, we devised the CI to be used by police to enhance witness recall of crime-related events.

When we first examined the problem, of witnesses failing to remember key elements of a crime, we thought about it mainly as a witness memory problem. As such, the original version of the CI (Geiselman et al., 1984) was composed exclusively of techniques that we believed would enhance witnesses retrieving information about past experiences (see Table 1.1: Active respondent participation; Report everything; Varied Retrieval). We later realized that witnesses' under-reporting criminal events was not only a reflection of their using inefficient memory-retrieval mechanisms, but also that the interviewers were not processing information efficiently (e.g., listening to and notating the witness's statements, keeping track of questions to be asked, developing a hypothesis of how the crime occurred, etc.). Moreover, other non-memory factors also contributed to witnesses' under-reporting events, including the social dynamics between the interviewer and the witness (e.g., inadequate rapport), and the difficulty of communicating some ideas (e.g., describing the odor of a fire). Thus, whereas the initial version of the CI was a simple collection of memory-enhancing mnemonics, the CI evolved into a more wide-ranging approach (the so-called "Enhanced CI") that addresses (a) the social dynamics between the interviewer and the witness, (b) the witness's memory, and other cognitive processes, and also the interviewer's cognitive processes, and also the interviewer's cognitive processes, and also (c) the witness and the interviewer communicating effectively with one another. The core elements of the CI and the psychological processes we intended to enhance are presented in Table 1.1. (For a complete description of the CI, see Fisher & Geiselman, 1992.)

As is documented in other chapters in this book and also in published reviews and meta-analyses (e.g., Fisher & Geiselman, 2018; Köhnken, Milne, Memon, & Bull, 1999; Memon, Meissner, & Fraser, 2010), the CI has been extremely successful in eliciting more information from witnesses to crime. The present chapter explores how the CI can be adapted to other, non-criminal investigations. Because the CI is a purely process-oriented approach, we expected – in truth, we hoped – that its effectiveness would extend to other kinds of investigation that depend on the same underlying psychological processes that the CI was intended to bolster, namely, (a) the social dynamics between the interviewer and the respondent,

TABLE 1.1 Elements of the Cognitive Interview

CI Element	Description	Psychological processes enhanced[1]
Rapport	Develop rapport between respondent and interviewer	Social Dynamics
Active respondent participation	Respondent actively to generate information (not merely to answer Interviewer's questions)	Social Dynamics
Report everything	Include all recollections in response; do not edit out unimportant details[2]	Memory & Communication
Reinstate context	Reinstate the context of the original experience	Memory
Describe in detail	Instruct respondents to provide a detailed account[3]	Communication
Close eyes	Instruct respondents to close their eyes[4]	Cognition
No interruptions	Do not interrupt the respondent's narration[5]	Social Dynamics & Cognition
Don't guess	Instruct respondents not to guess (OK to say "I don't know")	Cognition
Open-ended questions	Ask primarily open-ended questions (closed questions as follow-up)	Social Dynamics & Cognition
Multiple retrieval	Encourage respondents to search through memory more than once	Memory
Varied retrieval	Encourage respondents to search through memory in different ways	Memory
Respondent-compatible questions	Ask questions that are compatible with respondent's currently accessible information	Memory
Avoid suggestive questions	Avoid asking questions that suggest a specific answer	Memory
Code-compatible output	Allow respondents to output their knowledge in the same form as it is stored (often non-verbal)	Communication

1 These are the psychological processes we *intended* to enhance. We do not know which psycho-logical processes were *actually* enhanced. Some of the CI elements were intended to influence more than one process.

2 Sometimes this is misinterpreted to mean that respondents are encouraged to guess. Respondents are not encouraged to guess (see "Don't guess" instruction). This instruction encourages respondents to report all facts, whether the respondents consider the facts important or not.

3 This instruction can be embellished by the interviewer providing an example of a model (detailed) statement (see Leal, Vrij, Warmelink, Vernham, & Fisher, 2015).

4 Asking respondents to close their eyes should be implemented only after rapport has been developed.

5 This suggestion is relaxed if the respondent's narrative goes far afield of the critical event.

(b) the memory and cognitive processes of the respondent and the interviewer, and (c) communication between the interviewer and the respondent. Clearly, there are many kinds of investigative interviews that depend on these three underlying psychological processes, and which may benefit from the CI, including, debriefing military combatants after a mission, gathering human intelligence information from informants, interviewing drivers and passengers about vehicular accidents or interviewing workers about industrial accidents, interviewing patients about their medical histories, etc.

In exploring these non-criminal applications of the CI, we report both our own research efforts and also those of our colleagues, several of whom are contributors to this book. Most of these research studies, naturally, were conducted in controlled, laboratory environments with college students as the respondents in a simulated situation. Some research studies, however, were also conducted outside the laboratory, in the field, where the experimental participants were "real people" engaging in their normal, real-world (non-laboratory) lives. Finally, we describe a few instances in which high-ranking professional investigators incorporated elements of the CI into their investigations of real-world critical events.

Survey of Empirical Research

We take as our jump-off point into reporting the research on non-criminal events the most basic kind of experience: A single, external event that occurs in a specific episodic context (time and place) and the respondent is a cooperative, untrained observer. Within this basic experience, we examine both low-arousal events (e.g., memory for conversations) and high-arousal events (e.g., traffic accidents). From there, we explore events that vary systematically from the basic experience, either because they are collections of many similar events or because the respondent is a trained observer (e.g., police officer). We then examine a more common experience, in which a person's goal is to extract meaning (e.g., listening to a story). Finally, we explore internal, mental events (e.g., decisions, plans, and emotions), and we speculate on the CI's use in a therapeutic context.

Before presenting the experimental findings, let us describe the typical research paradigm, including the different variations. Generally, experimental participants experience an event, and then are interviewed about their memory for the event. The researcher typically measures how much the interviewee recalls and the accuracy of his/her recollection. Within this standard procedure there is considerable variation: (a) The experimental participants are usually college students, but in some studies they are young children, or older or non-student adults. (b) The experienced event is usually shown on videotape but sometimes it is experienced live; generally the participants observe the critical event passively, but sometimes they actively participate in the event; the event is usually fashioned by the experimenter, but in some studies, it is a naturally-occurring event from the participant's life. (c) The interviews are usually conducted immediately or within minutes of the critical event, but in some studies, several days, months, or years intervene. (d) The interview is conducted either as a CI or a "control" interview, which can either be a "Structured Interview" (a technique that incorporates generally accepted principles of interviewing, but does not include the memory-enhancing techniques unique to the CI) or a procedure that simulates a typical police interview. Many of the studies that claimed to conduct the CI used only some, but not all, of the CI elements (see Table 1.1), and so it is important when reading the individual studies to note exactly which CI elements were used. We address this issue later in the chapter (Retrospective Comments on the CI Research).

Single, external events

Low-arousal events: Laboratory studies using the CI have examined, among others, memory for innocuous events like blood donations and health-related events.

Blood donations: In some of the earliest studies on the CI, Köhnken and colleagues assessed the original version of the CI in a blood donation event. Experimental participants were shown a videotape of a typical blood donation event and then were interviewed with either a CI or a Structured Interview. In both Köhnken, Thürer, and Zoberbier (1994) and Mantwill, Köhnken, and Aschermann (1995), interviewees remembered more blood donation details when interviewed with the CI than with the Structured Interview, and at comparable levels of accuracy. This occurred both for participants who had donated blood in the past and for those who had not donated in the past (Mantwill et al., 1995). In Köhnken et al. (1994), not only were the interviewees tested for recall of the blood donation event, but also the interviewers were tested on their recollections of what the interviewees reported during the interview. Interviewers who had conducted a CI recalled more (of what the interviewees had reported) than interviewers who conducted a Structured Interview. Thus the CI not only facilitated observers' recollection of an external event, but also the interviewers' recollections of what transpired during the interview.

Accidents: A more common experience that should lend itself to the CI is one in which the witness is a passive bystander observer of either a vehicular or industrial accident. The CI was examined in at least four laboratory studies in which experimental participants watched a video of a car accident (Brock, Fisher, & Cutler, 1999; Chapman & Perry, 1995; Ginet & Verkampt, 2007; Milne, Clare, & Bull, 1999) and one in which the witnesses viewed a video of an industrial accident (MacLean, Stinson, Kelloway, & Fisher, 2011). In all four car accident studies, the CI elicited considerably more information than a Structured Interview, and at comparable accuracy rates. In the one study of memory for an industrial accident, the results were mixed, with the CI eliciting more information than the control interview, but at a lower accuracy rate. Given that the information-processing requirements for watching a video of an industrial accident should be similar to those of watching a car accident, what accounts for the different findings? We suspect that the more encouraging results of the car accident studies reflected that the CI and control interviews were conducted as interactive, face-to-face interviews, whereas the mixed results of the industrial accident reflected that the "interview" was a pre-printed set of instructions to which the witnesses wrote a written response. Moreover, in this study, several of the CI prompts were closed multiple-choice questions, which are prone to error and therefore generally discouraged when conducting a CI. Finally, a critical element of the CI, instructing witnesses not to guess if unsure, was missing from the written CI instructions. We will describe shortly, when discussing high-arousal events, a more compelling examination of the CI in which the witnesses were victims of real car accidents (Ginet, Teissedre, Verkampt, & Fisher, 2016).

Conversations: Relatively little research has been conducted on recalling conversations. It is unfortunate that memory for conversations has been overlooked, given its applied value in several domains: For national security, interviewers may want to learn what transpired during meetings of terrorist groups; business leaders or attorneys may want to know who said what during high-level business discussions; in current vogue in Washington politics, investigators want to know about conversations between American government officials and representatives of foreign governments. At least four studies have been conducted to examine the CI's effect on participants' recollections of earlier conversations. In Campos and Alonso-Quecuty (2008), Spanish college-aged students watched a video of two criminals discussing in detail their plans to commit a crime. The participants attempted to remember the conversation 15 minutes later, when they participated in either a CI or an interview modeled after a typical Spanish police interview. The CI-interviewed respondents recalled more elements of the conversation than the control-interview respondents, and at a slightly higher accuracy rate. Similar patterns (increased CI recall, although at comparable accuracy rates) were found by others when testing participants with mild intellectual disabilities (Clarke, Prescott, & Milne, 2013) and when testing older adults (young old: 60–74 and old-old: 75+) (Prescott, Milne, & Clarke, 2011). Fisher and Castano (2017) also examined college students' recollections of conversations, but in their study, the students participated actively in an engaging 15-minute group discussion (four to eight people per group) about an interesting, ethical business dilemma. Students who were interviewed (two days later) with a CI recalled almost twice as many facts about the group conversation as those interviewed with a Structured Interview. Interestingly, recall accuracy was extremely high for both conditions (0.98 in the CI; 0.99 in the Structured Interview). One need not think too hard to find implications of this research for real-life application to the legal, political, security, and business communities.

Public health events: The CI has also been assessed for recalling recent events that have implications for public health investigations, including memory for foods eaten, and physical contact with others. In an effort to simulate a food-poisoning investigation – without actually poisoning anyone – Fisher and Quigley (1992) "invited" students to select and eat from a smorgasbord of various (uncontaminated) party-type foods (chips, crackers, drinks, etc.) and then interviewed them between 4 and 14 days later (when victims of food poisoning would likely be contacted by public health officials) to find out what foods they had eaten earlier and what foods were available. Those interviewed with the CI recalled more than twice as many foods than those interviewed with a protocol designed to mimic a typical public health investigation (Mean foods recalled were 12.2 and 5.9, respectively). Even when asked to recognize the available and eaten foods from a menu of possible foods, participants interviewed with the CI outperformed the control group, although the differences were not as great as in the recall task (mean Hit Rates = 0.83 and 0.75, respectively). A conceptually parallel study, on memory for physical contact with others within the past few days, produced similarly encouraging results (see Mosser & Evans, this volume). We would expect comparable results for other public health matters, including remembering sexual contacts, using non-sterile syringes, traveling to mosquito-infested locations, etc. – but the research remains to be conducted (although see research by Devon Brewer for other cognitively based memory enhancers, e.g., Brewer & Garrett, 2001).

As opposed to the above studies, which examined a more-or-less complete version of the CI, many studies have attempted to isolate individual elements of the CI in health-related interviews, but with mixed results. On the positive side, Brewer, Garrett, and Kulasingam (1999) asked people to freely recall their sexual and injection partners. After the interviewees reported as many partners as they could recall, the interviewer provided the earlier-mentioned names (multiple retrieval), which prompted the interviewees to recall several new names. On the negative side, Cohen and Java (1995) asked people to freely recall various health-related experiences (e.g., symptoms, illnesses, injuries, medical visits) from the past three months. Follow-up instructions to reinstate the context of a specific month generated only a few additional experiences beyond those already elicited with a free narrative, and not as many as a recognition-based test. Similarly discouraging results were found by Armstrong and colleagues (2000) in a food recall study that focused on only one element of the CI (either context reinstatement, or reverse order, or multiple recall). It is difficult to interpret these studies with respect to the CI, as they limited themselves to testing only one element of the CI, and not the entire protocol (see also Milne & Bull, 2002). For the remainder of this chapter, therefore, we will consider only those studies that incorporated at least several elements of the CI.

High-Arousal Events

Car accident: We described earlier controlled laboratory experiments in which observers passively watched a videotape of a car accident (Brock et al., 1999; Chapman & Perry, 1995; Ginet & Verkampt, 2007). A more compelling test of the CI was conducted by Ginet et al. (2016) who interviewed adult victims of real traffic accidents, a considerably more arousing experience (van der Kolk, 1997). Within two years of their accident, the victims participated in either a CI or a Structured Interview about the details of the accident. Shortly before the interview, the accident victims indicated how aroused they were at the time of the accident, and their current state of psychological well-being. In general, those interviewed with the CI remembered many more accident details than those given a Structured Interview, and this held both for victims who rated the accident as a relatively low- or high-arousal event. (Only quantity of recall was assessed, because there was no reliable, independent measure of the accidents to assess accuracy.) The patterns of CI superiority, however, differed for central versus peripheral accident details. For central events, the CI superiority effect was greater for victims who reported the accident to be highly arousing; by comparison, for peripheral details, the CI superiority effect was greater for victims who reported the accident to be less arousing. That the CI was successful in recalling the central elements of a highly arousing experience is particularly important for many real-world investigations where it is critical to ferret out important details of life-threatening events (e.g., sexual assault and other serious crimes, police-officer-involved shootings, medical emergencies, military battles).

Not all studies have shown the CI to be superior to alternative interview protocols when retrieving high-arousal events. Peace and Porter (2004) asked community members to recall a traumatic experience or a positive experience either via a reduced version of the CI (context reinstatement, change order, change perspective), guided imagery, writing down a preliminary description, or via a free narrative that was similar to a Step-Wise interview (Yuille, Hunter, Joffe, & Zaparniuk, 1993). No differences were found across the four interview types. It is not clear to us why the CI was not more effective in the study other than that this was a simplified or incomplete version of the original CI.

Hostage-taking: Another kind of high-arousal event in which the success of the investigation depends heavily on the quantity and quality of information provided by victims is a hostage-taking. This kind of event might be considered a criminal investigation if the event is domestic, but a national-security event if the hostage taking occurs overseas, as was the case in 1979, when American civilians were taken hostage in Iran. We simulated such a scenario by having college students sign up for a different, innocuous study (Mosser, Fisher, Molinaro, Satin, & Manon, 2016). While waiting for their experimenter, two "bad guys" (confederates who were carrying look-alike, but obviously fake guns) barged into the waiting room, yelled at the student participants, and led them as a group to another room, where they were instructed to sit on the floor and not move. (As per the IRB approval, the participants were informed beforehand, when signing the consent forms, that, as part of the laboratory experiment, they may be exposed to a simulated violent event, with fake guns, and that they should just follow instructions and not interfere with the ongoing event.) The hostage takers yelled instructions to the hostages and also spoke amongst themselves about their detailed plan to lure police into a trap. The revealed details included, among others, the name of their renegade group and its anti-police philosophy, people they would later meet, and how, when, and where they would meet (with a map of the rendezvous area). The hostage-taking was disrupted by an "unexpected" event, and the hostage-takers fled. Shortly thereafter, the student hostages were interviewed by law enforcement officers either before or after they had received training in the CI. In comparison to other CI studies, in which we generally found that the CI elicited more information than the control interview, but at comparable accuracy rates, we found here that the CI interviews (after training) elicited the same amount of information as the control interviews (before training); however, the accuracy rates were higher for post-trained interviews (0.95) than pre-trained interviews (0.90) and the information was gathered more efficiently in the post-trained interviews (10.2 facts per minute) than in the pre-trained interviews (7.6 facts per minute).

Whereas the above study is only a laboratory simulation, the following account describes the CI's use in a real hostage-taking. Such real-world accounts obviously are limited by their subjective measurements, small numbers of participants, lack of experimental control, and a host of other traditional criteria; however, their realism captures features generally not available in laboratory research. We offer these real-world accounts to supplement, not to replace, the controlled laboratory studies and to enable real-world investigators to appreciate the potential of the CI in settings they are familiar with.

> After more than 30 years in federal law enforcement, counterintelligence and counterterrorism, I became an international security consultant in 2010 and now operate a strategic consultancy in which I often interview information sources to recall specific details of prior experiences. A client hired me to gather information about a hostage situation for the purpose of developing and executing a strategy for the safe return of the hostage. The hostage was taken from an area where al-Qaeda and affiliated groups operated. To ensure that my client was making informed decisions about their hostage, I interviewed two former hostages that had been safely released from captivity from the same area after being held for an extended period. I used the cognitive interview, in conjunction with other emerging research, including embodied cognition, and environmental priming. The interview was conducted in a comfortable setting to make the person interviewed as relaxed as possible, especially considering that I would be asking details of a traumatic experience. I also asked the persons interviewed to offer a birds-eye view and draw sketches of areas I was interested in, including where they were kidnapped from, areas held in, and conditions of captivity. On both occasions, the persons interviewed advised they were able to recall more information, about their captors, their locations, travel patterns and the mindsets of their captors, than they had previously provided during other interviews by trained interviewers. The reported details were

confirmed by others observing, who had also been privy to previous debriefings of the persons I interviewed. When the hostage was eventually released, I interviewed him/her in the same manner as the two former hostages. The now-freed hostage was surprised at the level of recall and specific details conveyed during the interview.

As described by Mark Fallon, Director of ClubFed,
LLC a strategic consultancy, and former NCIS Deputy
Assistant Director and Department of Homeland Security senior executive

Multiple events: In all of the above studies, the critical event occurred only once. Sometimes, however, critical events occur repeatedly (e.g., repeated sexual assault or frequent meetings of terrorist groups) and respondents are asked either to describe a general characteristic of the sequence (e.g., how often or where they occurred) or to isolate and describe a specific instance within the series.

One high-level context in which investigators need to learn about multiple events is when countries engage in espionage on their enemies to learn about potentially threatening developments. Such intelligence-gathering sessions might include debriefing spies or informants about their encounters with the enemy. Although we do not have direct access to spies or top-secret informants at our universities, we were able to simulate some of their debriefings by asking college students to recall their own family meetings, which, in common with terrorist meetings, occur periodically, with a set of core people attending many meetings, and where topics of discussion are repeated, but mixed in with new, upcoming events. As a test of the CI's application to such espionage, Leins, Fisher, Pludwinsky, Robertson, and Mueller (2014) interviewed students about family meetings they attended within the previous year. The study was conducted in two phases: In Phase I, the students provided brief labels (e.g., July 4th barbeque; cousin David's graduation) for various family meetings; in Phase II, the students described one of these family meetings in detail (see also later in this chapter Rivard, Fisher, Robertson & Mueller's, 2014, study on memory for the details of a specific meeting). In Phase I, the students attempted to recall as many family events as possible in a free recall format. After the students said that they could not remember any more events, they were provided several CI-related mnemonics, including varied retrieval (recall the events in different ways, e.g., local meetings and meetings requiring out-of-town travel), self-generated cues, and the use of non-verbal responding (time-line: see Hope, Mullis, & Gabbert, 2013). Of the 36 participants who recalled at least one event in the free report section of Phase I, 35 (97 percent) remembered at least one additional event when prompted with the mnemonic cues. Almost all of the family events reported in Phase I were corroborated by other family members. In Phase II, when students were asked to describe one family event in detail, those in the CI condition reported more than twice as many person, conversation, action, and setting details as did control participants. Obviously, the exact fashion of these Phase I and Phase II instructions will vary from one situation to the next, but the basic approach appears to have been validated, at least for a laboratory simulation.

Whereas the current chapter focuses on non-criminal investigations, the above study by Leins et al. (2014), on memory for several related events – and probing for one specific event in the series – can easily be translated in criminal investigations for repeated events, as in repeated sexual assaults on an individual. Here, the victim is asked to (a) convey the entire series of events, and also (b) to describe in detail one or more specific events. We expect that the general approach we used in Leins et al. will be effective in such cases, where successful prosecution depends on describing the general series of events and also on detailing one or more specific event. The general strategy that we recommend is to (a) use various CI-related mnemonics to elicit brief descriptors, or labels, of each event (e.g., at my uncle's house; with his friends) and then (b) isolate the most memorable event – as determined by the respondent – and then probe with the CI for details of the most memorable event, followed by other memorable events in turn.

The account below extends the Leins et al. (2014) laboratory study to a real-world investigation in which a terrorist who agreed to cooperate described earlier encounters with suicide bombers.

> The following describes an intelligence-gathering interview with a high ranked terrorist who had recruited many suicide bombers, and demonstrates the varied retrieval technique used in Phase I of Leins et al (2014). One of the first pieces of information that was needed was a full listing of as many terror actions he had planned and executed, and also the people who were involved. The interviewer incorporated the varied retrieval element of the CI by asking the terrorist to recall all the events that were conducted with people in the terrorist's family, but also to recall the events that were conducted with people outside the terrorist's family. Similarly, the terrorist was asked to recall the events that were conducted in an open area (e.g., park) and also those that were conducted in an enclosed area (e.g., building). This varied retrieval mnemonic was continued for an additional 20 dimensions. The terrorist succeeded in remembering many more events and related information compared to what he had revealed earlier when given a more traditional interview.
>
> *As described by Dr. Tzachi Ashkenazi, Israeli Prime Minister's Office*

Interviewing experts: Most of the studies we reported thus far entailed situations in which the respondent was a typical civilian, who had little experience or expertise in the domain of the investigation. In many interviews, however, the respondent is not a naïve civilian, but an expert in the investigative domain. This might occur, for instance, when interviewing police officers after a shooting or interviewing physicians after treating patients in an epidemic area. How does the CI fare when interviewing experts?

Law enforcement officers certainly receive training to be observant and to report relevant details. One might expect such training either to (a) increase the CI's effectiveness (because experts have encoded more efficiently, and hence have a larger pool of information that they might recall if interviewed properly) or (b) decrease the CI's effectiveness (because the experts have already been trained to report thoroughly). One recent study that examined the CI's effectiveness with law enforcement officers as respondents was conducted at the Federal Law Enforcement Training Center (FLETC; Rivard et al., 2014). In the study, "super-experts," FLETC instructors, who teach courses to law enforcement officers, were interviewed about a specific class they had taught within the past several days (4–43 days). Those interviewed with the CI recalled almost 80 percent more details of the target class than those interviewed with the 5-Step interview (the standard interview protocol taught at FLETC prior to their changing to the CI), and at high and comparable accuracy rates (almost 0.90).

If the CI is effective for debriefing experts, there may be many applications in real-world investigations, including (a) debriefing astronauts (or test pilots) after a space mission (experimental flight), (b) debriefing professional athletes, managers, and coaches after a game or competition, (c) debriefing surgeons and other medical staff after a medical procedure, (d) debriefing soldiers, and especially commanders, after a skirmish with the enemy, and (e) a host of other scenarios. Our experience is that these debriefing sessions are generally conducted by senior members within the domain (e.g., high-ranking members of the military), but whose expertise is in the content of the domain (e.g., military tactics) and not in the process of eliciting information from other experts. As such, they may know what facts to elicit, but they may not be skillful in the *process* of eliciting these facts from other people. Fortifying such content-experts with an efficient process of eliciting information may yield more information than they are currently eliciting.

The following portrays a real-world example of using the CI to elicit information from a soldier after an encounter with the enemy.

> The following portrays a real-world example of using the CI to elicit information from a wounded soldier. The interviewee was a soldier who survived an attack on his platoon while being in a vehicle that ended in many casualties. The surviving soldier was hospitalized in a military hospital located in a military base. Upon arriving at the hospital, the interviewer asked the physicians if he can interview the soldier in and around a similar vehicle (to reinstate context). After hearing the principles of the CI, the physicians agreed to the interview. The interview took place in and outside the vehicle, and it replicated the actual event, e.g., for the first 5 minutes of the real attack the soldier was sitting inside the vehicle and then got out and did a sort of 8-shape path around the vehicle that ended in hiding in the bushes. That space and time series of events were re-enacted exactly within the

interview, with the interviewer sitting with him at the beginning inside the vehicle, and then walking side by side with the soldier, and documenting his memories as he narrated them. Many new pieces of information were remembered by the soldier compared to an earlier conducted conventional military interview. These details, which helped to build up the intelligence picture and to take other actions, were corroborated later through additional pieces of intelligence. Also only in the CI it was found out exactly why the vehicle was separated from the other group of three other vehicles in the preliminary part of the event and consequently corrective actions were taken. Also holding the CI inside and around the vehicle helped the soldier to communicate clearly what he saw, from which distance and angle, what was hidden from him and why.

As described by Dr Tzachi Ashkenazi, Israeli Prime Minister's Office

The experimental CI study with experts that we reported earlier (Rivard et al., 2014) and the real-world instance of a soldier providing additional information with the CI demonstrate that the CI works with expert respondents, but the studies are mute on the issue of whether the CI will be more effective or less effective with expert than novice respondents. Given experts' greater memory for domain-relevant knowledge than novices, one might predict that either (a) the CI will be less effective for interviewing experts than novices, because experts have some, but not all, of the requisite skills to retrieve and communicate their knowledge, or (b) the CI will be more effective for experts than for novices, because experts have more information stored in memory than novices, and the CI increases by a constant amount the percentage of available information that is retrieved and reported. We know of only one CI study (Mosser et al., 2016) that allows us to assess the CI's effectiveness when interviewing experts (police) and novices (students). The study was not intended, and hence not designed formally, to compare police and students as witnesses to crime, but through a scheduling accident, we tested and hence were able to compare police and students. Moreover, there were only a limited number of police (N = 18) and student (N = 12) witnesses. As such, we offer these preliminary findings tentatively as suggestive of interesting trends and to stimulate others to pursue the matter. In the study, either police or students watched a video of a simulated crime scene and then were interviewed by an experienced police officer (whom they did not know) either before or after the interviewing police officer received training in the CI. As in other CI training studies in our lab, the interviewers elicited more information after CI training than before CI training and this held both for interviewing students and for interviewing police. The value of CI training, however, was greater when debriefing novices than when debriefing experts. We suspect that the CI was more valuable for interviewing novices, because their initial free narrative reports – in response to the opening question: What happened? – would have been considerably less extensive in a Structured Interview (pre-CI-training) than in the CI. By comparison, experts, who already realize the importance of providing a complete free narrative report, do not benefit as much by the CI's guidance to elicit an extensive, detailed narrative.

In the studies described thus far, the respondent was cooperative and responsive to the interviewer's instructions. Sometimes, however, respondents will be less than cooperative or even hostile, as when interviewing people who are affiliated with or have knowledge of terrorist or criminal groups. In such cases, the CI may be useful because respondents may be cooperative to provide some details (e.g., actions committed by people unknown to them) – even though they may withhold other details (e.g., actions committed by close friends or family). Second, an initially uncooperative respondent may become more willing to cooperate through effective rapport-building and other persuasion techniques. Research on such uncooperative respondents typically compares either a Structured Interview or an accusatory style of interview with a more information-gathering approach (often a combination of a CI plus other persuasion-related techniques) and generally finds that the information-gathering approach elicits more information (see Brandon & Wells, this volume.)

Memory for Non-Episodic, General Knowledge

The CI was originally designed to assist respondents to describe a specific episodic event that occurred in a particular autobiographical context. The principles of the original CI were therefore based on traditional episodic memory experiments in which words or other to-be-remembered events (e.g., details of a crime) were to be recalled. Sometimes, however, people are required to recall either the meaning of an event (e.g., listening to or reading a news report) or to abstract a general pattern that is common to many episodes.

The only study we know of that examined the CI's utility for memory of written narratives was conducted by Dornburg and McDaniel (2006). In the study, older participants read a brief story; three weeks later, they were provided in a group setting both written and oral instructions that incorporated several CI elements. Recall of the story elements was increased by the CI (compared to standard free recall instructions) without sacrificing accuracy. The study allows for several important implementations of the CI in that: (a) this was a test of memory for perceptually impoverished material – we shall extend this later in the chapter to memory for earlier thoughts and decisions, and (b) the CI techniques were conveyed as a standardized printed and oral set of instructions, which circumvents the social dynamics of a typical one-on-one, face-to-face interview and can thus be used to elicit information from larger groups of people or from remote locations.

In all of the studies described thus far, the investigator's or researcher's goal was to elicit information about one specific event. Sometimes the event was an isolated experience (e.g., memory for a hostage-taking, or memory for a story), and sometimes it was an experience within a series of related experiences (e.g., memory for a specific sexual assault that occurred within a series of many such assaults). On other occasions, however, investigators or researchers will be more interested in the general pattern of the series itself. For instance, aircraft engineers might want to learn from test pilots whether a plane behaved the same way on several test runs. Often, such patterns are important in the medical world, and especially in public health investigations, in which epidemiologists want to know whether people who typically engage in a particular life-style (e.g., sedentary job) are more likely to have specific health disorders (e.g., heart attacks). Establishing a person's life-style over several years might require thinking back many years in time, which far exceeds almost all CI – and other interviewing protocols – studies. One CI study, however, stands out. Fisher, Falkner, Trevisan, and McCauley (2000) interviewed people in 1995 about their daily activity schedules in 1960, 35 years in the past. Fortunately, we had access to a 1960 survey in which the same people listed their then-contemporaneous activity schedules, so we could determine how similar their 1995 estimates (of their 1960 schedules) were to what they reported originally in 1960. (Such comparisons of later recollections to earlier, contemporaneous assessments are often used to check the accuracy of flashbulb memories (e.g., Hornstein, Brown, & Mulligan, 2003).) Technically, this is a measure of consistency but in real-world situations where we do not have a perfect measure of accuracy, consistency with a contemporaneous report is a reasonably good approximation to accuracy). In our study, participants were asked, in 1995, to indicate the various activities they did in 1960 and how often they did the activities (weekly, less often, never, don't know). They were interviewed either via a CI that was modified for the task (e.g., extensive context reinstatement) or via a traditional epidemiological interview. The results showed that, in comparison to the traditional epidemiological interview, the CI-interviewed participants remembered many more activities, provided more precise answers, and their answers were slightly, but not significantly, more consistent with 1960 answers. Not surprisingly, people in 1995 underestimated how often they engaged in various activities in 1960, however, the degree of underestimation was lower for those in the CI than for those in the traditional epidemiological interview.

In concert with other applications of the CI for public health experiences (memory for foods eaten, Fisher & Quigley, 1992, or for physical contact with others, Mosser & Evans, this volume) we expect that, when adapted appropriately, the CI might be valuable for a variety of health-related investigations (see Brewer et al., 1999).

That the CI was successful after such a long retention interval also speaks to its relevance for conducting oral histories of historical events or for interviewing adults about experiences that may have occurred during childhood. It might also be adapted to cold-case criminal investigations (see, e.g., Amann, 2017, for a 14-year-old sexual assault in which the CI was instrumental to solving the case).

Memory for Internal, Mental Events

Thus far, all of the events that the CI has been applied to are external experiences, e.g., crimes, meetings, conversations, activities, etc. Oftentimes, however, people try to remember internal experiences, such as earlier thoughts or decisions. For the most part, research in these areas examines how such mental activities are made, with almost no research about how people later remember them – other than to show that people are sometimes unaware of, and hence cannot remember, how they made some decisions (Nisbett & Wilson, 1977). But, in our daily lives, we often try to remember how or why we made decisions – and, it seems, especially after we have made poor life decisions: What was I thinking when I gave $500 to Person X (or married person Y; or decided to pursue a career in Z)? Moreover, such recollections often take on monumental proportions: What were the generals and politicians thinking when we went to war in Vietnam? What was the physician thinking when she (incorrectly) diagnosed my medical condition as X and recommended therapy Y? What was the campaign manager thinking when he recommended running that outrageous advertisement? Our goal was to enhance memory for such internal, mental experiences.

Our research strategy to improving memory for internal, mental experiences was (a) to determine whether memory for internal mental experiences abide by the same rules as memory for external experiences, and, if so, (b) adapt and use the rules of external memory to recalling internal, mental experiences (Fisher, Mueller-Hirn, Carol, & Adika, 2017). It seems reasonable that memory for internal, mental events should abide by many of the same rules as memory for external events, as they both occur within specific autobiographical contexts – but empirical evidence always beats arguments that start off with "it seems reasonable." Hence, we examined two basic rules of memory for external events – memory degrades over time (Ebbinghaus, 1885/1964); preliminary testing enhances later memory (Bjork, 1988) – to see if they also held for memory of internal, mental events. The first two experiments showed that memory for earlier decisions (a) decreased with the passage of time, and (b) were improved by being tested earlier, just as were memory for external events. With this as our starting point, we then set out to examine whether the CI could be used to enhance memory for past decisions. In three laboratory experiments, participants engaged in an ethical decision-making task that they either (a) discussed aloud with another person or (b) decided alone in a think-aloud procedure. (We tape recorded the participants' overt comments and used the tape recorded statements as the criterion to assess accuracy when the participants were later asked to remember their earlier thoughts.) Across three studies, the retention intervals varied from immediate to two days. In all three studies, participants interviewed with the CI recalled considerably more of their original thoughts than those in the control condition, who were asked simply to recall their earlier decisions in as much detail as possible. Accuracy of the recalled decisions was extremely high in both conditions.

We know of at least two other studies conducted in other labs that examined the CI's ability to enhance memory for internal events, specifically for planning events and for emotions. Sooniste, Granhag, Strömwall, and Vrij (2015) instructed participants to engage in a lawful or unlawful activity – which they did not actually do – and then gave the participants 20–25 minutes to plan how they would implement the activity. (The study examined detecting deception, so some of the participants were instructed to lie about their activities and others to be truthful – but we shall not address those effects here.) The participants were then interviewed (either via a structured interview or elements within the CI: rapport, context reinstatement, report all) to describe their intentions and their mental preparations to implement the activity. Those interviewed with the CI were rated (by condition-blind raters) as providing more detailed descriptions of their intentions and planning than those interviewed with the Structured Interview – although note that some questions (how and why the intentions would be carried out) yielded no effect of interview type.

In the one other CI study on memory for internal experiences, Engelberg and Christianson (2000, Experiment 2) had participants watch a video of a highly arousing event (criminals terrorizing a person) and then rate their initial emotional reaction to the event. Two weeks later, the participants attempted to remember their earlier emotional reaction. Half of the participants were given a standard request (Unassisted Recall) to recall their original emotional reaction, and half were provided several elements of the CI (Memory-Enhancing Recall: context reinstatement, varied retrieval, close eyes instruction, social dynamics) before being asked to recall their original emotional reaction. In general, participants underestimated the magnitude of their original emotional reaction, but the underestimation was considerably lower for the Memory-Enhancing condition, i.e., when provided elements of the CI, participants' memory of their earlier emotional reaction was enhanced.

We note here that others have also developed knowledge-elicitation protocols that have been used for gathering information about people's earlier decisions. One such method, the Critical Decision Method (CDM), has been particularly effective in eliciting information about experts' decisions in naturalistic settings (see Crandall, Klein, & Hoffman, 2006, for a description of CDM, and Klein, 1998 for various implementations). The CDM procedure already contains some elements in common with the CI as described in Fisher and Geiselman (1992). We suspect that a revised CDM that incorporated some of the newer elements of the CI might yield an even more potent procedure.

Developing more effective interviewing protocols for remembering internal, mental events should have immeasurable application, given how often people think about their earlier thoughts, both for private reasons and also for high-powered investigations. It is unlikely that formal interview protocols will have much influence on one's self-reflective recollections, as these are likely to be done privately, but we can easily imagine how interviewing protocols might be used in a formal therapeutic context. Fisher and Geiselman (2010) speculated about why the CI might be valuable in such a context, but we have scant and mixed empirical evidence of the CI's therapeutic value. On the one hand, it appears to have been effective in a therapeutic session with a patient reliving an unwanted sexual advance (Shepherd, Mortimer, Turner, & Watson, 1999), but on the other hand, Ginet et al.'s (2016) car accident victims who were interviewed with the CI did not report any improved psychological well-being. We expect that the CI might make its way into more formal investigations following critical high-level decisions as exemplified by (a) military tribunals after a tactical decision that led to the loss of many soldiers, (b) legal cases after a physician's diagnosis of a patient who died, (c) chief executive officers' misguided decisions to invest millions of dollars in a failed project, (d) governmental investigations of politicians who were bribed by enemy agents to reveal top-secret information, (e) debriefing police officers after an officer-involved shooting (Geiselman, Wilson,& Artwohl, 2018), and a host of others.

Overview of Empirical Testing

In retrospect, the CI has been extremely successful in non-criminal investigations, replicating the effect in criminal investigations. Of the 24 studies described here – excluding those that examined only one component of the CI – 21 found the CI to be successful (increased quantity, at comparable or slightly higher accuracy rates than the comparison interview), two were not successful (no increase in quantity), and one showed mixed success (increase in quantity, but lowered accuracy). The three studies that were the least successful appeared to use relatively weak manipulations: In two of these, the CI was implemented as a set of pre-printed instructions and not as an interactive, face-to-face interview, and in the third study, the authors described the CI implementation as "simplified."

Perhaps more impressive than the sheer number of studies in which the CI was successful is the wide variety of to-be-recalled events: Blood donations, car accidents, conversations, health-related experiences, meetings, hostage-taking situations, and internal thoughts and emotions. The breadth of investigative domains in which the CI was successful is also reflected in the diversity across other experimental dimensions (retention interval, varying from immediate to 35 years; interviewers: student research assistants, police officers, and FLETC trainers; interviewees: community members, college students, elderly, and law enforcement officers). It would be irresponsible for us to argue, based on the studies cited here, that the CI was more potent for one of these situations than for another, as (a) the particular version of the CI that was used (specific elements incorporated) varied unsystematically across studies, (b) the comparison interview varied unsystematically across studies, and (c) in general, there were too few studies in each situation to have a reliable measure of the CI's effect in any one specific area. The global picture, however, suggests that the technique has considerable potential for many kinds of investigation.

There is always concern that artificial laboratory studies do not capture the essence of real-world investigations, and especially for highly arousing experiences. That the lab findings were replicated in field studies (car accidents: Ginet et al., 2016; robberies and other crimes: Fisher, Geiselman, & Amador, 1989; Colomb, Ginet, Wright, Demarchi & Sadler, 2013; George & Clifford, 1995) and supplemented by case studies of sexual assault (Amann, 2017; Shepherd et al., 1999) suggests that the findings are not confined to university laboratories.

Finally, and perhaps the most compelling for practitioners – but the least convincing for researchers – are the anecdotal accounts of the CI's perceived effectiveness in high-level military, hostage-taking, and security investigations. Obviously, such accounts suffer from the same limitations as all anecdotes. As such, they serve here not so much to provide scientific support for the CI's effectiveness, but rather to demonstrate its perceived utility in high-stakes investigations. Toward that goal, we provide one last real-world account, from a narcotics trafficking investigation, in which the goal was to determine the location of a narcotics operation center. Although this is, technically, a criminal investigation, one can easily imagine how zeroing in on a specific location might have many non-forensic applications, as in finding lost children and hikers, or perhaps determining an enemy's location, or a stolen or hidden or misplaced valuable object.

> My assignment as a federal investigator was to gather information about where an important narco-trafficker lived and operated from, and any activities planned for the future. As we later learned, these activities included developing future distribution routes and paramilitary style attacks against counter-narcotics investigators. I interviewed an informant who had worked with me in the past. The informant had been driven a few times to the critical location by two escorts, who discussed important details about other narco-traffickers who were visiting the same location. My informant only had limited spatial information, though, as the informant was blindfolded before each trip. Based on my understanding of the CI, I tried to recreate the context of the drive to elicit information about the escorts' conversations. I also used the CI concept of varied retrieval cues to gather information about the drive to the critical location. These (non-visual) cues targeted temporal details (the drive started in the afternoon and ended at dusk), olfactory details (smoggy odor initially, turning to cleaner air at the destination), auditory-proprioceptive details (sounds of other cars initially, but dissipated in time; road surface changed from paved to unpaved; speed of the car decreased considerably during the drive). Based on the

information I gathered from the informant, and other information gathered from another federal agency, we were able to find the target location.

As described by John Gervino, retired Special Agent with
Immigration and Customs Enforcement

Potential Costs of the CI

We have described the CI here in positive terms, as it elicits more information without reducing accuracy in comparison to other conventional interview protocols. But there are definitely costs to the CI, which make its use problematic in some situations. First, because the CI is a complex protocol and requires many on-line decisions, it likely takes longer to train investigators on the CI than to train them to conduct more conventional interviews. Second, the CI often takes longer to conduct than a more conventional interview, thereby precluding the CI's use – or at least the full version of it – if time is at a premium, as when many respondents have to be interviewed, and there is relatively little time available. In such instances, a shorter version of the CI, which does not incorporate all of the elements of the CI, may be preferable (see Davis, McMahon, & Greenwood, 2005, and Dando, Wilcock, Behnkle, & Milne, 2011 for shortened, but effective, versions of the CI; see also Brandon & Wells, this volume). Practically speaking, this probably makes use of the complete CI possible only for major investigations, when several investigators may be assigned to the case, or individual investigators have ample time to conduct complete CI interviews. We note, however, that in the context of the many person-hours that will be expended in a major investigation, the additional time to conduct a complete CI may be only a "drop in the bucket."

Third, because the CI is more respondent-centered than more traditional interviewer-centered approaches to interviewing – where the interviewer asks more directed questions about case-specific facts – it is likely that the CI will elicit, in addition to more relevant information, more irrelevant information. Such additional irrelevant information is potentially costly if analysts must sift through all of the information to decide which leads to pursue. Having said that, we suggest that it is usually better for analysts to have too much information, even if some is irrelevant, than to have too little information. Obviously, that depends on how much irrelevant information is generated. It is difficult to know in any case how much irrelevant information will be generated, but, presumably, that will depend on the respondent's knowledge of the investigative domain, with less irrelevant information being generated by knowledgeable respondents.

Where the CI Is Likely or Not Likely to Work Effectively

We explore here those instances in which the CI is most likely and least likely to be effective. Given the positive results across a wide array of domains, we expect the CI to be effective in almost any kind of investigative interview in which the respondent is asked to recall some prior experience, or to reveal his or her earlier thoughts or emotions about a topic. As we noted earlier, the CI is process-oriented, and so we expect the CI to be successful for any investigative interview that depends on either (a) the social dynamics between the interviewer and the respondent, (b) the memory and cognitive processes of the interviewer and the respondent, and (c) communication between the interviewer and the respondent. The topic of the to-be-recalled event should matter little, whether it is an indus-trial or vehicular accident, medical procedure, weather phenomenon, scientific expedition, military or security-related event, athletic or artistic performance, personal history, business transaction, group discussion, etc. So that we do not ignore the obvious, interviewers also need to be knowledgeable about the con-tent area of the investigation (e.g., aviation, medicine, baseball, military hardware, etc.), as merely understanding the underlying psychological processes will not provide any guidance about which specific facts to elicit (their importance to understanding the critical event), nor will it allow the interviewer to understand the respondent's use of technical language and jargon.

As a final note, the advantage conferred by conducting a CI depends on how efficiently the interviewer and respondent are functioning without explicit guidance from the CI. After all, some interviewers and respondents naturally engage effective social and cognitive principles even without formal training.

Although we expect the CI generally to be effective, we suspect that it will have reduced benefit in the following situations: (a) when the investigator needs to elicit only a limited amount of information (e.g., the investigator needs to determine only whether the perpetrator had a scar on his left forearm, or only whether the patient had taken a specific medication), and the investigator can target the requested information with a specific question. This, of course, assumes that the investigator has good metacognition and is correct in her assessment that this is the only bit of information that is required to complete the investigation; (b) when the respondent's recollection is driven mainly by the stimulus event provided (in psychology jargon, a "data-driven" process) as in asking a witness to *recognize* the perpetrator from a photograph – as opposed to *describing* the perpetrator (a "conceptually-driven" process); in general, the CI has not been effective to improve witnesses' recognizing people in photo-identification tasks (Fisher, Quigley, Brock, Chin, & Cutler, 1990) – although note that the CI did enhance people's recognizing foods eaten at an earlier meal (Fisher & Quigley, 1992); (c) when the respondent has insufficient knowledge of a technical domain and does not know which events to report, e.g., if an untrained lay person is describing his medical symptoms (swollen ankles), he may not realize, and there-fore not report, other symptoms that are medically related (e.g., itchy skin – both of which are symptoms of kidney failure); in such instances, more direct probing by a content-area expert may be required; (d) when the critical event was either not perceived or perceived very poorly or has been degraded or distorted over time or by other experiences so as to render the event irretrievable under any conditions. Whereas no interview protocol may give rise to retrieving such events, the CI instruction not to guess and permitting respondents to say "I don't know" should reduce false recollections.

Retrospective Comments on the CI Research

We were surprised to see how many recent CI studies were conducted with the original version of the CI (Geiselman et al., 1984), even though the enhanced CI (Fisher & Geiselman, 1992) had been shown many years ago to be superior to the original version (Fisher et al., 1987). Interestingly, some researchers, even though they cite Fisher and Geiselman (1992), still implemented only the four[1] mnemonics of the original CI. Unless one is conducting CI research for historical purposes, we strongly recommend that researchers use the most recent version of the CI.

In many publications, it is difficult to know exactly which elements of the CI were implemented. Sometimes, researchers cite Fisher and Geiselman (1992) as the source for how they conducted the CI, but it is obvious that they used only an unspecified subset of the elements described in Fisher and Geiselman. (This is not so much a critique of the research, as it would be almost impossible to incorporate all of the many CI elements within one interview; rather it is a critique of how the researchers report their research.) We recommend that researchers describe in each publication, even if only minimally, exactly which elements of the CI they used for the reported research project. That would allow other researchers to assess and replicate their studies, and also to shed some light on which elements of the CI are most or least effective.

The CI has often been described as a carpenter's toolbox (Fisher, Milne, & Bull, 2011), with many tools at the carpenter's disposal, and the skill of conducting the CI is to know which tools to use in any situation and how to adapt the tools for the specific case. Thus, no two CI interviews will be conducted exactly the same way, as, depending on the flow of the interview, the interviewer may opt to (a) include or exclude a CI element, (b) modify how the CI is implemented, (c) incorporate the CI element but in a different location within the interview, or (d) add an "extra-CI" technique because it is appropriate for the unique interview. As such, research on the CI is not so much an assessment of the interviewing technique that was actually used, but rather, the *training* that the interviewers received. Unless the researcher standardizes the CI's implementation, in which case it does not make effective use of the CI's inherent flexibility, the researcher is examining the effectiveness of training interviewers on the CI – which includes rules about when and how to implement the CI elements, and how doing so needs to be adapted to the unique properties of each interview.

Many CI studies have been conducted in novel settings, with different populations of respondents or with different to-be-remembered events or under various testing conditions, and found that the CI works in many contexts. Whereas such findings are satisfying – especially to us – and they have important applied value to practitioners in the targeted contexts, they are not terribly illuminating about the underlying psychological processes. Although we appreciate the importance of replication and examining the robustness of the CI, such research was probably more valuable in the 1980s and 1990s, in the CI's infancy, than it is now, in 2018. As such, we encourage researchers to take a more innovative approach, to explore and expand the CI's underlying psychological processes rather than to conduct yet more validation studies. We suggest various directions for future research below.

Future directions: We have made considerable progress in interviewing sources over the last few decades, but there is still much to be learned, in general, but also with respect to specific domains of investigation. Some lingering areas that still need guidance are:

1. The most valuable future goal, although conceptually the most difficult, is to generate new theory-based instructions to incorporate into the ever-evolving CI. The CI should not be thought of as a static procedure, as obviously we have not incorporated all of the possible memory-enhancing or reporting-enhancing techniques. The CI can always be improved by adding new techniques or refining already-existing techniques, and even, perhaps pruning away techniques that are not efficient. We invite our colleagues to generate such improvements. Below, we offer some suggestions about sub-areas that beg for new research.

2. When several respondents are available, as is often the case, should they be interviewed individually or collectively, as there is evidence both for individual interviews being superior (collaborative inhibition) and for group interviewing to be superior (collaborative facilitation: see Vredeveldt, Groen, Ampt, & van Koppen, 2017)? Are there conditions in which respondents can profitably be interviewed both as individuals and also within a group? If so, we will need guidance from the research on small group dynamics to devise interviewing principles unique to groups of respondents.

3. In many situations, people are interviewed by panels of interviewers rather than by a single interviewer. How does that change the social dynamics? To what degree do the various interviewers need to coordinate their efforts to create an efficient system?

4. Interviewers sometimes have incomplete or distorted recollections of what transpired during an interview (Köhnken et al., 1994 BIB-038). This is especially problematic when interviews are not video- or audio-recorded and we need to know what occurred within the interview. This is critical both for preserving the respondent's answers and also for improving the interviewer's techniques, or for training others to conduct effective interviewers. What guidance can we provide for interviewing the interviewers?

5. The CI has been shown to be effective when interviewing experts; however, the CI itself is not guided by any principles of expertise. Presumably the CI's ability to elicit information from experts could be improved by incorporating theoretical insights about the nature of expertise. Furthermore, the nature of expertise in one domain may differ from that in another domain. If so, then we should learn more about the nature of expertise within each domain so as to tailor the CI for a specific domain. Presumably, such domain-specific understanding will require researchers to interact more closely with knowledgeable people in each domain to learn about its unique properties.

As a final note, our experience has been that the various investigative domains (e.g., criminal, military, security, industrial and vehicular accidents) are largely independent of one another, with separate training facilities, different manuals, different personnel, different legal constraints, and, in general, different methods of conducting investigations. We suspect that their independence may hamper their learning from one another, and especially from developing techniques that are effective across domains. At some level, all investigative interviews have some, and perhaps even many, elements in common: A knowledgeable person is being interviewed by a curious, likely higher-status, person who wants to learn what the knowledgeable person knows. (Presumably, that is why the CI works, as it focuses on the general processes of eliciting information from a knowledgeable source, irrespective of the specific kind of knowledge to be gathered.) We encourage these various investigative domains to share their insights with one another, and in general to communicate more freely with the academic researchers (see Leps & Geiselman, 2014). Such interaction should benefit all concerned: Investigators can be exposed to a wider array of investigative techniques practiced by other kinds of investigators, and also to theory-guided techniques from academic researchers. In turn, academics should learn from experienced investigators who have developed unique, effective techniques. Academic researchers should avail themselves of the opportunity to test their theories in real-world situations, some of which are impossible to recreate in the laboratory. We use the present forum to promote such cross-fertilization.

Acknowledgments

Much of the research described was supported by grants from the U.S. Department of Justice (Federal Bureau of Investigation, High Value Detainee Interrogation Group (HIG)). Statements made in the present chapter reflect the authors' personal views and do not necessarily reflect the beliefs or policies of the HIG.

We are indebted to several research assistants whose dedicated work allowed us to complete many of the experiments described here: Drew Leins, Ali Mosser, Maggie Manon, Pete Molinaro, Geri Satin, Leonie Pludwinsky, Dana Hirn-Mueller, Jillian Rivard, David Raymond, Adam Adika, and Belinda Robertson.

Note

1 In the original version of the CI, two of the elements (Change Perspective, and Change Order) were listed separately. In the current accounting (Enhanced CI), these two elements are considered to be exemplars of one basic concept, Varied Retrieval.

References

Amann, W. (2017). *Cognitive interviewing brings cold case rapist to justice*. Air Force Office of Special Investigations Public Affairs. March 27, 2017. Downloaded March 12, 2018 from: https://urldefense.proofpoint.com/v2/url?u=http-3A__www.osi.af.mil_News_ Article-2DDisplay_Article_1130739_cognitive-2Dinterviewing-2Dbrings-2Dcold-2Dcase-2Drapist-2Dto-2Djustice_&d=DwIFAg&c=lhMMI368wojMYNABHh1g QQ&r=ypR12vpU5MrSJqa9GyToYg&m=MhlPSRWUD_zpt5o2Xyxv5Lg54wim zXy8iZFAFBfZijA&s=HwYkPwKdPRe6U2b0rJfoUe6KpiYOXOIYpz9b0G34h5 M&e=

Armstrong, A. M., MacDonald, A., Booth, I. W., Platts, R. G., Knibb, R. C., & Booth, D. A. (2000). Errors in memory for dietary intake and their reduction. *Applied Cognitive Psychology, 14*, 183–191.

Bjork, R. A. (1988). Retrieval practice and the maintenance of knowledge. In M. M. Gruneberg, P. E. Morris, and R. N. Sykes (Eds.), *Practical aspects of memory: Current research and issues. Vol. 1: Memory in everyday life* (pp. 396–401). New York: Wiley.

Brewer, D. D., & Garrett, S. B. (2001). Evaluation of interviewing techniques to enhance recall of sexual and drug injection partners. *Sexually Transmitted Diseases, 28*, 666–677.

Brewer, D. D., Garrett, S. B., & Kulasingam, S. (1999). Forgetting as a cause of incomplete reporting of sexual and drug injection partners. *Sexually Transmitted Diseases, 26*, 166–176.

Brock, P., Fisher, R. P., & Cutler, B. L. (1999). Examining the cognitive interview in a double-test paradigm. *Psychology, Crime & Law, 5*, 29–45.

Campos, L., & Alonso-Quecuty, M. L. (2008). Language crimes and the cognitive interview: Testing its efficacy in retrieving a conversational event. *Applied Cognitive Psychology, 22*, 1211–1227.

Chapman, A. J., & Perry, D. J. (1995). Applying the cognitive interview procedure to child and adult eyewitnesses of road accidents. *Applied Psychology: An International Review, 44*, 283–294.

Clarke, J., Prescott, K., & Milne, R. (2013). How effective is the cognitive interview when used with adults with intellectual disabilities specifically with conversation recall? *Journal of Applied Research in Intellectual Disabilities, 26*, 546–556.

Cohen, G., & Java, R. (1995). Memory for medical history: Accuracy of recall. *Applied Cognitive Psychology, 9*, 273–288.

Colomb, C., Ginet, M., Wright, D., Demarchi, S., & Sadler, C. (2013). Back to the real: Efficacy and perception of a modified cognitive interview in the field. *Applied Cognitive Psychology, 27*, 574–583.

Crandall, B., Klein, G., & Hoffman, R. R. (2006). *Working minds: A practitioner's guide to cognitive task analysis*. Cambridge, MA: MIT Press.

Dando, C. J., Wilcock, R., Behnkle, C., & Milne, R. (2011). Modifying the cognitive interview: Countenancing forensic application by enhancing practicability. *Psychology, Crime & Law, 17*, 491–511.

Davis, M. R., McMahon, M., & Greenwood, K. M. (2005). The efficacy of mnemonic components of the cognitive interview: Towards a shortened variant for time-critical investigations. *Applied Cognitive Psychology, 19,* 75–93.

Dornburg, C. C., & McDaniel, M. A. (2006). The cognitive interview enhances long-term free recall of older adults. *Psychology and Aging, 21,* 196–200.

Ebbinghaus, H. (1964). *Memory: A contribution to experimental psychology.* New York: Dover (Original work published in 1885).

Engelberg, E., & Christianson, S.-Ä (2000). Recall of unpleasant emotion using memory-enhancing principles. *Psychology, Crime & Law, 6,* 99–112.

Fisher, R. P., & Castano, N. (2017). The effectiveness of the cognitive interview in recalling group decision making. Unpublished manuscript, Florida International University, North Miami, FL.

Fisher, R. P., & Geiselman, R. E. (1992). *Memory-enhancing techniques in investigative interviewing: The cognitive interview.* Springfield, IL: Charles C. Thomas.

Fisher, R. P., & Geiselman, R. E. (2010). The cognitive interview method of conducting police interviews: Eliciting extensive information and promoting therapeutic jurisprudence. *International Journal of Law and Psychiatry, 33,* 321–328.

Fisher, R. P., & Geiselman, R. E. (2018). Investigative interviewing. In V. B. Van Hasselt & M. L. Bourke (Eds.), *Handbook of behavioral criminology* (pp. 451–465). Cham, Switzerland: Springer.

Fisher, R. P., & Quigley, K. L. (1992). Applying cognitive theory in public health investigations: Enhancing food recall with the cognitive interview. In J. Tanur (Ed.), *Questions about questions: Inquiries into the cognitive bases of surveys* (pp. 154–169). New York: Russell Sage Foundation.

Fisher, R. P., Geiselman, R. E., Raymond, D. S., Jurkevich, L. M., & Warhaftig, M. L. (1987). Enhancing enhanced eyewitness memory: Refining the cognitive interview. *Journal of Police Science and Administration, 15,* 291–297.

Fisher, R. P., Geiselman, R. E., & Amador, M. (1989). Field test of the cognitive interview: Enhancing the recollection of actual victims and witnesses of crime. *Journal of Applied Psychology, 74,* 722–727.

Fisher, R. P., Quigley, K. L., Brock, P., Chin, D., & Cutler, B. L. (1990). The effectiveness of the cognitive interview in description and identification tasks. Paper presented at the American Psychology-Law Society, Williamsburgh, VA.

Fisher, R. P., Falkner, K. L., Trevisan, M., & McCauley, M. R. (2000). Adapting the cognitive interview to enhance long-term (35 years) recall of physical activities. *Journal of Applied Psychology, 85,* 180–189.

Fisher, R. P., Milne, R., & Bull, R. (2011). Interviewing cooperative witnesses. *Currrent Directions in Psychological Science, 20,* 16–19.

Fisher, R. P., Mueller-Hirn, D., Carol, R., & Adika, A. (2017). What was I thinking about? Adapting the cognitive interview to remember earlier thoughts. Applied Cognition and the cognitive interview: A conference in honor of Ron Fisher. North Miami, FL.

Geiselman, R. E., Fisher, R. P., Firstenberg, I., Hutton, L. A., Sullivan, S. J., Avetissian, I. V., & Prosk, A. L. (1984). Enhancement of eyewitness memory: An empirical evaluation of the cognitive interview. *Journal of Police Science and Administration, 12,* 74–80.

Geiselman, R. E., Wilson, J. F., & Artwohl, A. (2018). Conducting the investigative interview. In D. L. Ross & B. M. Vilke (Eds.), *Guidelines for investigating officer-involved shootings, arrest-related deaths, and deaths in custody* (pp. 285–304). New York: Routledge.

George, R. C., & Clifford, B. R. (1995). The cognitive interview: Does it work? In G. Davies, S. Lloyd-Bostock, M. McMurran, & C. Wilson (Eds.), *Psychology, law, and criminal justice: International developments in research and practice* (pp. 146–154). New York: Walter de Gruyter.

Ginet, M., & Verkampt, F. (2007). The cognitive interview: Is its benefit affected by the level of witness emotion? *Memory, 15,* 450–464.

Ginet, M., Teissedre, F., Verkampt, F., & Fisher, R. (2016). When the criminal event is stressful: The benefit of the cognitive interview to improve the recall and the well-being of victims of road traffic accidents. European Association of Psychology and Law, 26th Annual Conference, Toulouse, France.

Hope, L., Mullis, R., & Gabbert, F. (2013). Who? What? When? Using a timeline technique to facilitate recall of a complex event. *Journal of Applied Research in Memory and Cognition, 2,* 20–24.

Hornstein, S. L., Brown, A. S., & Mulligan, N. W. (2003). Long-term flashbulb memory for learning of Princess Diana's death. *Memory, 11,* 293–306.

Klein, G. (1998). *Sources of power.* Cambridge, MA: MIT Press.

Köhnken, G., Thürer, C., & Zoberbier, D. (1994). The cognitive interview: Are the interviewers' memories enhanced, too? *Applied Cognitive Psychology, 8,* 13–24.

Köhnken, G., Milne, R., Memon, A., & Bull, R. (1999). A meta-analysis on the effects of the cognitive interview. *Psychology, Crime & Law, 5,* 3–27.

Leal, S., Vrij, A., Warmelink, L., Vernham, Z., & Fisher, R. P. (2015). You cannot hide your telephone lies: Providing a model statement as an aid to detect deception in insurance telephone calls. *Legal and Criminological Psychology, 20,* 129–146.

Leins, D., Fisher, R. P., Pludwinsky, L., Robertson, B., & Mueller, D. H. (2014). Interview protocols to facilitate human intelligence sources' recollections of meetings. *Applied Cognitive Psychology,* 28, 926–935.

Leps, C. & Geiselman, R. E. (2014). An interview protocol of experienced human intelligence collectors and counterintelligence agents: Implications for research. *American Journal of Forensic Psychology, 32,* 5–24.

MacLean, C. L., Stinson, V., Kelloway, E. K., & Fisher, R. P. (2011). Improving workplace incident investigations by enhancing memory recall. *International Journal of Workplace Health Management, 4,* 257–273.

Mantwill, M., Köhnken, G., & Aschermann, E. (1995). Effects of the cognitive interview on the recall of familiar and unfamiliar events. *Journal of Applied Psychology, 80,* 68–78.

Memon, A., Meissner, C. A., & Fraser, J. (2010). The cognitive interview: A meta-analytic review and study space analysis of the past 25 years. *Psychology, Public Policy, and Law, 16,* 340–372.

Milne, R., & Bull, R. (2002). Back to basics: A componential analysis of the original cognitive interview mnemonics with three age groups. *Applied Cognitive Psychology, 16,* 743–753.

Milne, R., Clare, I. C. H., & Bull, R. (1999). Using the cognitive interview with adults with mild learning disabilities. *Psychology, Crime & Law, 5,* 81–99.

Mosser, A., Fisher, R. P., Molinaro, P., Satin, G., & Manon, M. (2016). Train-the-trainer: Training law enforcement investigators in the CI. Paper presented at the meeting of the American Psychology-Law Society. Atlanta.

Nisbett, R. E., & Wilson, T. D. (1977). Telling more than we can know: Verbal reports on mental processes. *Psychological Review, 84,* 231–259.

Peace, K. A., & Porter, S. (2004). A longitudinal investigation of the reliability of memories for trauma and other emotional experiences. *Applied Cognitive Psychology, 18,* 1143–1159.

Prescott, K., Milne, R., & Clarke, J (2011). How effective is the enhanced cognitive interview when aiding recall retrieval of older adults including memory for conversations? *Journal of Investigative Psychology and Offender Profiling, 8,* 257–270.

Rivard, J. R., Fisher, R. P., Robertson, B., & Mueller, D. H. (2014). Testing the cognitive interview with professional interviewers: Enhancing recall of specific details of recurring events. *Applied Cognitive Psychology, 28,* 917–925.

Shepherd, E., Mortimer, A., Turner, V., & Watson, J. (1999). Spaced cognitive interviewing: Facilitating therapeutic and forensic narration of traumatic memories. *Psychology, Crime & Law, 5,* 117–143.

Sooniste, T., Granhag, P.-A., Strömwall, L., & Vrij, A. (2015). Statements about true and false intentions: Using the cognitive interview to magnify the differences. *Scandinavian Journal of Psychology, 56,* 371–378.

van der Kolk, B. (1997). Traumatic memories. In P. S. Applebaum, L. A. Uyehara, & M. R. Elin (Eds.), *Trauma and memory* (pp. 243–260). New York: Oxford University Press.

Vredeveldt, A., Groen, R. N., Ampt, J. E., & van Koppen, P. (2017). When discussion between eyewitnesses helps memory. *Legal and Criminological Psychology, 22,* 242–259.

Yuille, J. C., Hunter, R., Joffe, R., & Zaparniuk, J. (1993). Interviewing children in sexual abuse cases. In G. S. Goodman and B. L. Bottoms (Eds.), *Child victims, child witnesses: Understanding and improving testimony* (pp. 95–115). New York: Guilford Press.

2

THE IMPACT OF THE COGNITIVE INTERVIEW IN THE UK AND RECENT RESEARCH IN PORTUGAL

Ray Bull, Rui Paulo, and Pedro Albuquerque

This chapter briefly overviews some early/foundational research on the Cognitive Interview (CI) involving the first author – RB. It then describes our very recent research conducted in Portugal. Crucially, it also mentions some real-world impacts of the cognitive interview.

Even though, with several colleagues, in the 1990s the first author of the current chapter (i.e., RB) published a number of studies on the Cognitive Interview, he has repeatedly failed to recall when he first met Ronald P. Fisher many years ago. However, RB does remember a few things about when he first met Ron's CI co-originator – Ed Geiselman. This was at a conference in the USA. Being then 'early career' and taking his mentor's advice, RB sat at the back so as not to disturb the presenters by his reading of journal articles if their presentation happened to be boring. Ed began to present and after a while said 'the CI improved recall by around 40%'. RB had never heard of anything in the whole of psychology that had been associated with a 40 per cent improvement! So he listened to the rest of this 'early/decades ago' presentation and then read the few publications available at that time on the CI – all, of course, written by Ron and Ed. As with almost all research, their studies/experiments were not perfect, and so with others in England RB successfully applied for funding to conduct in the early/mid 1990s several better experiments expecting to find the claimed very large CI effect to be spurious. (For more on this see later in this chapter.)

Later on RB did met Ron and was told by Ron that in the USA few, if any, investigative agencies/police seemed interested in the CI in the late 1980s and early 1990s. But in England RB thought that the police could possibly be interested, because in 1992 nationally they had just developed (with the help of psychologists/psychology) the 'PEACE' model of investigative interviewing that could incorporate the CI procedures/techniques.

The (audio) taping of interviews with suspects became common practice in England and Wales in 1986. Research on interviews conducted soon after 1986 revealed a lack of interviewer skills (for an overview of this research see Milne & Bull, 1999) and therefore the national Association of Chiefs of Police and the relevant government ministry decided to improve the training that interviewers received. A working party of experienced detectives was set up in 1990 to develop training and principles of interviewing. While these detectives were having their working party meetings the senior London police officer Tom Williamson convened a different small working party of detectives and psychologists (including Eric Shepherd, Stephen Moston, and RB) that produced in 1991 an (unpublished) overview of aspects of psychology that might be useful to the improving of such interviewing. This overview was made available to the national team of detectives that was developing PEACE. Once that team of detectives had drafted their guidance documents they sent drafts of these to RB asking if they had 'got the psychology correct'? They indeed had. Indeed, due to the fact that these experienced detectives had decided to base their recommendations on psychology, what they were advocating could incorporate the CI because the CI is also based on psychology (for inclusion of the CI within the PEACE approach see Milne & Bull, 1999).

Thus, RB invited Ron to present a one-day workshop at his university in England. When advertised, that day soon sold out – and so another was added on the next day, which also sold out. Ron kindly invited RB to assist him with this first-ever CI workshop in the UK and thus RB 'first-hand' learned how to conduct a CI properly.

Early Research on the CI

One issue that blights many scientific studies involving humans rather than, for example, chemicals is that whichever part of an experiment human beings participate in they bring unknown, uncontrolled factors to the study. For example, in Ron and Ed's early studies (for an overview of these see Milne & Bull, 1999) some of the participant interviewers were trained by Ron and Ed in the original CI techniques whereas other participant interviewers received no training (Geiselman, Fisher, MacKinnon, & Holland, 1985, 1986). Thus, these CI interviewers, because they had received greater attention from the researchers (and for other reasons) may have been more motivated to gather accounts from the interviewees compared to those interviewers who had not received any training. This motivation, RB thought, could at least in part explain why their interviewees produced more information independent of any CI effect. (As with any pioneering research, with the benefit of hindsight such constructive criticisms can be made of Ron and Ed's early work.)

Indeed, Ed and Ron realized from their analyses of the interviews in the pioneering 1980s studies that although the 'original' CI was based on cognitive psychology (hence the 'cognitive interview'), what was lacking in such interviews, on the part of the interviewers, were skills found to be important by research within social psychology (Milne & Bull, 1999; Walsh & Bull, 2012a). Therefore in their seminal 1992 book (Fisher & Geiselman, 1992) they proposed (what others refer to as) the 'enhanced cognitive interview' that included some aspects of these social/communication skills.

In the light of the possibility that Ron and Ed's findings in the 1980s might have been artefactual, in collaboration with my then Portsmouth colleague Günter Köhnken and with Amina Memon from nearby Southampton University, we successfully applied to a UK research council for funding to conduct several studies of the CI in which our designs sought to improve upon Ron and Ed's pioneering studies (for example, by training all of the interviewers – some of them in the CI and others to conduct a comparison interview that did not contain the original CI mnemonics – this we called an 'SI' for 'Structured Interview,' which was in line with recommendations in the 1992 *Memorandum of good practice* (see below). The results of our teamwork are available in 15 publications that are provided in the reference list – below is a brief mention of some of what we found.

However, before that should be mentioned a UK study conducted in 1991 (see Clifford & George, 1996) that involved a (rather small) sample of experienced police officers interviewing real-life witnesses to/victims of crime. Some of the interviewers were for the purposes of the study trained in the enhanced CI. The effect of the training was compared with a (control) group of police (in a before/after design). Both the nature of the interviewers' behaviour (number, rate, and type of questions asked) and the amounts of relevant information elicited were assessed. It was found that the interview behaviour of the CI-trained officers improved (but that of the control group did not) and that the CI interviews elicited more information.

In our research in the early 1990s we found (details are available in the relevant publications) that

1. An appropriate version of the CI does assist children.
2. A modified version of the CI can help adults and children with learning disabilities.
3. Some of the CI techniques are more effective than others.
4. Using the CI can reduce the negative effects of subsequently asked suggestive questions.
5. Training police officers to use the CI also needs to address their ingrained 'bad habits'.

The First Meta-Analysis of CI Studies

In 1999 we published what was the first meta-analysis of CI studies (Köhnken, Milne, Memon, & Bull, 1999). The database comprised 42 studies with 55 individual comparisons involving nearly 2,500 interviewees. A strong overall effect was found for the increase in correctly recalled details (41 per cent) with the Cognitive Interview compared to a control interview ($d = 0.87$). The overall effect for the increase in incorrect details (25 per cent) was also significant for the Cognitive Interview ($d = 0.28$). However, the accuracy rates (proportion of correct details relative to the total amount of details reported) were almost identical in both types of interview (85 per cent for the Cognitive Interview and 82 per cent for Standard Interviews). Taking methodological factors into consideration, it was found that effect sizes for correct details were larger if staged events were used as the to-be-remembered episode (as compared to video films) and if the interviewees actively participated in the event.

Official Government Guidance in England and Wales

In 1990, RB was commissioned by the Government in England and Wales to draft what became the 1992 *Memorandum of good practice on video recorded interviews with child witnesses for criminal proceedings.* The main purpose of this groundbreaking guidance document was to provide real-world investigative/forensic interviewers with an evidence/research-based set of guidelines. At that time there was no or almost no published work on the possible benefits of the CI with children and thus it was not possible to recommend the CI in that document. However, when the government commissioned a team led by Graham Davies at Leicester University to write guidance on how to achieve best evidence from vulnerable witnesses in the year 2000, RB wrote the chapter giving guidance on how to interview vulnerable people. In this, in light of the then available research RB was able to recommend use of the CI by those who had received appropriate training. This 2002 document, *Achieving best evidence in criminal proceedings: Guidance on interviewing victims and witnesses,* has been updated a few times in the intervening 15 years and the CI remains recommended within it. (See www.cps.gov.uk/publications/docs/best_evidence_in_criminal_proceedings.pdf.)

Having, along with others, made contributions to best practice for interviewing victims and witnesses, RB then turned his attention to the under-researched topic of how best to gather information from people suspected of crime/wrongdoing. (Some of this is summarized in Bull, 2013, 2014; Dando & Bull, 2011; Dando, Bull, Ormerod, & Sandham, 2015; Walsh & Bull, 2010; 2012a, 2012b, 2015.)

Some Real-World Cases in the UK

Having published our experimental studies, which demonstrated that Ron and Ed were correct to assert that the CI was indeed noticeably effective, a number of developments occurred in the UK. For example, (i) national training of police gave prominence to the CI as part of the (1992) PEACE approach and (ii) in 1997

RB was commissioned to write a report on the CI and its effectiveness that was used in a case before the national Court of Appeal (i.e., *R v. Hill*, 1995) in which a person now claiming to have committed a murder (rather than the man in prison for it) had recently been interviewed using the CI (within the PEACE approach). The man in prison was released.

With regard to vulnerable interviewees, this 'PEACE + CI' approach seems to make good sense. For example, in the early 1990s, RB and Becky Milne were asked by a major police force to assist them in their interviewing of residents in a home for vulnerable adults who may have been physically abused by the owners/directors of that residence. Within this investigation first of all the police asked a clinical/forensic psychologist to advise them as to which of the residents would likely be able to communicate in an investigative interview setting. The police then interviewed the most likely person and immediately couriered by police motorcycle that video recorded interview to the University of Portsmouth where we worked. Later on that same day we sent feedback on the quality of the interviewing (including aspects of the CI) to the investigative team who did their best to take it on board when interviewing another resident the next day. Again that video recording was promptly sent to us for comment – and so on. The outcome of this investigation was that the director of the care home was sent to prison and others were implicated.

In the UK most investigative psychologists agree that an important aspect of their role is to convey to investigators/interviewers in an appropriate/comprehensible way the findings of relevant research. Over the last 45 years (since RB started as a university employee working with the police) this has become 'custom and practice' so that it is almost always the case that a psychologist does not conduct the investigative interviews. Some 'police approved' psychologists are 'on hand' to advise on interviews but they very rarely 'sit in' during the actual interviews (which are by law electronically recorded).

Just under 15 years ago RB received a telephone call from a Senior Investigative Officer (SIO) within the London Metropolitan Police Service. The SIO asked RB to travel to London to assist with the interviewing of a woman who had been raped some days prior. In her earlier police interview she had recalled rather little of the rape, saying to the police that she did not wish to recall much detail because she feared that later in court she might be cross-examined on any (even minor) errors that she might make. The SIO wanted (with her agreement) a further interview to take place to obtain as much detail as possible (partly because the rapist may also have raped at least one other woman). The SIO asked RB, as a 'police recognized' psychologist, to have an extensive chat with the female officer selected (with some guidance comments from RB) for this further interview about 'advanced' versions of the PEACE model within which RB included a lot on the CI. The interviewee was fully aware of RB's role and agreed that at moments that the interviewer or interviewee wished there would be pauses in the interview while RB (who was observing the interview in an adjacent room through a one-way mirror) offered further advice to the interviewer. The outcome was that the interviewee provided a lot of detailed information. She also thanked the interviewer and RB, later thanking RB again in an item in a magazine. In 2005 the small team of police officers who dealt sensitively with this case and RB at a ceremony received 'commendations', RB's being for 'Innovation and professionalism while assisting a complex rape investigation which supported a successful prosecution'.

Very Recent Studies of the CI in Portugal

Having 'moved on' to researching/writing about how to effectively yet ethically interview suspects from research on improving the interviewing of witnesses/victims (Bull, 2010), it was with considerable interest to RB to be approached by a student in Portugal who was thinking about conducting doctoral research on the CI in Portugal. This bright young man successfully applied in his country for a fully funded Ph.D. studentship that involved regular visits to Portsmouth University, England to be supervised by RB. Aided by Becky Milne, we assisted him to grasp a deep understanding of the CI. Then, together with his main supervisor in Portugal, RB helped him design, conduct, analyse, write up, and publish several studies that brought new techniques to be part of the CI. These new contributions are in the spirit always advocated by Ronald P. Fisher who has successfully and repeatedly made the point that the constantly-evolving CI should be seen as a toolbox from which techniques are chosen for use as appropriate. Both Ronald P. Fisher and Ed Geiselman have always stressed that what they innovatively developed can be enhanced by further research. Generously and appropriately they did not seek to obtain copyright or in any other way prevent what they produced via research (often funded by the taxpayer) from being further developed by others in a variety of countries. Our initial studies conducted in Portugal required no revising of the Cognitive Interview – other than, of course, translating its instructions (Paulo, Albuquerque, & Bull, 2013).

In 2017, the studies conducted in Portugal resulted in a Ph.D. successfully being defended in public. (In Portugal successful Ph.D.s receive one of three grades and this outstanding thesis received the highest grade.) In our first study (Paulo, Albuquerque, Saraiva, & Bull, 2015), participants watched a recording of a (mock) robbery and were interviewed with either the (new) Portuguese version of the Enhanced Cognitive Interview (ECI) or a Structured Interview (SI). (In our 1999 meta-analysis it was found that effect sizes for correct details were larger if staged events were used as the to-be-remembered episode (as compared to video films) and if the interviewees actively participated in the event, so using in our Portugal studies a video recording might underestimate any CI effect.) Participants interviewed with the ECI provided more information without compromising accuracy, particularly in free recall. A higher perception of interview appropriateness (i.e., how witnesses evaluated the appropriateness of the procedure used) was associated with more detailed recall.

ECI research has mainly focused on increasing report size and has somewhat overlooked how to improve or evaluate report accuracy. Our second ECI study (Paulo, Albuquerque, & Bull, 2016a) seems to be the first that has evaluated if witnesses' spontaneous verbal expressions of uncertainty while recalling (e.g. saying 'I think', 'maybe', 'I believe', etc.) are associated with the accuracy of the directly associated information being recalled. Such spontaneous provision (while recalling) of being uncertain was related to lower accuracy of what was being recalled at that time in the interview. Also, participants' self-ratings of motivation were significantly associated with recall accuracy. In a follow-up study (Paulo, Albuquerque, & Bull, 2017) we also found that information which interviewees recalled with high certainty was more accurate. In sum, we found participants to be capable of monitoring their interview recall in a holistic and time-saving manner.

In another study (Paulo, Albuquerque, & Bull, 2016b), we focused on increasing CI recall with a new strategy, category clustering recall (CCR). This recall strategy consists in asking witnesses to recall everything they can remember about the crime episode one more time, but this time witnesses are asked to organize their recall into broad information categories. Witnesses to a (video-recorded mock) crime were interviewed with either (i) the ECI; (ii) a revised enhanced cognitive interview (RECIa) – using CCR instead of the change order mnemonic during the second recall; or (iii) another revised enhanced cognitive interview (RECIb) – also with CCR but conjunctly used with 'eye closure' and additional open-ended follow-up questions. Participants interviewed with CCR (RECIa and RECIb) produced more information without compromising accuracy. Eye closure and additional open-ended follow-up questions did not further enhance recall. We then tested if this technique could, in some situations, be also more effective than witness-compatible questioning (Paulo, Albuquerque, Vitorino, & Bull, 2017). We found participants who were interviewed with CCR were able to recall a higher number of correct details without compromising report accuracy. Thus, CCR might be a very important technique for investigative professionals, allowing the interviewer to obtain more correct information without additional questioning.

'Improper' Use of the CI?

A 'Very Early' Field Study

In the early 1990s having found that our training of graduate students was successful in conducting a CI (or a comparison interview that did not contain the original CI mnemonics – the SI), we decided to see if this CI training (which had led to increased recall) would benefit police interviewers (Memon, Holley, Milne, Köhnken, & Bull, 1994; Memon, Bull, & Smith, 1995). With the assistance of a police organization in England we staged what looked like an armed robbery in the car park of the training school. Witnesses (clerical staff and probationers – new police recruits in the first weeks of their career in the force) were gathered prior to the event and located at various points in the vicinity. A hidden camera recorded the entire event which began with two 'security guards' arriving in a car to drop off some cash. Two armed robbers leapt out of a van and ambushed them. A 'gardener' came to the assistance of the security guards and was shot. A 'get-away car' picked up the robbers. The incident lasted two minutes. Witnesses were interviewed a few hours after the event. They were asked to discuss the event with no one. The interviewers in this study were 33 police officers attending various training courses at the training school during 1992. They had an average of ten years' experience in the force. Prior to the study they had not received any 'formal' training regarding witness interviewing.

The training session given for the purposes of this study lasted for approximately four hours and was similar to that which we had successfully used with graduate interviewers. All trainees were first of all given a brief lecture on the importance of interviewing and told that the focus of the day was going to be on witness interviews. This involved general principles of communication and elicited examples of good and bad questioning techniques from the group. Open questions were described as the most reliable and leading questions the least reliable. The effects of different types of questions were discussed. After a short break the group was randomly divided into two. One group received training in what was referred to as 'investigative' techniques (the SI – see above) and the other in the extra CI techniques. This was followed by role-plays. Due to time constraints, officers had the opportunity to take part in only one role-play. The training session ended with officers receiving handouts summarizing all the information and a one page summary sheet for them to take into the interview.

After lunch, each officer individually interviewed a witness and made it clear to the witness that they had no information other than that a robbery had taken place. There were no particular constraints placed on the length of the interviews. The mean length of CI interviews was 36.02 minutes and the SI interviews 36.10 minutes. Each interview was audio-recorded.

For the free recall phase there were no significant differences for total correct information (CI: mean = 53.89; and SI: mean = 52.33), for errors (CI: mean = 3.73; SI: mean = 3.61), for suppositions (CI: mean = 6.80; SI: mean = 5.66), or for accuracy (CI: mean = 0.86; SI: mean = 0.89). For the questioning phase there also were no significant differences in total correct information, errors or suppositions.

The following CI techniques were used in some of the cognitive interviews: context reinstatement (100 per cent of the interviews), report everything (43 per cent), witness compatible questioning (10 per cent), transfer of control (10 per cent), focused retrieval (70 per cent), change perspective (55 per cent), and change order (18 per cent). Some of these techniques were also applied by the SI interviewers (e.g., context reinstatement 26 per cent, report everything 48 per cent). This suggests that some of the CI techniques were already part of standard practice.

In the study, an expert on the CI examined each application of the three most frequently used techniques and rated them on a seven-point scale for: (1) clarity of each instruction; and (2) appropriate use of the technique (with 1 = very clear/appropriate use and 7 = not at all clear/inappropriate use). The mean ratings for the clarity and appropriate use of the context technique were 3.65 and 4.50; for the change perspective technique were 3.11 and 3.33; and use of focused techniques were 3.42 and 3.57. Thus, these instructions were at best moderately clear and were not always used appropriately. Indeed, some of the CI-trained police were able to conduct a CI but many of them were not.

That the CI-trained interviewers did not use all of the CI techniques covered in the training (unlike our graduate student interviewers in our other studies) and when they did employ them did not use them properly could explain why we found no differences in between the CI and SI groups in what the witnesses remembered. This study was one of the first to assist UK police to realize (i) that for training to be effective it needs to take a large number of factors into account and (ii) that not all police officers can become good interviewers (for more on this see Griffiths & Milne, 2006).

Change Perspective

One of the original mnemonics included within the CI since the 1980s has been the 'change perspective' instruction. Although in and of itself this instruction (when properly used) rarely provides a lot of extra information (Milne & Bull, 2002), it can sometimes gather information of investigative relevance. However, police interviewers rarely use it (Dando, Wilcock, Milne, & Henry, 2009), one possible reason being that much of the training in the CI advocates that the witness/victim now try to recall what another person present saw – this can potentially be criticized by lawyers (Milne & Bull, 1999). Instead, it is better to assist the interviewee to change perspective 'within themselves' – for example, if the witness while inside a bank experienced an armed robbery and thus recalled the actual robbery from an emotional/frightened perspective, she/he could now (i.e., late on in the interview) be asked to recall what she saw inside and outside the bank before she realized that a robbery was taking place (i.e., from a more relaxed perspective) (Paulo, Albuquerque, & Bull, 2016a).

Remembering when RB First Met Ron

To try to help RB to recall his first 1980s meeting with Ronald P. Fisher he used the 'original' mnemonic CI techniques. He started with the 'context reinstatement' but the problem with this was that RB couldn't recall the context in which he and Ron had first met! Then RB realized that at their first meeting there was some indeed visual context – which was Ron himself! So RB found on the internet a photo of Professor Ronald P. Fisher to provide (somewhat changed by the passage of time?) possible visual context reinstatement. Unfortunately, the correct photo of Ron did not help to recall that first meeting. So RB then tried the other three of the 'original' four CI mnemonic techniques – change order, change perspective, recall everything – but still failed to recall when he first met Ron because these essential techniques could not work due to RB not being able to recall anything at all about this event.

A Worldwide Influence

Not only the current chapter but also other chapters in this book testify to the importance of the CI and its seminal role in the shift towards effective and ethical investigative interviewing. Furthermore, in light of psychological research such as that described above, a growing number of countries/organizations have decided to adopt the CI and the PEACE model of investigative interviewing. Indeed, recently in 2016 the United Nations' 'Special Rapporteur on torture and other cruel, inhuman or degrading treatment or punishment' (Juan E. Mendez) submitted his report that was then transmitted by the UN Secretary-General to the UN General Assembly. In this publicly available report (available at https://digitallibrary.un.org/record/839995/files/A_71_298-EN.pdf) its summary stated that

> The Special Rapporteur…advocates the development of a universal protocol identifying a set of standards for non-coercive interviewing methods and procedural safeguards that ought, as a matter of law and policy, to be applied at a minimum to all interviews by law enforcement officials, military and intelligence personnel and other bodies with investigative mandates.

When mentioning this 'universal protocol' the UN Special Rapporteur noted that

> Encouragingly, some States have moved away from accusatorial, manipulative and confession-driven interviewing models with a view to increasing accurate and reliable information and minimizing the risks of unreliable information and miscarriages of justice.

And that

> The essence of an alternative information-gathering model was first captured by the PEACE model of interviewing adopted in 1992 in England and Wales . . . investigative interviewing can provide positive guidance for the protocol.

Furthermore the Special Rapporteur stated that

> investigative interviewing . . . comprises a number of essential elements that
> are key to the prevention of mistreatment and coercion and help to guar-
> antee effectiveness. Interviewers must, in particular, seek to obtain accurate
> and reliable information in the pursuit of truth; gather all available evidence
> pertinent to a case before beginning interviews; prepare and plan interviews
> based on that evidence; maintain a professional, fair and respectful attitude
> during questioning; establish and maintain a rapport with the interviewee;
> allow the interviewee to give his or her free and uninterrupted account of
> the events; use open-ended questions and active listening; scrutinize the
> interviewee's account and analyse the information obtained against previ-
> ously available information or evidence; and evaluate each interview with a
> view to learning and developing additional skills.

In our opinion the Special Rapporteur has recommended to the United Nations a
model of interviewing (replacing 'interrogation') that is firmly based on the available research evidence largely derived from psychological research such as that on
the PEACE method and the CI.

Closing Comment

Here in the UK all universities' disciplines/departments (e.g., psychology) are
assessed every five years in a national exercise that is crucially important regarding
funding in the ensuing five years. A main aspect of this assessment is the quality
of the research conducted as evidenced by articles in peer-reviewed journals. In
these crucial assessments the 'impact' on the 'real world' of the published research
is also considered important, being defined as 'an effect on, change or benefit to
the economy, society, culture, public policy or services, health, the environment or
quality of life, beyond academia'. Clearly, research on the cognitive interview has
had and continues to have this type of impact – due to the pioneering work of
Ronald P. Fisher and Ed Geiselman.

References

Bull, R. (2010). The investigative interviewing of children and other vulnerable
    witnesses: Psychological research and working/professional practice. *Legal and
    Criminological Psychology*, *15*, 5–23.
Bull, R. (2013). What is 'believed' or actually 'known' about characteristics that may con-
    tribute to being a good/effective interviewer? *Investigative Interviewing: Research and
    Practice*, *5*, 128–143.
Bull, R. (2014). When in interviews to disclose information to suspects and to challenge
    them? In R. Bull (Ed.), *Investigative interviewing* (pp. 167–181). New York: Springer.

Clifford, B., & George, R. (1996). A field investigation of training in three methods of witness/victim investigative interviewing. *Psychology, Crime & Law, 2,* 241–248.

Dando, C., & Bull, R. (2011). Maximising opportunities to detect verbal deception: Training police officers to interview tactically. *Journal of Investigative Psychology and Offender Profiling, 8,* 189–202.

Dando, C., Wilcock, R., Milne, R., & Henry, L. (2009). A modified cognitive interview procedure for frontline police investigators. *Applied Cognitive Psychology, 23,* 698–716.

Dando, C., Bull, R., Ormerod, T., & Sandham, A. (2015). Helping to sort the liars from the truth-tellers: The gradual revelation of information during investigative interviews. *Legal and Criminological Psychology, 20,* 114–128.

Fisher, R. P., & Geiselman, R. E. (1992). *Memory-enhancing techniques in investigative interviewing: The cognitive interview.* Springfield, IL: Charles C. Thomas.

Geiselman, E., Fisher, R., MacKinnon, D., & Holland, H. (1985). Eyewitness memory enhancement in the police interview: Cognitive retrieval mnemonics versus hypnosis. *Journal of Applied Psychology, 70,* 401–412.

Geiselman, E., Fisher, R., MacKinnon, D., & Holland, H. (1986). Enhancement of eyewitness memory with the cognitive interview. *American Journal of Psychology, 99,* 385–401.

Griffiths, A., & Milne, R. (2006). Will it all end in tiers? In T. Williamson (Ed.), *Investigative interviewing: Research rights and regulation* (pp. 167–189). Cullompton: Willan.

Köhnken, G., Milne, R., Memon, A., & Bull, R. (1999). The cognitive interview: A meta-analysis. *Psychology, Crime & Law, 5,* 3–28.

Memon, A., Bull, R., & Smith, M. (1995). Improving the quality of the police interview: Can training in the use of cognitive techniques help? *Policing and Society, 5,* 53–68.

Milne, R., & Bull, R. (1996). Interviewing children with mild learning disability with the cognitive interview. In N. Clark and G. Stephenson (Eds.), *Investigative and forensic decision making* (pp. 44–51). Leicester: British Psychological Society.

Milne, R., & Bull, R. (2002). Back to basics: A componential analysis of the cognitive interview. *Applied Cognitive Psychology, 16,* 743–753.

Paulo, R., Albuquerque, P., & Bull, R. (2013). The enhanced cognitive interview: Towards a better use and understanding of this procedure. *International Journal of Police Science and Management, 15,* 190–199.

Paulo, R., Albuquerque, P., Saraiva, M., & Bull, R. (2015). The enhanced cognitive interview: Testing appropriateness perception, memory capacity, and estimate relation with rapport quality. *Applied Cognitive Psychology, 29,* 536–543.

Paulo, R., Albuquerque, P., & Bull, R. (2016a). The enhanced cognitive interview: Expressions of uncertainty, motivation and its relation with report accuracy. *Psychology, Crime & Law, 22,* 366–381.

Paulo, R., Albuquerque, P., & Bull, R. (2016b). Improving the enhanced cognitive interview with a new interview strategy: Category clustering recall. *Applied Cognitive Psychology, 30,* 775–784.

Paulo, R., Albuquerque, P., & Bull, R. (2017). Witnesses' verbal evaluation of certainty and uncertainty and its relationship with report accuracy. Manuscript submitted for publication.

Paulo, R., Albuquerque, P., Vitorino, F., & Bull, R. (2017). Enhancing the cognitive interview with an alternative procedure to witness-compatible questioning: Category clustering recall. *Psychology, Crime & Law, 23,* 967–982.

Walsh, D., & Bull, R. (2010). What really is effective in interviews with suspects? A study comparing interview skills against interview outcomes. *Legal and Criminological Psychology, 15,* 305–321.

Walsh, D., & Bull, R. (2012a). Examining rapport in investigative interviews with suspects: Does its building and maintenance work? *Journal of Police and Criminal Psychology, 27,* 73–84.

Walsh, D., & Bull, R. (2012b). How do interviewers attempt to overcome suspects' denials? *Psychiatry, Psychology and Law, 19,* 151–168.

Walsh, D., & Bull, R. (2015). The association between interview skills, questioning and evidence disclosure strategies, and interview outcomes. *Psychology, Crime & Law, 21,* 661–680.

3

EXPANDING THE LEGACY OF THE COGNITIVE INTERVIEW

Developments and Innovations in Evidence-Based Investigative Interviewing

Lorraine Hope and Fiona Gabbert

Prior to the seminal work by Fisher and colleagues and the publication of the *Memory-Enhancing Techniques for Investigative Interviewing: The Cognitive Interview* (Fisher & Geiselman, 1992), investigative interviews with witnesses had largely been considered a routine policing task, as much informed by 'gut' or intuition as experience, with little if any consideration of systematic, psychologically-informed techniques or protocols. With the exception of early work on the misinformation effect that highlighted the dangers of leading and repeated questioning (e.g., Loftus & Palmer, 1974; Poole & White, 1991) and other influential work on eyewitness suggestibility (e.g., Lindsay & Johnson, 1989), research had yet to focus on the applied memory and social interaction features of investigative interviewing. Thus, the development of the Cognitive Interview (CI) essentially offered investigators and researchers a route to achieve a step-change in investigative interviewing practice and a scientific evidence-base to support that change.

Capitalizing on the nature of episodic memory and memory retrieval processes, and incorporating the principles of social dynamics, cognition, and communication, the CI provides investigators with a psychologically-informed approach to eliciting detailed and reliable accounts from memory. Although heavily reliant on investigator resources, including time and high-quality training, evidence suggests the CI is effective across investigative domains (e.g., crimes, accidents, health-related experiences), interviewees (e.g., children, adults, older adults, witnesses, and suspects), and nationalities (e.g., US, UK, Brazilian; for a review, see Fisher, 2010; see also Vrij, Hope, & Fisher, 2014). However, as well as benefiting investigators and other end-users, the emergence of the CI also provided academic researchers with a framework for thinking about the task of investigative interviewing from a psychological perspective. For example, the CI draws on (at least) two principles of memory. The first is the notion that a memory trace consists of a network of related information. The second principle is that there are several possible ways of retrieving an encoded event, so information that cannot be retrieved initially, may become accessible using a different retrieval approach (see Fisher, 2010).

Capitalizing on these theoretical principles, the original CI comprised several techniques to facilitate the accurate retrieval of witnessed events (*report everything, mental reinstatement of context, change temporal order,* and *change perspective*). Strategies aimed at optimizing both the retrieval process and the social and communication aspects of an investigative interview (e.g., *rapport building, transferring control of the interview to the witness, focused retrieval,* and *witness compatible questioning*) were more explicitly integrated in a revised version of the CI (the 'Enhanced CI'; Fisher, Geiselman, Raymond, Jurkevich, & Warhaftig, 1987). As such, the contemporary CI comprises several different memory-facilitating techniques. However, it is critical to note that, as advised by Fisher and colleagues (Fisher, Schreiber Compo, Rivard, & Hirn, 2014), the CI is not a 'recipe' but rather a collection of techniques, only some of which might be used in any given interview.

In taking this systematic approach to applying principles of memory to the task of eliciting information from witness memory in the course of an investigative interview, Fisher and Geiselman (1992) provided a blueprint for psychology researchers to apply theory and findings in the basic experimental literature to the applied context. In this chapter, we will examine the legacy of the CI and explore developments and innovations that have stemmed directly from its development and introduction to the field.

Extending the Legacy: Developments and Innovations

Over the past two decades police forces across the world have trained their officers in the use of the CI which has, broadly, led to enhanced investigative practice and better quality interviews with victims and witnesses. However, during this time, a number of pragmatic or logistical obstacles to the wholesale use of the CI have been noted. For example, concerns have been raised that the CI is not appropriate for use in time-critical situations, particularly when there is limited access to trained personnel or resources are otherwise restricted (Dando, Wilcock, & Milne, 2008). Furthermore, the CI is not the most efficient or economical method of obtaining witness accounts in certain investigative contexts (e.g., volume crime). To address the challenge of obtaining reliable witness and victim accounts in these particular investigative contexts, researchers have been informed and, indeed, inspired by the structure and content of the CI, resulting in the development of a range of derivative context-appropriate tools and techniques.

Variants of the CI: Successful Modifications and Contextual Adaptations

Reflecting the very real demands on police investigators, surveys with police officers have revealed that, in many investigations, there is rarely time available to interview witnesses using a full CI (see Dando et al., 2008; Kebbell & Milne, 1998; Kebbell, Milne, & Wagstaff, 1999). Furthermore, some officers have expressed discomfort with using particular mnemonics, such as 'change-order' and 'change-perspective' instructions (Dando et al., 2008). Some of this resistance likely reflects a fundamental misunderstanding of the principles underlying the CI (i.e., that varied retrieval methods can effectively cue memory). Almost certainly, misunderstandings are due to ill-informed training, attempts to use the CI as a 'tick box' protocol, or the use of supplementary techniques in an inappropriate manner.

Nevertheless, to respond to practical challenges, researchers have worked to develop time-critical short-form versions of the CI when obtaining eyewitness evidence is a priority, but where available time to conduct interviews is limited. For example, to determine whether a shortened form of the CI might deliver equivalent information from witnesses in time-critical situations, Davis, McMahon, and Greenwood (2005) tested a modified version of the CI, in which the 'change order' and 'change perspective' mnemonics were omitted. Their findings suggested that the short-form modified version of the CI performed as well as a full CI and outperformed a standard Structured Interview.

In a comprehensive review of the CI literature, Memon, Meissner, and Fraser (2010) noted that short-form versions of the CI typically retain the 'mental reinstatement of context' and 'report everything' initial components but omit the 'change order' and/or 'change perspective' components (e.g., Wright & Holliday, 2007; see Memon et al., 2010, Table 2). Research examining the efficacy of the different components of the CI confirms that the mental context reinstatement and report everything mnemonics are most effective for promoting detailed and accurate recall (Milne & Bull, 2002).

Another more recent modification of the CI that also addresses the need for shorter interview procedures involves use of a sketch instruction at the outset of the interview (see Dando, Wilcock, & Milne, 2009a; Dando, Wilcock, Milne, & Henry, 2009b). This approach indirectly places the onus on the witness to 'self-generate' retrieval cues while drawing a detailed sketch plan of the witnessed incident. Dando and colleagues (2009a, 2009b) found that asking witnesses to draw a detailed sketch of what they saw, and to talk while doing so, was as effective as an instruction to mentally reinstate context in terms of the amount of information correctly recalled.

Shorter versions of the CI are certainly valuable in time critical contexts. However, even a shortened CI requires police resources in terms of time and manpower. For incidents involving multiple witnesses to a crime, it is highly unlikely that sufficient interviewers will be available at the scene of an incident. For example, consider the likely chaos in the aftermath of a terrorist attack in a busy city location. For emergency responders, including the police, the obvious key priority will be to recover injured victims and secure the scene against secondary attacks. However, at that scene, there may also be a large number of witnesses who hold important information about the incident. Many witnesses may be lost because follow-up enquiries can take months (by which time the witness may no longer be able to report fine-grained details about the incident). Even relatively common criminal incidents such as a knife-fight outside a nightclub, a violent mugging on a train platform or a fatal hit-and-run, may have been seen by many potentially cooperative witnesses.

With limited resources, officers are unlikely to be able to capitalize on multiple witnesses and will instead typically attempt to identify a smaller number of key witnesses. There are at least two problems with this strategy. First, officers arriving at a chaotic scene may find it difficult to identify key witnesses. Where multiple witnesses are present, discriminating among witnesses may be based on simple heuristics, such as how vocal someone is. In reality, officers need to discriminate between informative and uninformative witnesses and assess which witnesses to interview as a priority and whom to contact at a later date. Second, limiting the focus of the investigation to only a small number of witnesses at such an early stage is problematic, particularly if the selected witnesses fail to provide detailed or reliable accounts.

In response to the serious challenge faced by investigators when an incident occurs for which there are numerous eyewitnesses, Gabbert, Hope, and Fisher (2009) developed the Self-Administered Interview (SAI©). The SAI© is a generic response tool that is suitable for obtaining information about a wide range of different incidents. It takes the form of a standardized protocol of instructions, open-ended questions and non-leading cues that enable witnesses to provide their own statement, and is therefore ideal for use when restricted resources mean that a traditional interview is not possible. The SAI© draws on a number of key features of the Cognitive Interview. For instance, the initial open-ended free recall instruction is preceded by a mental reinstatement of context (MRC) instruction, which guides the witness through the process of mentally revisiting the scene with instructions to focus on different aspects of their experience and information about how this activity will assist them with recalling their account. Witnesses are encouraged to 'Give yourself plenty of time to concentrate, and visualize what happened in your mind' and, in order to fully support the self-generated context reinstatement procedure, it is suggested they consider the following: Where were you? What were you doing? Who were you with? How were you feeling? What was happening? Who was involved? What could you see? What could you hear? Witnesses are also advised they may find it helpful to shut their eyes while engaging in this procedure. Witnesses are then asked to 'Report Everything' and provide the most complete and accurate account possible, but avoid guessing about details they cannot remember. The next section of the SAI© focuses on eliciting detailed person descriptor information and, using non-leading prompts, asks witnesses to provide as much detail as possible about the perpetrator's appearance (e.g., hair, complexion, build, distinguishing features, etc.).

Integrating the varied and repeated retrieval features of the CI protocol, the next SAI© section asks witnesses to generate a sketch of the scene to preserve important spatial information, including details relating to direction of movement or travel (which may be particularly pertinent for the investigation of road traffic incidents or direction of escape routes). The remaining sections instruct witnesses to describe any persons who may have been present and who may have seen what happened, even if they were not directly involved (e.g., other witnesses), provide information about any vehicles which may have been present or involved in the incident, and describe the witnessing conditions (e.g., weather conditions, time of day, lighting, obstructions, length of time).

Empirical testing suggests that the SAI© elicits significantly more information from witnesses than open-ended requests for information while maintaining high accuracy rates. Furthermore, results indicate that initial completion of an SAI© is associated with an increase in the amount of information provided by witnesses in a delayed CI (Hope, Gabbert, Fisher, & Jamieson, 2014). Research has also shown that witnesses who complete an SAI© are more resistant to misleading information encountered after an incident (Gabbert, Hope, Fisher, & Jamieson, 2012). In an examination of whether completing an SAI© might provide witnesses with more general reporting skills, Gawrylowicz, Memon, and Scoboria (2013) observed an interesting transfer effect, such that reporting about one event using the SAI© enhanced subsequent reporting about another unrelated event. This apparent reporting advantage was also observed for a sample of older witnesses (Gawrylowicz, Memon, Scoboria, Hope, & Gabbert, 2014).

A recent meta-analysis (Pfeil, 2017) of 15 empirical studies reported a substantial increase in the reporting of correct details for the SAI© with a large summary effect size ($d = 1.20$), comparable to the benefit found for the CI (see Memon et al., 2010). Analyses also suggested that this increase in reporting of correct details also transfers to a subsequent witness interview about the same event ($d = 0.92$).

Despite being a relatively new investigative tool for officers tasked with eliciting initial witness accounts, the SAI© has been used to prioritize witnesses and facilitate the identification of additional witnesses in a range of contexts, including investigations of murder, shootings, and assaults (see Hope, Gabbert, & Fisher, 2011). To date, the SAI© has also been embedded within national guidelines relating to investigative policy and practice in the Netherlands and Norway.

Extending the CI 'Toolbox'

To date, the majority of research pertaining to the CI has focused on validating the procedure as a whole, testing the existing component parts, or conducting the interview via different modalities. However, a number of researchers have examined the potential of new theory-based mnemonics that may contribute to the CI 'toolbox'. For example, Colomb and Ginet (2012) tested a *guided peripheral focus* mnemonic. The mnemonic instruction invites witnesses to (i) divide the memory of the event into a set of main actions; (ii) form a mental image of each main action he/she has remembered; (iii) close their eyes to help access the mental images; and (iv) transfer the focus from the retrieval of central elements to the recall of peripheral ones such as secondary actions, person descriptors, location descriptors, objects, and sounds. Across two studies, the use of this mnemonic enhanced the completeness of witness statements. Colomb and Ginet (2012) suggested this technique might be used as a cognitive aid towards the end of an interview to prompt additional recollections.

A second example of an innovation developed with a view to extending the techniques available for use with a CI is the *category clustering recall mnemonic* developed and tested by Paulo, Albuquerque, and Bull (2016). The theoretical rationale underlying this mnemonic is that recalling in 'category clusters' is compatible with the way in which we use semantic categories to encode, organize, and recall information and, as a result, a related mnemonic might be an effective method to cue memories. The technique involves asking people to organize their recall into information categories (person details, person location details, object details, object location details, action details, conversation details, and sound details). To evaluate the mnemonic, Paulo et al. (2016) showed participants a simulated crime event on video, and then interviewed them 48 hours later with either (i) an enhanced CI; (ii) a modified enhanced CI featuring the category clustering recall mnemonic (instead of the change order mnemonic); or (iii) a modified enhanced CI featuring the category clustering recall mnemonic, in addition to an 'eye closure' instruction and additional open-ended follow-up questions. Participants interviewed with the category clustering recall mnemonic reported more information without compromising accuracy (eye closure and follow-up questions were not found to further benefit recall).

A third example of mnemonic development in the investigative interviewing context is reflected in research on the use of *self-generated cues* to facilitate retrieval from memory. A self-generated cue is defined as any detail salient to the individual, and generated by the individual themselves, which is intended to facilitate more complete retrieval of a target memory (Wheeler & Gabbert, 2017). Such a self-generated cue might be any idiosyncratic detail of an experienced event that is in some way salient or memorable to the interviewee. The theory underpinning this technique draws on Anderson's (1983) spreading activation theory, Tulving and Thomson's (1973) cue overlap theory, and Nairne's (2002) cue distinctiveness theory, all of which endorse the notion that the quality of the overlap between encoded information and retrieval cue predicts the likelihood of successful retrieval. Across two experiments, Wheeler, Gabbert, Jones, Hope, and Valentine (2017) demonstrated that self-generated cues enhanced recall performance of mock witnesses. Specifically, compared to control participants, or those who received standard mental reinstatement of context instructions, participants who generated their own cues reported more accurate information. Similarly, Kontogianni, Hope, Vrij, Taylor, and Gabbert (2018) found a beneficial effect of the self-generated cues mnemonic for promoting additional recall across both timeline and free recall interview formats.

Other developments have focused on extending the utility of individual techniques or instructions described as part of the original CI. For example, as a means of facilitating focus and retrieval, eye-closure has been an integral feature of CI instructions. Drawing on the efficacy of the eye-closure procedure for retrieval (Perfect et al., 2008; Wagstaff et al., 2004), Vredeveldt et al. (2015) examined whether an eye-closure interview instruction alone might be beneficial in an investigative interviewing context. In a field study, police investigators administered the eye-closure instruction with witnesses to serious crimes. Although witnesses who closed their eyes did not report more information overall, the information they did provide was independently judged to be of greater forensic relevance than information provided by witnesses who did not receive the eye-closure instruction.

Recent work has also focused on the psychological needs of witnesses and victims who may need additional support in the course of an interview. Investigators in international law enforcement, security, and other response agencies are increasingly faced with the challenge of interviewing distressed or traumatized victims or witnesses to war, genocide, and human trafficking. However, investigative interview approaches have not explicitly incorporated techniques to address the psychological needs of distressed or traumatized individuals; nor have therapeutic approaches addressed the investigative need for accurate and detailed information. Therefore, a major challenge for investigators and other professionals (e.g., asylum assessors, frontline or receiving NGOs) working to build evidence for reporting or tribunal purposes, lies in eliciting detailed and reliable accounts from such traumatized individuals (Sandick, 2012).

To address the needs of both witnesses and investigators in this context, Castelfranc-Allen (2014) devised the Visual Communication Desensitization (VCD©) interview procedure, which is designed to rapidly secure accurate accounts while reducing distress. The VCD© interview procedure comprises a two-part cognitive-behavioural approach to eliciting information from a cooperative but traumatized victim or witness. The VCD© allows the interviewee to initially communicate the level of their distress across a timeline of the incident. Understanding the varying levels of distress of the interviewee across the experienced or witnessed incident allows the interviewer to plan the subsequent interview. For example, by learning which topics may be distressing for the witness, the interviewer may first ask open questions around low-distress topics that might be easier for the interviewee to discuss. Accessing information about the least distressing topics allows the interviewer to identify entry points to discuss more substantive topics with sensitivity to the distress of the interviewee. Early stage testing (Castelfranc-Allen

& Hope, 2018), and use in practice suggests the VCD© may offer investigators an additional technique for use with traumatized or distressed individuals.

Investigative Interviewing Innovations Motivated by the CI

Following the pioneering work of Fisher and Geiselman (1992), researchers have sought to advance the field of investigative interviewing in new directions, leading to the development of novel, flexible, theory-driven approaches for eliciting information in increasingly complex and dynamic investigative contexts. In this section we describe some of the more recent tools and techniques that emerged from our labs as a direct result of having worked with Ronald P. Fisher on earlier projects, including the SAI©.

Timeline Technique

Crimes involving multiple perpetrators pose a significant problem for investigators and the courts, particularly if an individual suspect does not dispute being present at the scene of a crime but denies involvement (Roberts, 2003). Successful prosecutions typically require evidence demonstrating a direct link between perpetrators and their criminal actions. Recalling and reporting details of complex, dynamic events involving multiple perpetrators is often a challenge for witnesses and it may be difficult for interviewers to elicit information about 'who did what' and the specific sequence of actions and events.

By definition, a perpetrator's actions are temporally associated with both the perpetrator-actor and the sequence in which the actions took place. Given that contextual information in episodic memory is associated with the temporal-spatial context in which it was encoded, retrieval can rely heavily on reinstating the appropriate contextual representations (Tulving, 1983). Unsurprisingly, the basic memory literature also confirms that episodic memory is temporally ordered and that temporal context plays an important role in the retrieval process during free recall (Howard & Kahana, 1999; Kahana, 1996; Unsworth, 2008). Indeed, phenomena such as the temporal contiguity effect (whereby items encoded in close temporal proximity tend to be recalled in close proximity) suggest the temporal clustering of items is a 'ubiquitous property' of sequence recall (Polyn, Norman, & Kahana, 2009, p. 130; see Kahana, Howard, & Polyn, 2008).

Many police interviewing approaches oblige witnesses to 'start at the beginning' and produce, initially at least, a linear narrative account of what they saw. While this type of linear reporting provides an organizing narrative structure, it may not be an optimal approach for facilitating the reporting of complex events involving multiple perpetrators. Providing such an account necessarily involves selecting which information to provide first (e.g., descriptions, actions, sequence of events) and switching between elements at different times when reporting information about different perpetrators and differentiating between who did what and when.

Furthermore, in verbal interviews, conversational maxims may make it difficult for the witness to suddenly introduce an item which has been retrieved spontaneously but is unrelated to the current phase of the narrative. In written accounts, it may be pragmatically difficult to add additional information at the relevant point without extensive editing. In either case, adding information which is out of sequence will disrupt the narrative flow of the 'story' and may be resisted.

Unlike many interviews that simply involve this kind of linear question-and-answer exchange determined by the interviewer, the CI actively promotes witness-compatible questioning and implicitly draws on temporal context and ordering to facilitate recall (i.e., mental reinstatement of context and reverse order recall mnemonics) with no constraints on the order of the witness's account. Dispensing with the linear verbal narrative common to most interviewing formats discussed so far, and drawing on the witness-led approach established in the CI, the Timeline Technique is a multi-modal format designed to facilitate witness reporting about complex event sequences, particularly events involving multiple actors (Hope, Mullis, & Gabbert, 2013; Kontogianni et al., 2018).

Drawing on social survey methodologies (e.g., event history calendars) used previously to elicit information about autobiographical events (e.g., Belli, Stafford, & Alwin, 2009), the Timeline Technique is a self-administered recall and reporting technique designed to optimize an interviewee's ability to recall information within a particular time period in sequence, identify people involved, and link those people with their specific actions. Hope et al.'s (2013) participants used a timeline-based reporting format and reported their account of a witnessed event on a timeline of the relevant time period for the target event. Additional retrieval support was provided through the use of instructions and interactive reporting materials. Mock witnesses who provided their accounts about a multi-perpetrator event using a timeline provided more (i) person-description details (ii) person-action details, and (iii) sequence details than requesting a free report at no cost to accuracy. Testing also included the comparison of component elements of the Timeline Technique (i.e., instructions, reporting cards, visual timeline; Experiment 2) but optimal performance was observed when the full timeline format was used. More recently, Kontogianni et al. (2018) noted a beneficial effect of self-generated cues to further enhance reporting in the Timeline Technique, while Hope et al. (submitted) observed beneficial effects of reporting using a timeline approach when eliciting information about 'who said what' in conversational recall (see also Leins, Fisher, Pludwinski, Rivard, & Robertson, 2014).

As a self-report approach, the Timeline Technique may also be beneficial in other reporting contexts where a cooperative interviewee wishes to provide a comprehensive account. For example, in an intelligence gathering context, eliciting information in the course of debriefing with a cooperative source is a challenge exacerbated by the fact that the interviewee may have *several* critical experiences to report but may not be in a position to discriminate which experiences are of interest to the interviewer and which are not. Furthermore, information may have been gained over an extended period of time, often years. Such information may be difficult to recall in the absence of supportive or helpful retrieval cues. The interviewer is also at a disadvantage in that, unlike investigations following a crime or incident, there is no outcome information or evidence available around which to plan the interview. Therefore, the task for the interviewer is to facilitate high quality and extensive recall during the debriefing.

Traditionally, approaches to interviewing in intelligence gathering contexts have focused on extended interviews, using various question-and-answer techniques. Such approaches are unlikely to maximize the amount of information reported by even the most compliant interviewee. One way to address this problem is to provide the interviewee with optimal retrieval support, through the use of retrieval strategies, and appropriate cueing with the aim of eliciting as much information as possible in the course of a phased debriefing procedure. In addition to providing retrieval support, the Timeline Technique also incorporates a number of activities known to be synonymous with positive interviewing outcomes, including an emphasis on rapport building, interviewee-led accounts, and limited interviewer input. As the Timeline Technique is largely self-administered, the interviewee has autonomy over the reporting process. The transfer of control from the interviewer to the interviewee is an important feature of other effective interview techniques, such as the CI.

Structured Interview Protocol

Concerns over the quality of investigative interview skills is particularly acute for frontline uniformed officers who have a lack of policing experience coupled with demanding and multi-faceted work priorities. The provision of interview training for these officers is already limited, and this situation is likely to worsen as workloads increase and opportunities for training decrease.

In response to the need for appropriate investigative interviewing training for frontline officers who typically receive minimal training with respect to communicating with victims, witnesses or suspects (and critically, who do not receive CI training), researchers have recently developed a 'Structured Interview Protocol', designed to complement the PEACE interview framework (Gabbert et al., 2016). Specifically, the protocol, and associated training, incorporates context-appropriate evidence-based interview techniques into each of the stages of PEACE (Preparation and Planning, Engage and Explain, Account, Clarify and Challenge, and Evaluation of the interview). As such, it promotes best practice interview skills to elicit high quality, reliable evidence via effective research-based guidelines and techniques. For example, for the 'Engage and Explain' stage of PEACE, the protocol draws from a broad theoretical understanding of memory and human interaction, as well as more specific empirical research on building rapport, and influencing reporting thresholds (amongst other relevant research), to produce guidelines on how to effectively engage and build trust with a victim/witness, and how to best set expectations for the interview context. Further, for the 'Account' stage of PEACE, the protocol draws from theoretical work on memory and meta-memory (including source monitoring), as well as from empirical research on the use of specific question types (Oxburgh, Myklebust, & Grant, 2010), focusing techniques such as eye-closure (Perfect, Andrade, & Eagan, 2011), and the use of 'don't know' responses (Scoboria & Fisico, 2013).

Results of laboratory and field trials indicate that the Structured Interview Protocol promotes high quality, efficient, and effective interview performance via skilled use of rapid rapport techniques, enhanced 'Engage and Explain' skills, and a clear increase in appropriate question types used in a structured manner (Gabbert et al., 2016). As with the CI, the collection of recommended instructions and retrieval techniques incorporated within the Structured Interview Protocol can be used together or separately, depending on the goals of the interviewer.

Conclusion

Since the introduction of the CI to the field, research efforts have focused on validating and extending work on the CI, as well as advancing the field in new and innovative directions. The examples outlined in this chapter highlight the ongoing development of novel, flexible, theory-driven approaches for eliciting information in increasingly complex and dynamic investigative contexts. There is still much to be done, however, and we urge greater exploration of the wider requirement of ethical, efficient, and effective information elicitation techniques beyond policing contexts, such as elicitation of patient histories by medical professionals, investigation of occupational incidents, debriefing of intelligence sources, and reporting by operational staff, such as law enforcement personnel and emergency responders. As researchers, we are fortunate in having the blue-print for tackling these challenges so clearly elucidated in the development of the CI by Ronald P. Fisher and colleagues.

References

Anderson, J. R. (1983). A spreading activation theory of memory. *Journal of Verbal Learning and Verbal Behavior, 22,* 261–295.

Belli, R. F., Stafford, F. P., & Alwin, D. F. (Eds.). (2009). *Calendar and time diary methods in life course research.* Thousand Oaks, CA: Sage.

Castelfranc-Allen, J. M. (July, 2014). The VCD: An innovative procedure that helps address both therapeutic and evidentiary concerns for trauma victims. Paper presented at the 7th Annual Conference of the International Investigative Interviewing Research Group (iIIRG), Lausanne, Switzerland.

Castelfranc-Allen, J. M., & Hope, L. (2018). Visual Communication Desensitization (VCD©): A novel two-phased approach to interviewing traumatised individuals in investigative contexts. *Psychiatry, Psychology and Law, 25,* 589–601.

Colomb, C., & Ginet, M. (2012). The cognitive interview for use with adults: An empirical test of an alternative mnemonic and of a partial protocol. *Applied Cognitive Psychology*, *26*, 35–47.

Dando, C. J., Wilcock, R., & Milne, R. (2008). The cognitive interview: Inexperienced police officers' perceptions of their witness/victim interviewing practices. *Legal and Criminological Psychology*, *13*, 59–70.

Dando, C., Wilcock, R., & Milne, R. (2009a). The cognitive interview: The efficacy of a modified mental reinstatement of context procedure for frontline police investigators. *Applied Cognitive Psychology*, *23*, 138–147.

Dando, C., Wilcock, R., Milne, R., & Henry, L. (2009b). A modified cognitive interview procedure for frontline police investigators. *Applied Cognitive Psychology*, *23*, 698–716.

Davis, M. R., McMahon, M., & Greenwood, K. M. (2005). The efficacy of mnemonic components of the cognitive interview: Towards a shortened variant for time-critical investigations. *Applied Cognitive Psychology*, *19*, 75–93.

Fisher, R. P. (2010). Interviewing cooperative witnesses. *Legal and Criminological Psychology*, *15*, 25–38.

Fisher, R. P., & Geiselman, R. E. (1992). *Memory-enhancing techniques for investigative interviewing: The cognitive interview*. Springfield, IL: Charles C. Thomas Publisher.

Fisher, R. P., Geiselman, R. E., Raymond, D. S., Jurkevich, L. M., & Warhaftig, M. L. (1987). Enhancing eyewitness memory: Refining the cognitive interview. *Journal of Police Science and Administration*, *15*, 291–297.

Fisher, R. P., Schreiber Compo, N., Rivard, J., & Hirn, D. (2014). Interviewing witnesses. In T. Perfect & S. Lindsay (Eds.), *Handbook of applied memory* (pp. 559–578). Los Angeles, CA: Sage.

Gabbert, F., Hope, L., & Fisher, R. P. (2009). Protecting eyewitness evidence: Examining the efficacy of a self-administered interview tool. *Law and Human Behaviour*, *33*, 298–307.

Gabbert, F., Hope, L., Fisher, R. P., & Jamieson, K. (2012). Protecting against susceptibility to misinformation with the use of a Self-Administered Interview. *Applied Cognitive Psychology*, *26*, 568–575.

Gabbert, F., Hope, L., La Rooy, D., McGregor, A., Ellis, T., & Milne, R. (June, 2016). Introducing a PEACE-compliant 'Structured Interview Protocol' to enhance the quality of investigative interviews. Paper presented at the 9th Annual Conference of the International Investigative Interviewing Research Group (iIIRG), London, UK.

Gawrylowicz, J., Memon, A., & Scoboria, A. (2013). Equipping witnesses with transferable skills: The Self-Administered Interview©. *Psychology, Crime & Law*, *20*, 315–325.

Gawrylowicz, J., Memon, A., Scoboria, A., Hope, L., & Gabbert, F. (2014). Enhancing older adults' eyewitness memory for present and future events with the Self-Administered Interview. *Psychology and Aging*, *29*, 885–890.

Hope, L., Gabbert, F., & Fisher, R. P. (2011). From laboratory to the street: Capturing witness memory using a Self-Administered Interview. *Legal and Criminological Psychology*, *16*, 211–226.

Hope, L., Mullis, R., & Gabbert, F. (2013). Who? What? When? Using a timeline technique to facilitate recall of a complex event. *Journal of Applied Research in Memory and Cognition*, *2*, 20–24.

Hope, L., Gabbert, F., Fisher, R. P., & Jamieson, K. (2014). Protecting and enhancing eyewitness memory: The impact of an initial recall attempt on performance in an investigative interview. *Applied Cognitive Psychology*, *28*, 304–313.

Hope, L., Gabbert, F., Kinninger, M., Kontogianni, F., Bracey, A., & Hanger, A. (submitted). Who said what and when? A timeline approach to eliciting information and intelligence about conversations, plots and plans.

Howard, M. W., & Kahana, M. J. (1999). Contextual variability and serial position effects in free recall. *Journal of Experimental Psychology: Learning, Memory and Cognition, 25,* 923–941.

Kahana, M. J. (1996). Associative retrieval processes in free recall. *Memory & Cognition, 24,* 103–109.

Kahana, M. J., Howard, M. W., & Polyn, S. M. (2008). Associative retrieval processes in episodic memory. In H. L. Roediger, III (Ed.), *Cognitive psychology of memory. Vol. 2 of Learning and memory: A comprehensive reference* (pp. 476–490). Oxford: Elsevier.

Kebbell, M., & Milne, R. (1998). Police officers' perception of eyewitness factors in forensic investigations. *Journal of Social Psychology, 138,* 323–330.

Kebbell, M. R., Milne, R., & Wagstaff, G. F. (1999). The cognitive interview: A survey of its forensic effectiveness. *Psychology, Crime & Law, 5,* 101–115.

Kontogianni, F., Hope, L., Vrij, A., Taylor, P. J., & Gabbert, F. (2018). The benefits of a self-generated cue mnemonic for timeline interviewing. *Journal of Applied Research in Memory and Cognition, 7,* 454–461.

Leins, D. A., Fisher, R. P., Pludwinski, L., Rivard, J., & Robertson, B. (2014). Interview protocols to facilitate human intelligence sources' recollections of meetings. *Applied Cognitive Psychology, 28,* 926–935.

Lindsay, D. S., & Johnson, M. K. (1989). The eyewitness suggestibility effect and memory for source. *Memory & Cognition, 17,* 349–358.

Loftus, E. F. & Palmer, J. C. (1974). Reconstruction of auto-mobile destruction: An example of the interaction between language and memory. *Journal of Verbal Learning and Verbal Behaviour, 13,* 585–589.

Memon, A., Meissner, C. A., & Fraser, J. (2010). The cognitive interview: A meta-analytic review and study space analysis of the past 25 years. *Psychology, Public Policy, and Law, 16,* 340–372.

Milne, R., & Bull, R. (2002). Back to basics: A componential analysis of the original cognitive interview mnemonics with three age groups. *Applied Cognitive Psychology, 16,* 743–753.

Nairne, J. S. (2002). The myth of the encoding-retrieval match. *Memory, 10,* 389–395.

Oxburgh, G. E., Myklebust, T., & Grant, T. D. (2010). The question of question types in police interviews: A review of the literature from a psychological and linguistic perspective. *International Journal of Speech, Language and the Law, 17,* 45–66.

Paulo, R. M., Albuquerque, P. B., & Bull, R. (2016). Improving the enhanced cognitive interview with a new interview strategy: Category clustering recall. *Applied Cognitive Psychology, 30,* 775–784.

Perfect, T. J., Wagstaff, G. F., Moore, D., Andrews, B., Cleveland, V., Newcombe, S., Brisbane, K. A., & Brown, L. (2008). How can we help witnesses to remember more? It's an (eyes) open and shut case. *Law and Human Behavior, 32,* 314–324.

Perfect, T. J., Andrade, J., & Eagan, I. (2011). Eye-closure reduces the cross-modal memory impairment caused by auditory distraction. *Journal of Experimental Psychology: Learning, Memory and Cognition, 37,* 1008–1013.

Pfeil, K. (2017). The effectiveness of the Self-Administered Interview: A meta-analytic review and empirical study with older adult witnesses. Unpublished doctoral thesis. University of Cambridge, UK.

Polyn, S. M., Norman, K. A., & Kahana, M. J. (2009). A context maintenance and retrieval model of organizational processes in free recall. *Psychological Review, 116*, 129–156.

Poole, D. A., & White, L. T. (1991). Effects of question repetition on the eyewitness testimony of children and adults. *Developmental Psychology, 27*, 975–986.

Roberts, A. (2003). Questions of who was there and who did what: The application of Code D when a suspect disputes participation but not presence. *Criminal Law Review* (October), 709–716.

Sandick, P. A. (2012). Speechlessness and trauma: Why the International Criminal Court needs a public interviewing guide. *Northwestern Journal of International Human Rights, 11*, Article 4.

Scoboria, A., & Fisico, S. (2013). Encouraging and clarifying 'don't know' responses enhances interview quality. *Journal of Experimental Psychology: Applied, 19*, 72–82.

Tulving, E. (1983). *Elements of Episodic Memory*. Oxford: Clarendon Press.

Tulving, E., & Thomson, D. M. (1973). Encoding specificity and retrieval processes in episodic memory. *Psychological Review, 80*, 352–373.

Unsworth, N. (2008). Exploring the retrieval dynamics of delayed and final free recall: Further evidence for temporal–contextual search. *Journal of Memory and Language, 59*, 223–236.

Vredeveldt, A., Tredoux, C. G., Northje, A., Kemptn, K., Puljevic, C., & Labuschagne, G. N. (2015). A field evaluation of the eye-closure interview with witnesses of serious crimes. *Law and Human Behavior, 39*, 189–197.

Vrij, A., Hope, L., & Fisher, R. P. (2014). Eliciting reliable information in investigative interviews. *Policy Insights from the Behavioral and Brain Sciences, 1*, 129–136.

Wagstaff, G. F., Brunas-Wagstaff, J., Cole, J., Knapton, L., Winterbottom, J., Crean, V., & Wheatcroft, J. (2004). Facilitating memory with hypnosis, focused meditation, and eye closure. *International Journal of Clinical & Experimental Hypnosis, 52*, 434–455.

Wheeler, R. L., & Gabbert, F. (2017). Using self-generated cues to facilitate recall: A narrative review. *Frontiers in Psychology*. https://doi.org/10.3389/fpsyg.2017.01830

Wheeler, R. L., Gabbert, F., Jones, S. E., Hope, L., & Valentine, T. (2017). The effectiveness of self-generated retrieval cues in facilitating eyewitness recall. Individual paper presentation at Society for Applied Research in Memory and Cognition (SARMAC XII), January 2017, Sydney, Australia.

Wright, A. M., & Holliday, R. (2007). Enhancing the recall of young, young-old and old-old adults with cognitive interviews. *Applied Cognitive Psychology, 21*, 19–43.

4

THE COGNITIVE INTERVIEW

A Tiered Approach in the Real World

Becky Milne, Andy Griffiths, Colin Clarke, and Coral Dando

This chapter will examine how the Cognitive Interview (CI) has been applied in the real world of policing. We will consider the impact the CI has had on everyday policing, ranging from frontline communication, to being utilized within a visually recorded interview, which may replace live evidence in the courtroom (depending on the legislative framework of the country it is being applied to). As the CI is utilized in a multitude of different types of information and evidence gathering scenarios the way in which the CI needs to be applied, and thus trained, should reflect the context within which it is to be used in the field. Accordingly, the UK has developed the 'Tiered approach' to interview training (Clarke, Milne, & Bull, 2011), whereby interviewers learn interviewing skills (including the CI) incrementally, across a police investigator's career span. This approach has been adopted in numerous countries and the chapter will explain the approach, outline a model of training to maximize transference of skills into the workplace, and the research base examining its effectiveness in the field.

The Beginnings

The CI is one of the glowing examples of research-based innovation founded in psychology, as is well documented in this book and elsewhere (e.g. Fisher & Geiselman, 1992; Milne & Bull, 1999; Fisher, Milne, & Bull, 2011). The CI first emerged in 1984 (Geiselman et al., 1984). Since then its evolution demonstrates how academic research adapts, refines, and morphs concepts across time, adding to the growing set of tools that have now become part of the CI. Many researchers, ourselves included, have examined the CI in different guises, in an attempt to countenance the application of the constituent components in the real world of policing. There is no doubt that the CI is a successful forensic tool because it enhances memory, increasing the amount of accurate investigation relevant detail (Milne & Bull, 2016). As information is at the heart of establishing the answers to the two core investigative questions: (1) What happened? (if anything did happen) and (2) Who did it? (Milne & Bull, 2016), it is no surprise that the CI has become one of the most prominent tools in any investigator's armoury for combating crime. Indeed, over the past 25 years many law enforcement organizations, worldwide, have recognized the importance of the CI and have incorporated it into their training as one of the main interview frameworks (e.g., the UK, Norway, Australia, Ireland, and New Zealand; see Fisher et al., 2011). Nevertheless, researchers continue to be baffled by the fact that the CI in its *entirety* is rarely implemented in the field. This begs the question, why? We will attempt to answer this question in this chapter, and give workable solutions to help both practitioners and academics realize the full potential of the CI, and establish how techniques developed in the laboratory can then be applied into the field (see also Griffiths & Milne, in prep. – Investigative Interviewing Impact Framework [IIIF] – for a full discussion of the necessary elements required for research-based investigative interviewing skills transference and Lamb, 2016 for similar issues with respect to child forensic interviewing).

Early studies examining the applicability of the CI to the field were very promising in that they demonstrated that police officers could be readily trained in a very short period and the resultant interview behaviour improved, substantially (Fisher, Geiselman, and Amador, 1989; Clifford & George, 1996). However, it was not until the police in England and Wales developed a national approach to interviewing, following a public outcry due to miscarriage of justice cases which had poor interviewing at the heart of the acquittals (see Poyser & Milne, 2011, 2015; Poyser, Nurse, & Milne, in prep. for a review), that the CI was for the first time adopted by police organizations nationwide. The government and police response in the UK to the backlash of the miscarriages was to professionalize the police with regard to investigation and interview training. As a result, the investigative interviewing ethos, and the PEACE (an acronym for the stages of an investigative interview – see below) approach to interviewing was established (Milne & Bull, 2016; see also Milne, Shaw, & Bull, 2007; Griffiths & Milne, 2005).

It was a team of practitioners and academics working together in 1992 who coined the term PEACE and created a new era of research-based investigative interviewing (Griffiths & Milne, in prep.). A strategic decision to remove the term 'interrogation' from the UK police vernacular marked the start of a culture shift towards an investigative information gathering mind-set, away from the prevalent, but now outdated, confession culture. Within the PEACE framework of communication (P – planning and preparation; E – engage with and explain the interview process to the interviewee; A – gaining an account; C – closure of the interview; and E – evaluation of the information attained and interviewer skill level), two models of interviewing from the research literature were adopted by the British police service in its entirety (all 43 areas which make up the UK Police Service, plus Northern Ireland and Scotland [the latter in the form of PRICE]). The two models that emerged as best practice were: (i) conversation management (CM) which was deemed useful for interviewing more resistant interviewees and (ii) the CI (Fisher & Geiselman, 1992) which was useful for interviewing cooperative interviewees – interviewees who were willing to speak (however truthfully; for a fuller description see Milne & Bull, 1999; Shepherd & Griffiths, 2013; Fisher & Geiselman, 1992). For the first time, a whole country was to train all operational officers (N = 127,000) in the use of the CI (using police officers as trainers; Milne & Bull, 2016). This was a giant step in the evolution of the CI from the laboratory to the field.

PEACE training started to be rolled out to forces in England and Wales in 1993 as a week-long course. This then continued across the UK for over ten years. In 1998 the Home Office commissioned Clarke and Milne to examine the effectiveness of PEACE – Had it worked? – i.e., produced skilled interviewers who conducted ethical and legal interviews. This first national evaluation of PEACE in the UK examined the standard and legal compliance of real-life police interviews of suspects, witnesses, and victims of crime. The resultant research report, now known as the Clarke and Milne (2001) report, found that the interview training which officers had received was not being fully transferred into the workplace, i.e., interviewers were not using all elements of PEACE, including the components of the CI. Several reasons were put forth for the lack of adherence to the training and PEACE framework (see Clarke & Milne, 2001, 2016; Clarke et al., 2011), including a lack of supervision in the workplace. The Clarke and Milne report made several recommendations for police interviewing. Many of the recommendations have since been implemented nationally (Clarke & Milne, 2001, 2016; Clarke et al., 2011). Amongst the most apparent changes was the adoption of the recommended Tiered approach to developing an interviewer's skill level, learning skills incrementally across an individual's career, which was fully adopted by the UK police and formed part of the then UK government's 'Professionalising the Investigative Process' (PIP) agenda and associated National Occupation Standards. The '5-tiered approach' to interview training starts from Tier 1 – basic communication skills for recruits to – Tier 5 – highly skilled interview managers who create interview strategy in high-profile and complex cases (Griffiths & Milne, 2005). The Tiered approach has also been adopted by many countries (e.g., Australia, Canada, Ireland, New Zealand, Norway). With regard the CI, in the UK, the essence of the CI is taught at Tier 1 and then techniques are added to the CI 'toolbelt' across the tiers/levels.

Research specifically examining the perceived practical utility of the CI found that police officers (both experienced and less experienced frontliners) generally found the CI to be a worthwhile approach, although some techniques were preferred and used more frequently than others (e.g., the report everything instruction; Kebbell, Milne, & Wagstaff, 1999; Dando, Wilcock, Milne, & Henry 2009c; Dando, Wilcock, & Milne, 2009a, 2009b). For example, the instruction to report everything, never guess, and mental reinstatement of context technique already a well-established body of knowledge about 'what works' in skills transference of complex skills (Hoffman et al., 2014). Knowledge of the cognitive processes that underpin communication is only part of the equation; the remainder being knowledge about training methods that successfully embed the required skills and resist fade. The skills fade phenomenon was developed from military training research that indicated gradual performance decline (Hoffman et al., 2014). This finding corroborates Griffiths et al. (2011) who identified significant skills fade in complex interview skills learnt by Tier 3 interviewers only one year after training.

Griffiths et al. (2011) examined whether the Tiered approach worked and specifically focused on Tier 3, the Advanced interview training programme. It was found that if we 'select' the correct individuals and give them intensive training in small groups, with lots of hands-on practice and constructive feedback then we can get officers up to a good standard of interviewing suspects in high stakes cases (e.g., murder). One of the interesting findings that emerged from this work concerned the 'who' that is selected, as it was found that not everyone could reach (or may never be able to reach) the Tier 3/Advanced level, i.e., it is thought that some people did not have the innate ability that could be honed through training (see more later). Thus, with respect to suspect interviewing we seem to have the formula of how to create and maintain good interviewers (see Griffiths & Milne, in prep. for the full formula). However, the interviewing of suspects is only one half of the investigative coin; what about witnesses/victims? This part of investigative interviewing business is not so clear cut.

So, one key to getting the training right is to get the right people into the training room in the first place, especially for the more advanced levels of training. Is there an 'X' factor of interviewing? Or can all people be trained?

Ability/Skill Sets of Interviewers: The 'X' Factor of Interviewing

As has been outlined, there is now a comprehensive academic and practitioner literature regarding what constitutes best practice for investigative interviewing. There is an evidence base that dictates what interview methods are most suitable dependent upon the types of interviewee, i.e., interviewees are sometimes compliant, sometimes resistant, some are vulnerable, and others are motivated to be dishonest (Milne & Powell, 2010), and for specific types of crime (e.g., sex offenders; Westera, Kebbell, & Milne, 2016c). Research has also started to examine the context in which the techniques are to be used; from frontline policing, which requires fast and efficient methods, to visually recorded interviews where often more time can be afforded (Milne & Bull, 2016; Dando, Wilcock, Milne & Henry, 2009c; Dando, Wilcock, Benkle, & Milne, 2011b − also see later in this chapter). Nevertheless, how *able* interviewers are at utilizing such dictum, each having differing levels of natural ability, different levels of skill, and under different pressures is an area ripe for work. Indeed, as mentioned the majority of research examining the impact of interview training in the real world and the transference of skills into the field has found variable and disappointing results (e.g. Dando, Wilcock, & Milne, 2009a, 2009b; Griffiths et al., 2011; MacDonald et al., in press; Walsh & Milne, 2008). A further factor in the application of good practice is individual differences across interviewers.

Prior to 1984 in the UK (and still existing in many countries) interviewing by police officers was considered to be an inherent skill that all officers possessed and which could be developed merely by learning from more experienced colleagues. As previously noted, PACE (and the associated Codes of Practice) for the first time laid down that all interviews with suspects must be recorded. This resulted in the working practices within the police interview room being opened to public scrutiny on a grand scale; evaluative research could begin (Milne & Powell, 2010). The first ever such study found, perhaps not surprisingly due to the lack of structure, investment, and the haphazard approach to interview training, that there were severe shortcomings in the skills demonstrated by the police during such interviews (Baldwin, 1992). A direct result was the PEACE approach to interviewing being developed and associated training regime created as already outlined (Milne et al., 2007 and see earlier). Nevertheless, field studies of police interviews have shown that most real-life interviews still contain some undesirable practices (e.g., Clarke & Milne, 2001, 2016; Schreiber Compo, Hyman Gregory, & Fisher, 2012; Snook, Luther, Quinlan, & Milne, 2012).

Perhaps one reason for lack of transference is due to individual differences/ potential. In 2006, Griffiths and Milne evaluated 60 interviews conducted by 15 police officers trained in the basic PEACE protocol. After coding 96 criteria for level of skill and presence of interviewing techniques, Griffiths and Milne found that skill level was *below* that expected for basic PEACE-trained officers (Tier 2). However, interviewers who were identified as '*having potential*' and who went on to receive three weeks of advanced interview training (Tier 3) showed improvement across all criteria measured, though the skills that were deemed complex as opposed to simple (e.g., building rapport versus stating those present in the interview room respectively) depreciated when the interviewers went back into the field and this dissipated further over an 18 month period (see skills fade discussion earlier: Griffiths & Milne, 2010; Griffiths et al., 2011). 'Having potential' is an interesting concept, and raises the question – what is this potential? The discrepancy between best practice methods and actual investigative interviewer behaviour revealed by nearly all these previous evaluations tells only part of the story of how well police interview suspects and witnesses.

Some people are perceived as 'natural' communicators/interviewers; is this what we see as potential? Being a natural communicator stems from the belief that communication skills are an aspect of an individual's personality and thus have an inherited element. Horvath (1995) presented a coherent argument for the biological origins of 'communicator style'. Further, McCroskey, Heisel, and Richmond (2001) mapped correlations between Eysenck's big three personality recorded (Milne & Bull, 2016). However, the real world is far from ideal, as has already been shown in this chapter.

Conclusion

Thus, for the CI to be fully realized in the field, researchers and practitioners alike need to endeavour to put the aforementioned in place to enable the use of these innovative techniques that have already had such an impact on the investigative and interviewing world around the globe. It is imperative that rather than responding to mistakes exposed by the criminal justice system, training implements change proactively as reliable empirical evidence emerges. Global collaborations between academics and practitioners provide ample opportunity for this if the research agenda is forward thinking and not reactive.

References

Ambler, C., & Milne, R. (2006). Call handling centres: An evidential opportunity or threat? Paper presented at the Second International Investigative Interviewing Conference, Portsmouth, July.

Baldwin, J. (1993). Police interview techniques: Establishing truth or proof? *British Journal of Criminology, 33,* 325–352.

Clarke, C., & Cherryman, J. (2010). Improving the transfer of communication skills training: Links between communication skills, personality and communicator style. Paper accepted for the International Conference on Communication in Healthcare 2010 (ICCH), Verona, Italy (4–7 September).

Clarke, C., & Milne, R. (2001). *National evaluation of the PEACE investigative interviewing course.* Police Research Award Scheme, PRAS/149. London: Home Office.

Clarke, C., & Milne, R. (2016). Interviewing suspects in England and Wales: A national evaluation of PEACE interviewing one decade later. In D. Walsh, G. Oxburgh, A. Redlich, & T. Mykleburst (Eds.), *International developments and practices in investigative interviewing and interrogation, vol 2: Suspects* (pp. 21–44). London: Routledge.

Clarke, C., Milne, R., & Bull, R. (2011). Interviewing suspects of crime; The impact of PEACE training, supervision and the presence of a legal advisor. *Journal of Investigative Psychology and Offender Profiling, 8,* 149–162.

Clifford, B., & George, R. (1996). A field investigation of training in three methods of witness/victim investigative interviewing. *Psychology, Crime & Law, 2,* 241–248.

Dalton, G., Milne, R., Hope, L., & Pike, G. (in prep.). Body worn video cameras: An evaluation of police frontline communication.

Dando, C., Wilcock, R., & Milne, R. (2008). The cognitive interview: Inexperienced police officers' perceptions of their witness/victim interviewing practices. *Legal and Criminological Psychology, 13,* 59–70.

Dando, C. J., Wilcock, R., & Milne, R. (2009a). The cognitive interview: Novice police officers' witness/victim interviewing practices. *Psychology, Crime & Law, 15,* 679–696.

Dando, C. J., Wilcock, R., & Milne, R. (2009b). The cognitive interview: The efficacy of a modified mental reinstatement of context procedure for frontline police investigators. *Applied Cognitive Psychology, 23,* 138–147.

Dando, C. J., Wilcock, R., Milne, R., & Henry, L. (2009c). A modified cognitive interview procedure for frontline police investigators. *Applied Cognitive Psychology, 23,* 698–716.

Dando, C., Omerod, T., Wilcock, R., & Milne, R. (2011a). Eyewitness memory and change temporal order retrieval: Help or hindrance? *Cognition, 121,* 416–421.

Dando, C., Wilcock, R., Benkle, C., & Milne, R. (2011b). Modifying the cognitive interview: Countenancing forensic application by enhancing practicability. *Psychology, Crime & Law, 17,* 491–511.

Davies, G., Bull, R., & Milne, R. (2016). Analysing and improving the testimony of vulnerable witnesses interviewed under the 'Achieving Best Evidence' protocol. In P. Radcliffe, A. Heaton-Armstrong, G. Gudjonsson, & D. Wolchover (Eds.), *Witness testimony in sexual cases: Investigation, law and procedure.* Oxford: Oxford University Press.

Fahsing, I., & Ask, K. (2013). Decision making and decisional tipping points in homicide investigations: An interiew study of British and Norwegian detectives. *Journal of Investigative Psychology and Offender Profiling, 10,* 155–165.

Fahsing, I., & Ask, K. (2016). The making of an expert detective: The role of experience in English and Norwegian police officers' investigative decision making. *Psychology, Crime & Law, 22,* 203–223.

Fisher, R. P., & Geiselman, R. E. (1992). *Memory-enhancing techniques for investigative interviewing: The cognitive interview.* Springfield, IL: Charles Thomas.

Fisher, R. P., Geiselman, R. E., & Amador, M. (1989). Field test of the cognitive interview: Enhancing the recollection of actual victims and witness of crime. *Journal of Applied Psychology, 74,* 722–727.

Fisher, R., Milne, R., & Bull, R. (2011). Interviewing cooperative witnesses. *Current Directions in Psychological Science, 20,* 16–19.

Fresch, P. A., & Funke, J. (Eds.). (1995). *Complex problem solving: The European perspective.* Mahwah, NJ: Lawrence Erlbaum Associates.

Gabbert, F., Hope, L., La Rooy, D., McGregor, A., Milne, R., & Ellis, T. (2016). Introducing a PEACE-compliant 'Structured Interview Protocol' to enhance the quality of investigative interviews. International Investigative Interviewing Research Group conference, London (June).

Geiselman, R. E., Fisher, R. P., Firstenberg, I., Hutton, L. A., Sullivan, S. J., Avetissian, I. V., & Prosk, A. L. (1984). Enhancement of eyewitness memory: An empirical evaluation of the cognitive interview. *Journal of Police Science and Administration, 12,* 74–80.

Griffiths, A., & Milne, R. (2005). Will it all end in tiers? Police interviews with suspects in Britain. In T. Williamson (Ed.), *Investigative interviewing: Rights, research, regulation* (pp. 167–189). Cullompton: Willan Publishing.

Griffiths, A., & Milne, B. (2010). Application of cognitive interview techniques. In C. Ireland & M. Fisher (Eds.), *Consultancy and advising in forensic practice: Empirical and practical guidelines* (pp. 71–80). Chichester: British Psychological Society.

Griffiths, A., & Milne, R. (Eds.). (in prep). *Investigation: Psychology into practice.* London: Routledge.

Griffiths, A., Milne, R., & Cherryman, J. (2011). A question of control? The formulation of suspect and witness interview question strategies by advanced interviewers. *International Journal of Police Science and Management, 13,* 1–13.

Hoffman, R. R., Ward, P., Feltovich, P. J., DiBello, L., Fiore, S. M., & Andrews, D. H. (2014). *Accelerated expertise: Training for high proficiency in a complex world.* New York: Psychology Press.

Pierce, 2014; Rape, Abuse, and Incest National Network [RAINN], 2016; Testa, Hoffman, & Livingston, 2010; Testa & Livingston, 2009).

Given the prevalence of this potentially vulnerable witness and victim group, surprisingly little is known about if, and how, alcohol intoxication affects memory under conditions that are similar to real-world eyewitness contexts (see also Soraci et al., 2007). That is, relatively few studies have examined how alcohol affects eye-witness memory (see Appendix). Given the prevalence of intoxicated witnesses in the criminal justice system, it is crucial to understand how intoxicated indi-viduals encode, store, and retrieve memories of crimes to better assess the quality of evidence they provide. For example, are intoxicated witnesses/victims cap-able of providing accurate and plentiful information to investigators? What is the relationship between a witness's intoxication level and their memory? What role do investigative techniques play when collecting information from intoxicated witnesses? The aim of the present chapter is to summarize the scientific literature that has examined how alcohol affects witnesses' memory, starting with the effects of alcohol on "basic" cognitive processes and then examines the extent to which these findings translate to alcohol's effects on witness memory.

Alcohol and "Basic" Memory Research

The relationship between alcohol and memory has been studied since the early 1900s (Clouston, 1911; Hollingworth, 1923). Research on this topic was limited however until the 1970s and 1980s when the number of published studies increased considerably. A substantial portion of these early studies examined memory and cognitive functioning of people who chronically consumed alcohol (i.e., alcohol-dependent persons; Allen, Faillace, & Reynolds, 1971; Goodwin, Hill, Powell, & Viamontes, 1973; Tamerin, Weiner, Poppen, Steinglass, & Mendelson, 1971; see Mello, 1973 for review). Many studies also examined animals' (mainly rats) ability to complete various tasks after short- and long-term exposure to different doses of alcohol (see e.g., Gibson, 1985; Hodges, Thrasher, & Gray, 1989; MacInnes & Uphouse, 1973; Walker & Hunter, 1978). Although these early tests on alcohol-dependent persons and animals provide an important initial understanding of alcohol's effects on cognitive processes in specific populations, they allow for only tangential inferences regarding alcohol's potential effects on witness memory.

More relevant to the relation between alcohol and witness memory, research examining the effects of alcohol on social drinkers' memory also burgeoned in the 1970s and 1980s (see Echeverria, Fine, Langolf, Schork, & Sampaio, 1991; Mintzer, 2007 for reviews). Most of these studies manipulated participants' intoxication levels experimentally and took place in three stages. In the first stage, participants would be randomly assigned to a non-alcohol or alcohol group upon entering the lab. Depending on their assigned group, participants would drink one or more beverages that contained either no alcohol or a predetermined dose of alcohol. These doses were often adjusted based on the participants' Body Mass Index

(BMI) and gender to ensure that each person reached approximately the same blood alcohol concentration (BAC) level. Some studies also incorporated a placebo condition in which participants were led to believe they were consuming alcohol but in fact consumed very little or no alcohol. This allowed researchers to examine the effects of expecting to consume alcohol compared to the effects of actually consuming alcohol (i.e., expectancy vs. physiological effects) on memory processes (see Rohsenow & Marlatt, 1981; Testa et al., 2006). After consuming their assigned beverage (or sometimes during consumption), participants entered the second stage of the experiment and were presented with different types of stimuli to encode. These stimuli varied across studies but typically involved digit span tasks (e.g., Dougherty, Marsh, Moeller, Chokshi, & Rosen, 2000; Nordby, Watten, Raanaas, & Magnussen, 1999), word lists (e.g., Fillmore, Vogel-Sprott, & Gavrilescu, 1999; Maylor & Rabbit, 1987; Tracy & Bates, 1999), word pairs (e.g., Curran & Hildebrandt, 1999; Lombardi, Sirocco, Andreason, & George, 1997; Weissenborn & Duka, 2000), or pictures (e.g., Goodwin, Powell, Bremer, Hoine, & Stern, 1969; Parker, Birnbaum, & Noble, 1976). After a predetermined retention interval participants entered the third stage of the experiment which was the memory test (i.e., retrieval). Retention intervals ranged from seconds to weeks, and occasionally months, depending on the studies' focus on short-term/working memory or long-term memory. Retrieval tasks also varied considerably across studies; that is, participants have been asked to retrieve information via free recall, cued recall, multiple choice responding, recognition, or many other alternatives.

Experimentally manipulating intoxication levels in these controlled settings allowed researchers to directly compare intoxicated individuals' memory for a controlled stimulus to that of participants who were intoxicated to a different degree, sober, or falsely believed that they were intoxicated. In line with popular belief, the bulk of this research showed that alcohol can have a negative effect on all stages of the memory process (i.e., encoding, storage, and retrieval) across a variety of basic cognitive tasks (see e.g., Birnbaum & Parker, 1977; Josephs & Steele, 1990; Maylor & Rabbit, 1987, 1993; Mintzer, 2007; Tracy & Bates, 1999).

Theoretical Underpinnings

Across research fields, researchers have developed and used different theoretical approaches when explaining and predicting alcohol's effect on cognitive processes. Both alcohol-dependent and non-dependent individuals may experience complete or partial memory loss if consuming alcohol *before* encoding, known as anterograde alcohol-induced amnesia (White, 2003). These impairments are noticeable after alcohol consumption due to alcohol's disruption of cellular activity in the brain (White, 2003; White, Matthews, & Best, 2000), which primarily affects the hippocampus (White et al., 2000). Alcohol therefore has a larger impact on the encoding phase of new information given the importance of the hippocampus in the formation of new autobiographical memories (White, 2003).

In contrast to the potentially negative effects of alcohol-induced antero-grade amnesia on memory, some research suggests that alcohol consumed *after* encoding may *enhance* memory performance, which is known as the retrograde enhancement/facilitation effect (e.g., Bruce & Phil, 1997; Knowles, 2005; Tyson & Schirmuly, 1994). This enhancing effect might be explained by the fact that alcohol intoxication can lead to a decrease in retroactive interference (Mann, Cho-Young, & Vogel-Sprott, 1984) by suppressing cognitive activity, which other-wise would have interfered with the formation of new memories (Moulton et al., 2005). Alcohol's retrograde enhancement effect and anterograde impairment effect have been found in a number of studies (e.g., Bruce & Phil, 1997; Garfinkel, Dienes, & Duka, 2006; Knowles & Duka, 2004).

Memory loss linked to alcohol-induced amnesia can either be total (i.e., blackout/en bloc blackout), or more commonly fragmentary (i.e., grayout/frag-mentary blackout) (Lee, Roh, & Kim, 2009; Perry et al., 2006; White, 2003). Blackouts and grayouts occur in both alcohol-dependent individuals and social drinkers. The probability of experiencing a blackout or grayout increases as BAC levels rise. Blackouts usually occur when there is a combination of two factors, that is, (1) fast consumption of (2) a large amount of alcohol (Perry et al., 2006). However, minor memory impairments can occur even after con-sumption of relatively small amounts of alcohol (i.e., one to two glasses) (e.g., Breitmeier, Seeland-Schulze, Hecker, & Schneider, 2007). It is important to point out that alcohol-induced memory impairments can depend on several other factors, including the type of retrieval task (e.g., recall or recognition), the memory system involved (e.g., episodic or semantic memory), and whether the BAC is increasing or decreasing (Söderlund, Parker, Schwartz, & Tulving, 2005). For example, alcohol is more likely to affect explicit (conscious) memory than implicit (unconscious) memory (Lister, Gorenstein, Fisher-Flowers, Weingartner, & Eckardt, 1991; Ray, Bates, & Ely, 2004). Some research further suggests that the effects of alcohol are also moderated by individual differences. For example, not all individuals who rapidly consume a large amount of alcohol experience an alcohol-induced blackout (White, Signer, Kraus, & Swartzwelder, 2004). This might be due to variations in genetic factors that affect the central nervous system (Lee et al., 2009). As such, it is difficult to predict which individuals will experi-ence an alcohol-induced blackout or grayout. It is also difficult to predict when memory impairments will occur within the same person given that one person can experience memory impairments one day but not the next even though the same amount of alcohol was consumed (Knowles, 2005).

Alcohol myopia theory: Alcohol myopia theory (AMT) suggests that alcohol-intoxicated individuals are in a state of myopia (i.e., near-sightedness) and pri-marily encode central information about a to-be-remembered stimulus or event, at the expense of peripheral details. The AMT was originally proposed by Claude Steele and Robert Josephs in 1990 to explain how alcohol reduces inhibition and causes intoxicated individuals to make impulsive and rash decisions such as driving under the influence or starting a bar fight (Josephs & Steele, 1990; Steele & Josephs, 1990). The theory posits that intoxicated individuals are cognitively impaired and thus have limited resources and cannot pay attention to as many stimuli as sober individuals. Consequently, drinkers are forced to concentrate on more salient aspects of a situation at the expense of less salient/peripheral aspects. In the original version of AMT, the reduced ability to focus on peripheral information was predicted to lead drinkers to make irrational decisions, because they are unable to consider alternative consequences for their actions (i.e., focus on the feelings of comfort of driving to get home fast but fail to recognize the dangers of driving under the influence) (e.g., Abbey, Saenz, & Buck, 2005; George, Rogers, & Duka, 2005). Some eyewitness memory researchers have used AMT to explain how witnesses perceive and encode information (e.g., Dysart, Lindsay, MacDonald, & Wicke, 2002). Researchers have argued that drinkers' reduced ability to perceive peripheral information in the environment also reduces their ability to provide a plentiful and accurate account of the event relative to sober or less intoxicated individuals (Harvey, Kneller, Campbell, 2013a, 2013b; Schreiber Compo et al., 2011).

Perceptions of Intoxicated Witnesses

Personal experiences and numerous "basic" alcohol and memory studies highlighting the negative relationship between alcohol and memory have led many people to associate alcohol consumption with memory impairments. This includes members of the criminal justice system (e.g., jurors, investigators) who believe alcohol distorts witness memory and diminishes both its reliability and credibility (Evans & Schreiber Compo, 2010; Evans et al., 2009; Kassin, Tubb, Hosch, & Memon, 2001). For example, Evans and Schreiber Compo (2010) asked mock jurors to read hypothetical crime reports given by witnesses and victims reported to be sober, moderately intoxicated, or highly intoxicated during the incident. Regardless of crime type and level of intoxication, witnesses who consumed alcohol were rated as more cognitively impaired, less credible, and less able to make accurate line-up identifications than those who were sober. Kassin and colleagues (2001) found this opinion was also held by legal experts. They surveyed 64 psychological experts on an array of topics pertaining to eyewitness memory and found that 90 percent agreed that the literature at that time was reliable enough to endorse the statement "alcohol intoxication impairs an eyewitness's later ability to recall persons and events." Most of the experts (61 percent) also stated they would testify in court about the topic and almost every expert (95 percent) agreed the negative relationship between alcohol and memory could be considered common sense. It is important to note, however, that when asked about impairments the experts were not provided a specific intoxication level, making it hard to interpret their answers. Interestingly, at the time of the survey (2001) there was only one published study that had examined the effects of alcohol on witness memory (Yuille & Tollestrup, 1990). Since the survey, a considerable amount of research regarding alcohol's effect on memory in general and witness memory in particular has been published that casts doubt on the extent to which the experts' opinions are warranted. For example, a handful of recent studies have revealed a variety of situations (e.g., implicit tasks, emotional episodic events) in which alcohol does not affect memory (e.g., Brown, Brignell, Dhiman, Curran, & Kamboj, 2010; Garfinkel et al., 2006; Jarosz, Colflesh, & Wiley, 2012; Molnár, Boha, Czigler, & Gaál, 2010) or can even facilitate memory (e.g., Colflesh & Wiley, 2013; Gawrylowicz, Ridley, Albery, Barnoth, & Young, 2017; Molnár et al., 2010; Moulton et al., 2005). More importantly, recently emerging work regarding alcohol's effects on *witness* memory raises doubt as to whether alcohol has any negative effect on witness memory when tested using stimulus material likened to investigative contexts, at least at low to moderate levels of intoxication.

Alcohol and Witness Memory Research

To date, there are 17 published studies that have directly examined how alcohol affects witness memory (see Appendix). Most of these studies follow the same procedure outlined above in that participants are randomly assigned to an alcohol or control condition, and sometimes also to a placebo condition, within a laboratory setting. Participants are then either presented with a live-staged interaction (e.g., Schreiber Compo et al., 2011; Schreiber Compo et al., 2012; Yuille & Tollestrup, 1990), a video of a mock crime (e.g., Hagsand, Roos af Hjelmsäter, Granhag, Fahlke & Söderpalm Gordh, 2013a, 2013b, 2017; Hildebrand Karlén, Roos af Hjelmsäter, Fahlke, Granhag, & Söderpalm Gordh, 2017; Schreiber Compo et al., 2017), or a slide show that depicts a staged interaction or mock crime (e.g., Harvey et al., 2013a, 2013b). Participants are then asked to recall information about the witnessed event and/or asked to identify an individual from the event. Recall formats and face identification procedures vary considerably across studies. For example, whereas some researchers choose written retrieval tasks (Crossland, Kneller, & Wilcock, 2016; La Rooy, Nicol, & Terry, 2013; Schreiber Compo et al., 2011), others use live mock interviews in which participants answer free, cued, multiple choice and/or yes/no questions provided by an interviewer (Hagsand et al., 2013a, 2017; Yuille & Tollestrup, 1990). Identification procedures consist of show-ups (Dysart et al., 2002), simultaneous line-ups (Hagsand et al., 2013b; Harvey et al., 2013b; Kneller & Harvey, 2015), or face recognition paradigms (Colloff & Flowe, 2016; Harvey 2014; Hilliar, Kemp, & Denson, 2010).

Studies examining the relationship between alcohol and witness memory can be categorized in various ways. This chapter will divide the research into memory for events versus memory for faces. Most studies have examined intoxicated witnesses' ability to remember events (e.g., actions, conversations, objects) while fewer studies have concentrated on intoxicated individuals' ability to recognize faces (i.e., make a line-up identification of a perpetrator seen during the crime scene or event). A few studies have tested both witnesses' memory for events and faces within the same experiment.

Memory for events: Studies examining the effect of alcohol on event memory generally center around two aspects of participants' recall: the quantity and quality of information provided by a witness. That is, researchers are interested in the amount of information intoxicated individuals recall relative to their less intoxicated/sober counterparts (e.g., quantity of recalled details) and the accuracy of this information (e.g., quality of recalled details).

Some studies suggest that alcohol negatively affects participants' recall quantity (e.g., Harvey et al., 2013a, 2013b; Hildebrand Karlén et al., 2017; Yuille & Tollestrup, 1990). That is, intoxicated individuals report fewer units of information than those who are less intoxicated and/or sober. This effect appears across different delays (e.g., immediately, 1 day, 1 week), recall formats (e.g., free, cued, multiple choice responses), and intoxication levels. However, it is important to note that specific deficits in memory quantity are not consistent between, or within, studies. For example, Hildebrand Karlén et al. (2017) found participant gender to be an important moderator, such that intoxicated females recalled less information than sober females but intoxicated males recalled the same amount of information as sober males. Another study found that question type was critical (Hagsand et al., 2017) in that intoxicated witnesses' responses to free recall questions contained less information than sober participants' responses, yet when participants' overall recall (free and cued recall combined) was taken into consideration, no differences were found between sober and intoxicated individuals. However, Hagsand et al. (2017) showed that both sober and intoxicated witnesses recalled more details and more accurately in free recall compared to cued recall. In sum, there is considerable support that alcohol can affect the amount of information reported in some fashion, even at moderate to low levels of intoxication (i.e., BACs $\leq 0.08\%$). However, the boundary conditions of the effect remain unclear.

In contrast to quantity, a negative effect of alcohol on memory quality has proven to be rather evasive, that is, only about half (i.e., six) of the studies that have examined alcohol's effect on witness memory quality have found differences between intoxicated participants and less intoxicated and/or sober participants (e.g., Yuille & Tollestrup, 1990; Schreiber Compo et al., 2012; Flowe, Takarangi, Humphries, & Wright, 2015). When significant differences do emerge, they are inconsistent. For example, Schreiber Compo et al. (2012) found that intoxicated individuals reported more inaccurate information than those who were sober. However, this effect was only apparent when participants were interviewed using cued questions compared to open-ended questions or a mixture of the two question formats (open-ended and cued). This finding suggests that investigators following the funnel approach recommended by the CI may be less likely to elicit inaccurate information from intoxicated individuals than those relying solely on cued questions. Regardless of question type, alcohol had no effect on the amount of accurate information reported by participants or the number of misinformation items incorporated into participants' reports. Flowe et al. (2015) also found that alcohol had a negative effect on participants' recall quality. This effect only appeared, however, when "*I don't know*" (IDK) responses were classified as inaccurate; it is worth noting most investigative interviewers and researchers would not consider IDK responses to be inaccurate statements. When "*I don't know*" responses were excluded from participants' statements, alcohol had no effect on participants' recall quality. Similarly, Crossland et al. (2016) found that higher levels of intoxication increased the number of "*I don't know*" responses given to cued questions. However, alcohol had no effect on the number of accurate or inaccurate details reported by participants and did not affect the quality of responses elicited from open-ended questions. In sum, the existing literature cautiously suggests that alcohol may have a stronger impact on the quality of witnesses' memory in responses to cued questions as opposed to open-ended questions. That is, open-ended questions seemingly decrease the amount of inaccurate information (fabricated or modified) reported by intoxicated individuals compared to cued questions. Cued questions, on the other hand, appear to lower intoxicated individuals' reporting threshold and lead to speculation, possibly increasing the number of false details provided. This assumption is in line with research on other witness populations (Benia, Hauck-Filho, Dillenburg, & Stein, 2015; Lamb, Orbach, Hershkowitz, Esplin, & Horowitz, 2007); however, more studies examining the relationship between alcohol and question format are needed before concrete claims can be made, especially given the variability across methods and findings in the literature thus far. That is, given the various ways in which participants have been asked to retrieve information across studies and the different ways in which that information has been scored, it is not surprising that results regarding alcohol's effect on event memory have been inconsistent. Varying methodologies are likely causes of inconsistent findings in any newly-emerging research field. It is therefore expected that as research in this area continues to grow, commonalities between studies and findings will emerge more consistently, yielding a clearer picture of the relationship between alcohol and event memory.

Given the practical implications and benefits to law enforcement, researchers have also explored how retention intervals (i.e., time between encoding and retrieval) affect intoxicated individuals' recall (e.g., Hagsand et al., 2017; La Rooy et al., 2013; Schreiber Compo et al., 2017; Yuille & Tollestrup, 1990). In these studies, memory is still assessed via the quantity and/or quality of information provided by intoxicated individuals relative to those who are sober or less intoxicated. In add-ition, comparisons are made between intoxicated individuals who provide infor-mation immediately (while intoxicated) and those who provide information after a delay (while sober; but see Schreiber Compo et al. 2017 for witnesses recalling intoxicated after a delay. Participants are also sometimes interviewed repeatedly, once immediately after witnessing the event and again after a delay, allowing researchers to examine the consistency of information provided by intoxicated individuals across time and multiple interviews. These studies show that a delay negatively affects the quantity of information provided by witnesses, regardless of intoxication (La Rooy et al., 2013; Flowe et al., 2015; Yuille & Tollestrup, 1990). Recall quality, however, often remains intact across retention intervals, suggesting that witnesses who view a crime while intoxicated will provide less overall information but accurately so even after a delay. Hagsand et al. (2017) and La Rooy et al. (2013) further found that intoxicated individuals interviewed twice incorporated new information that was not provided in their first account into their second account, much of which was accurate (around 80 percent), showing the benefits of repeated interviewing. However, to better understand how multiple interviews and retention intervals affect witness recall, future studies should test participants at different retention intervals and examine how other factors potentially moderate the relationship between alcohol and memory. For example, Schreiber Compo et al. (2017) examined how state-dependent learning may affect intoxicated individuals' ability to recall information across a retention interval. In contrast to their hypotheses, the authors found no state-dependent learning effect. That is, participants were not better when recalling information in the same state they originally encoded it in, regardless of intoxication condition. The authors point out, however, that the alcohol levels induced in the lab (BAC of around 0.08%) may have been too low to yield a state-dependent learning effect.

Taken together, empirical findings on alcohol's effect on event memory are too inconsistent to allow for a clear prediction regarding the context in which alcohol clearly affects witness memory. However, it is apparent from the data collected thus far that alcohol does not consistently impair eyewitness memory, especially at low-to-moderate BAC levels, a somewhat surprising data pattern given both lay-persons' and experts' general beliefs regarding intoxicated witnesses.

Memory for faces: Studies examining the relationship between alcohol and witnesses' facial memory typically use one of two identification procedures: a face recognition paradigm or a standard police identification procedure. In a face recognition paradigm, participants view faces displayed on a screen one at a time. Following a delay these faces are shown to participants a second time (old faces) along with faces not previously viewed (new faces). Participants' task during this second viewing is to state whether each face displayed is old or new. Findings from these studies are mixed in that one found that intoxicated participants recognized fewer old faces than those in the placebo and control conditions (Hilliar et al., 2010), while others indicate alcohol may have no effect on participants' ability to remember old and new faces (i.e., Colloff & Flowe, 2016; Harvey, 2014). It is important to note, however, that studies using the face recognition paradigm do not closely mimic line-up identifications made by witnesses in the real world (thus not listed in the Appendix). For example, although some eyewitnesses view crimes with multiple perpetrators, it is unlikely that a witness has a direct view of each perpetrator's face for a predetermined period of time. The actions performed by perpetrators of real crimes also impair witnesses' ability to remember facial features; for example, the perpetrator may never face the witness squarely but instead remain in profile. This aspect of the encoding process is not accounted for by the facial recognition paradigm. Regarding the identification phase of these studies, decisions made using this paradigm are not independent of each other given the similarities across the various faces in the stimulus set. Specifically, overlapping features among faces make it more difficult for participants to distinguish old and new faces. For example, participants in Colloff and Flowe (2016) focused on distinguishing features of old faces but were hesitant to state faces were "old." This conservative decision-making criterion suggests that participants recognized certain features of "old" faces but were unable to distinguish whether it was unique to an "old" face or an overlapping feature with a "new" face. Given these encoding and retrieval differences between the face recognition paradigm and real-world eyewitness conditions, the face recognition paradigms are considered less transferable to the memory processes of eyewitnesses (e.g., Colloff & Flowe, 2016).

Studies that use a standard police identification procedure expose witnesses to an event in which only one individual (i.e., the perpetrator) must later be identified (e.g., Hagsand et al., 2013b; Harvey et al., 2013b; Kneller & Harvey, 2015; Yuille & Tollestrup, 1990). The identification procedure used most often in these studies is the simultaneous line-up, which is frequently used in US police departments (National Institute of Justice [NIJ], 2013). Here, witnesses are shown photos simultaneously (typically six to eight) and asked to identify a previously seen face (often accompanied with the warning that the face may or may not be in the line-up). Half the witnesses in these studies view target-present line-ups, in which the perpetrator's photo is included amongst the others which should resemble the perpetrator on core physical characteristics (i.e., fillers). The remaining witnesses view target-absent line-ups, in which the perpetrator's photo is absent and all photos depicted are of individuals who simply resemble the perpetrator. The only exception in the literature is Dysart et al. (2002), who used a show-up identification procedure rather than a line-up. In a show-up, witnesses view one photo in which the perpetrator is pictured (target-present) or is not pictured (target-absent). Witnesses are then asked to state whether the individual pictured is or is not the perpetrator from the event.

Unlike the findings regarding alcohol's effect on event memory, the handful of studies on alcohol's effects on memory for faces have been more uniform in that alcohol has not been found to affect identification accuracy. For example, Yuille and Tollestrup (1990) exposed participants to a live-staged interaction. One week later participants returned to the lab and viewed either a target-present or target-absent. When the perpetrator was not pictured, intoxicated participants made slightly more false identifications than those who were sober; however, this increase was not significant. Furthermore, no intoxication-related differences were found in the choosing rates from target-present line-ups. Similarly, Hagsand and colleagues (2013b) exposed participants to a video-taped mock crime, asked participants to return to the lab one week later and to identify the perpetrator from a target-present or target-absent line-up. Again, alcohol had no effect on participants' identification accuracy rom either line-up type. Harvey et al. (2013b) yielded the same results using a shorter retention interval (1 day) and a slideshow of a mock theft. Thus, alcohol has not been found to affect identification rates in target-absent or target-present line-ups. That is, intoxicated individuals are just as likely as those who are less intoxicated and/or sober to correctly identify a perpetrator from a target-present line-up and falsely identify a suspect from a target-absent line-up. The only exception to these null findings is those reported by Dysart et al. (2002) in which alcohol increased false identifications from a target-absent show-up. It is important to note, however, that in addition to using a show-up identification procedure, Dysart et al. (2002) also tested participants at higher BAC levels than other studies (BACs as high as 0.21 percent), possibly suggesting that impairments in identification recall might not be noticeable until elevated BAC levels are reached. Dysart et al. (2002) also tested witnesses quite immediately (i.e., a 12-minute retention interval) while they were still intoxicated in contrast to the 24-hour or one-week delay used in other studies. These methodological differences suggest that Dysart et al.'s (2002) significant findings may not be a function of alcohol alone but the result of a combination of factors. To examine the impact each of these methodological differences (e.g., line-up format, retention interval before identification task, high intoxication levels) have on witness memory, more studies examining the relationship between alcohol and facial memory using standard eyewitness identification procedures are needed.

Challenges with Alcohol and Witness Memory Research

Low intoxication levels: One challenge in particular that has been discussed as a likely contributor to the null effects and inconsistent findings across studies is the low-to-moderate BAC level at which participants are frequently tested (e.g., Schreiber Compo et al., 2017). With the exception of two studies (i.e., Crossland et al., 2016; Dysart et al., 2002), every study in this area has been conducted inside laboratories where ethical and safety restrictions prohibit administering high doses of alcohol to participants. The ethically approved alcohol dose in most laboratories is 0.08g ethanol/kg, with the aim of reaching a BAC level of 0.08–0.10 percent, although some participants can fall outside of this BAC range. Although the 0.08 percent level marks the legal US driving limit and has been shown to produce consistent motor impairments (Harrison & Fillmore, 2005; Laude & Fillmore, 2015; Marczinski, Harrison, & Fillmore, 2008), it does not fully capture the range of BAC levels encountered by law enforcement (Evans et al., 2009; Palmer et al., 2013). Furthermore, these BAC levels do not allow for adequate tests of participants likely to experience an alcohol-induced blackout or grayout. Therefore, one important recommendation is that future research should examine intoxicated witnesses' memory in contexts that allow for higher BAC levels, such as in field settings (i.e., bars and restaurants).

Field versus laboratory studies: The alcohol dose restrictions associated with laboratory studies can be avoided if quasi-experimental studies are conducted in a field setting and test participants voluntarily consuming large quantities of alcohol. However, quasi-experiments in the field present their own unique challenges. For example, by testing participants who are voluntarily consuming alcohol, the experimenter loses the ability to control/manipulate the amount of alcohol participants consume, or the rate at which alcohol is consumed, possibly accentuating pre-existing differences between participants who consume large versus small amounts of alcohol. In addition to losing experimental control, finding a bar or other field setting that will allow researchers to approach patrons and utilize space to test participants can be challenging. An additional concern with field research is that individuals recruited from drinking environments such as bars may not be representative of the general population of social drinkers. Furthermore, obtaining informed consent from already intoxicated participants can raise concern about the degrees to which their consent is in fact informed.

Of course, laboratory studies are far from challenge-free. Ethical and medical safety constraints, although of immense importance, limit not only the dose of alcohol that can be administered, but also place restrictions on who can be a participant. While the exact restrictions and procedures may vary depending on the institutional review/ethics board, participants must generally be in good physical and mental health, without any problematic drinking or drug habits. Extensive screening must therefore be conducted before someone participates and potentially consumes alcohol. This limits the participant pool considerably, arguably rendering the included sample non-representative of the student drinking population and the student population in general. Adding to the time-consuming nature of laboratory-based alcohol research, participants may not leave the laboratory until they have reached an acceptably low level of intoxication (typically below 0.02 and 0.05 percent depending on study). This may require that participants be supervised during detox in the laboratory for many hours prior to release.

State of intoxication and recall delay: Another issue encountered in research on alcohol and witness memory, whether it be laboratory or field research, is the natural confound between recall delay and intoxication level/state-dependent learning. That is, when interviewed after a delay, participants who were intoxicated at encoding must now recall the event in a different state (sober, or at a different level of intoxication), whereas sober participants are in the same state of intoxication at encoding (sober) and retrieval (sober). As such, differences between groups may be due to the state of intoxication at encoding *or* a difference in states between encoding and retrieval (see Schreiber Compo et al., 2017). Given that this confound is of practical importance ("Should investigators delay interviews to let intoxicated witnesses sober up?"), researchers should focus on the importance of testing different sobering delays after different levels of intoxication are reached. Researchers must also be vigilant of how similarities across encoding and recall states might affect intoxicated individuals' accounts and consider the potential effects of re-intoxicating participants after retention intervals (Schreiber Compo et al., 2017).

Conclusions and Future Directions

Taken together, the initial wave of research on alcohol's effects on witness memory suggests that intoxicated witnesses may in fact be better than their reputation – a finding somewhat at odds with "basic" research on alcohol and memory processes (i.e., remembering word lists and syllables). Importantly, data do not suggest that low to moderate doses of alcohol (BAC below 0.10 percent) affect witnesses' memory for faces. Concerning mildly to moderately intoxicated witnesses' memory for events, findings cautiously suggest that this witness group may report less overall information. Furthermore, a handful of studies suggest that under certain conditions witness accuracy can also be negatively affected, although specific conditions have yet to be clearly identified. The next important steps in this research are therefore to systematically disentangle the relative importance of BAC level, question format, identification format, state-dependent learning, retention interval, and repeated interviews in alcohol's potential role in eyewitness memory. Future research should also examine how established interviewing techniques affect intoxicated individuals. For example, in addition to open-ending questioning, the CI recommends investigators build rapport with the witness and mentally recreate the context of the crime before attempting to elicit information (e.g., Fisher & Geiselman, 1992). These techniques may also benefit intoxicated individuals and should therefore be empirically examined. Furthermore, researchers need to effectively address real-world concerns and assist investigators in collecting the strongest evidence possible, focusing on system variables that are under the investigators' control (Wells, 1978) and including scenarios where real-world witnesses and victims are common such as domestic violence and sexual assault.

Appendix

Alcohol and Witness Memory Studies

(Chronological Order)

1. Yuille & Tollestrup (1990)
2. Dysart, Lindsay, MacDonald, & Wicke (2002)
3. Schreiber Compo, Evans, Carol, Kemp, Villalba, Ham, & Rose (2011)
4. Schreiber Compo, Evans, Carol, Villalba, Ham, Garcia, & Rose (2012)
5. Hagsand, Roos af Hjelmsäter, Granhag, Fahlke, & Söderpalm Gordh (2013a)
6. Hagsand, Roos af Hjelmsäter, Granhag, Fahlke, & Söderpalm Gordh (2013b)
7. Harvey, Kneller, & Campbell (2013a)
8. Harvey, Kneller, & Campbell (2013b)

9. La Rooy, Nicol, & Terry (2013)
10. Flowe, Takarangi, Humphries, & Wright (2015)
11. Hildebrand Karlén, Roos af Hjelmsäter, Fahlke, Granhag, & Söderpalm Gordh (2015)
12. Kneller & Harvey (2015)
13. Crossland, Kneller, & Wilcock (2016)
14. Hagsand, Roos af Hjelmsäter, Granhag, Fahlke, & Söderpalm Gordh, (2017)
15. Hildebrand Karlén, Roos af Hjelmsäter, Fahlke, Granhag, & Söderpalm Gordh (2017)
16. Schreiber Compo, Carol, Evans, Pimentel, Holness, Nichols-Lopez, Rose, & Furton (2017)
17. Flowe, Colloff, Karoglu, Zelek, Ryder, Humphries, & Takarangi (2017)

Note: This list and the chapter excludes three studies that examined the effects of alcohol on offender/suspect memory (i.e., Read, Yuille, & Tollestrup, 1992; Van Oorsouw & Merckelbach, 2012; Van Oorsouw, Merckelbach, & Smeets, 2015).

References

Abbey, A. (2002). Alcohol-related sexual assault: A common problem among college students. *Journal of Studies on Alcohol*, *14*, 118–128.

Abbey, A., Saenz, C., & Buck, P. O. (2005). The cumulative effects of acute alcohol consumption, individual differences and situational perceptions on sexual decision making. *Journal of Studies on Alcohol*, *66*, 82–90.

Abbey, A., Wegner, R., Woerner, J., Pegram, S. E., & Pierce, J. (2014). Review of survey and experimental research that examines the relationship between alcohol consumption and men's sexual aggression perpetration. *Trauma, Violence, & Abuse*, *15*, 265–282.

Allen, R. P., Faillace, L. A., & Reynolds, D. M. (1971). Recovery of memory functioning in alcoholics following prolonged alcohol intoxication. *Journal of Nervous and Mental Disease*, *153*, 417–423.

Benia, L. R., Hauck-Filho, N., Dillenburg, M., & Stein, L. M. (2015). The NICHD investigative interview protocol: A meta-analytic review. *Journal of Child Sexual Abuse*, *24*, 259–279.

Birnbaum, I. M., & Parker, E. S. (1977). *Alcohol and human memory*. Oxford: Lawrence Erlbaum Associates.

Breitmeier, D., Seeland-Schulze, I., Hecker, H., & Schneider, U. (2007). The influence of blood alcohol concentrations of around 0.03% on neuropsychological functions: A double-blind, placebo-controlled investigation. *Addiction Biology*, *12*, 183–189.

Brown, J., Brignell, C. M., Dhiman, S. K., Curran, H. V., & Kamboj, S. K. (2010). Acute effects of alcohol on memory: Impact of emotional context and serial position. *Neurobiology of Learning and Memory*, *93*, 428–434.

Bruce, K. R., & Phil, R. O. (1997). Forget "drinking to forget": Enhanced consolidation of emotionally charged memory by alcohol. *Experimental and Clinical Psychopharmacology*, *5*, 242–250.

Clouston, T. S. (1911). Alcohol and particular brain poisons as causes of unsoundness of mind. In *Unsoundness of mind* (pp. 108–115) London: Methuen & Co.

Colflesh, G. J. H., & Wiley, J. (2013). Drunk, but not blind: The effects of alcohol intoxication on change blindness. *Consciousness and Cognition: An International Journal, 22,* 231–236.

Colloff, M. F., & Flowe, H. D. (2016). The effects of acute alcohol intoxication on the cognitive mechanisms underlying false facial recognition. *Psychopharmacology, 233,* 2139–2149.

Crossland, D., Kneller, W., & Wilcock, R. (2016). Intoxicated witnesses: Testing the validity of the alcohol myopia theory. *Applied Cognitive Psychology, 30,* 270–281.

Curran, H. V., & Hildebrandt, M. (1999). Dissociative effects of alcohol on recollective experience. *Consciousness and Cognition, 8,* 497–509.

Dougherty, D. M., Marsh, D. M., Moeller, F. G., Chokshi, R. V., & Rosen, V. C. (2000). Effects of moderate and high doses of alcohol on attention, impulsivity, discriminability, and response bias in immediate and delayed memory task performance. *Alcoholism: Clinical and Experimental Research, 24,* 1702–1711.

Dysart, J. E., Lindsay, R. C. L., MacDonald, T. K., & Wicke, C. (2002). The intoxicated witness: Effects of alcohol on identification accuracy from showups. *Journal of Applied Psychology, 87,* 170–175.

Echeverria, D., Fine, L., Langolf, G., Schork, T., & Sampaio, C. (1991). Acute behavioural comparisons of toluene and ethanol in human subjects. *Occupational and Environmental Medicine, 48,* 750–761.

Evans, J. R., & Schreiber Compo, N. (2010). Mock jurors' perceptions of identifications made by intoxicated eyewitnesses. *Psychology, Crime & Law, 16,* 191–210.

Evans, J. R., Schreiber Compo, N., & Russano, M. (2009). Intoxicated witnesses and suspects: Procedures and prevalence according to law enforcement. *Psychology, Public Policy, and Law, 15,* 194–221.

Fillmore, M. T., Vogel-Sprott, M., & Gavrilescu, D. (1999). Alcohol effects on intentional behavior: Dissociating controlled and automatic influences. *Experimental and Clinical Psychopharmacology, 7,* 372–378.

Fisher, R. P., & Geiselman, R. E. (1992). *Memory-enhancing techniques for investigative interviewing: The cognitive interview.* Springfield, IL: Charles C. Thomas.

Fisher, R. P., & Schreiber, N. (2007). Interview protocols for improving eyewitness memory. In M. P. Toglia, J. D. Read, D. F. Ross, & R. C. L. Lindsay (Eds.), *The handbook of eyewitness psychology,* Vol. 1: *Memory for events* (pp. 53–80). Mahwah, NJ: Lawrence Erlbaum Associates.

Flowe, H. D., Takarangi, M. K. T., Humphries, J. E., & Wright, D. S. (2015). Alcohol and remembering a hypothetical sexual assault: Can people who were under the influence of alcohol during the event provide accurate testimony? *Memory, 24,* 1042–1061.

Flowe, H. D., Colloff, M. F., Karoğlu, N., Zelek, K., Ryder, H., Humphries, J. E., & Takarangi, M. (2017). The effects of alcohol intoxication on accuracy and the confidence–accuracy relationship in photographic simultaneous line-ups. *Applied Cognitive Psychology, 31,* 379–391.

Garfinkel, S. N., Dienes, Z., & Duka, T. (2006). The effect of alcohol and repetition at encoding on implicit and explicit false memories. *Psychopharmacology, 188,* 498–508.

Gawrylowicz, J., Ridley, A. M., Albery, I. P., Barnoth, E., & Young, J. (2017). Alcohol-induced retrograde facilitation renders witnesses of crime less suggestible to misinformation. *Psychopharmacology, 234,* 1267–1275.

George, S., Rogers, R. D., & Duka, T. (2005). The acute effect of alcohol on decision making in social drinkers. *Psychopharmacology, 182,* 160–169. doi: 10.1037/t00696-000

Gibson, W. E. (1985). Effects of alcohol on radial maze performance in rats. *Physiology & Behavior, 35,* 1003–1005.

Goodwin, D. W., Powell, B., Bremer, D., Hoine, H., & Stern, J. (1969). Alcohol and recall: State-dependent effects in man. *Science, 163*, 1358–1360.

Goodwin, D. W., Hill, S. Y., Powell, B., & Viamontes, J. (1973). Effect of alcohol on short term memory in alcoholics. *British Journal of Psychiatry, 122*, 93–94.

Granhag, P. A., Ask, K., & Mac Giolla, E. (2013). Eyewitness recall: An overview of estimator-based research. In T. J. Perfect & D. S. Lindsay (Eds.), *The SAGE handbook of applied memory* (pp. 541–558). London: Sage Publications.

Hagsand, A., Roos af Hjelmsäter, E., Granhag, P. A., Fahlke, C., & Söderpalm Gordh, A. (2013a). Bottled memories: On how alcohol affects eyewitness' recall. *Scandinavian Journal of Psychology, 54*, 188–195.

Hagsand, A., Roos af Hjelmsäter, E., Granhag, P. A., Fahlke, C., & Söderpalm Gordh, A. (2013b). Do sober eyewitnesses outperform alcohol intoxicated eyewitnesses in a lineup? *European Journal of Psychology Applied to Legal Context, 5*, 23–47.

Hagsand, A. V, Roos af Hjelmsäter, E., Granhag, P. A., Fahlke, C., & Söderpalm Gordh, A. (2017). Witnesses stumbling down memory lane: The effects of alcohol intoxication, retention interval, and repeated interviewing. *Memory, 25*, 531–543.

Harrison, E. L. R., & Fillmore, M. T. (2005). Are bad drivers more impaired by alcohol? Sober driving precision predicts impairment from alcohol in a simulated driving task. *Accident Analysis and Prevention, 37*, 882–889.

Harvey, A. J. (2014). Some effects of alcohol and eye movements on cross-race face learning. *Memory, 22*, 1126–1138.

Harvey, A. J., Kneller, W., & Campbell, A. C. (2013a). The effects of alcohol intoxication on attention and memory for visual scenes. *Memory, 21*, 969–980.

Harvey, A. J., Kneller, W., & Campbell, A. C. (2013b). The elusive effects of alcohol intoxication on visual attention and eyewitness memory. *Applied Cognitive Psychology, 27*, 617–624.

Hildebrand Karlén, M., Roos af Hjelmsäter, E., Fahlke, C., Granhag, P. A., & Söderpalm Gordh, A. (2015). Alcohol intoxicated witnesses: Perception of aggression and guilt in intimate partner violence. *Journal of Interpersonal Violence, 32*, 3448–3474.

Hildebrand Karlén, M., Roos af Hjelmsäter, E., Fahlke, C., Granhag, P. A., & Söderpalm Gordh, A. (2017). To wait or not to wait? Improving results when interviewing intoxicated witnesses to violence. *Scandinavian Journal of Psychology, 58*, 15–22.

Hilliar, K. F., Kemp, R. I., & Denson, T. F. (2010). Now everyone looks the same: Alcohol intoxication reduces the own-race bias in face recognition. *Law and Human Behavior, 34*, 367–378.

Hodges, H., Thrasher, S., & Gray, J. A. (1989). Improved radial maze performance induced by the benzodiazepine antagonist ZK 93 426 in lesioned and alcohol-treated rats. *Behavioural Pharmacology, 1*, 45–55.

Hollingworth, H. L. (1923). The influence of alcohol. *Journal of Abnormal Psychology and Social Psychology, 18*, 204–237.

Jarosz, A. F., Colflesh, G. J. H., & Wiley, J. (2012). Uncorking the muse: Alcohol intoxication facilitates creative problem solving. *Consciousness and Cognition: An International Journal, 21*, 487–493.

Josephs, R. A., & Steele, C. M. (1990). The two faces of alcohol myopia: Attentional mediation of psychological stress. *Journal of Abnormal Psychology, 99*, 115–126.

Kassin, S. M., Tubb, V. A., Hosch, H. M., & Memon, A. (2001). On the "general acceptance" of eyewitness testimony research: A new survey of the experts. *American Psychologist, 56*, 405–416.

Kneller, W., & Harvey, A. J. (2015). Lineup identification accuracy: The effects of alcohol, target presence, confidence ratings, and response time. *European Journal of Psychology Applied to Legal Context, 8*, 11–18.

Knowles, S. K. Z. (2005). The effect of alcohol on memory for emotionally significant events (Doctoral dissertation). Retrieved from database of Gothenburg University Library, Sweden.

Knowles, S. K. Z., & Duka, T. (2004). Does alcohol affect memory for emotional and non-emotional experiences in different ways? *Behavioural Pharmacology, 15*, 111–121.

Lamb, M. E., Orbach, Y., Hershkowitz, I., Esplin, P. W., & Horowitz, D. (2007). A structured forensic interview protocol improves the quality and informativeness of investigative interviews with children: A review of research using the NICHD investigative interview protocol. *Child Abuse & Neglect, 31*, 1201–1231.

La Rooy, D., Nicol, A., & Terry, P. (2013). Intoxicated eyewitnesses: The effects of alcohol on eyewitness recall across repeated interviews. *Open Journal of Medical Psychology, 2*, 107–114.

Laude, J. R., & Fillmore, M. T. (2015). Simulated driving performance under alcohol: Effects on driver-risk versus driver-skill. *Drug and Alcohol Dependence, 154*, 271–277.

Lee, H., Roh, S., & Kim, D. J. (2009). Alcohol-induced blackout. *International Journal of Environmental Research and Public Health, 6*, 2783–2792.

Lister, R. G., Gorenstein, C., Fisher-Flowers, D., Weingartner, H. J., & Eckardt, M. J. (1991). Dissociation of the acute effects of alcohol on implicit and explicit memory processes. *Neuropsychologia, 29*, 1205–1212.

Lombardi, W. J., Sirocco, K. Y., Andreason, P. J., & George, D. T. (1997). Effects of triazolam and ethanol on proactive interference: Evidence for an impairment in retrieval inhibition. *Journal of Clinical and Experimental Neuropsychology, 19*, 698–712.

MacInnes, J. W., & Uphouse, L. L. (1973). Effects of alcohol on acquisition and retention of passive-avoidance conditioning in different mouse strains. *Journal of Comparative and Physiological Psychology, 84*, 398–402.

Mann, R. E., Cho-Young, J., & Vogel-Sprott, M. (1984). Retrograde enhancement by alcohol of delayed free recall performance. *Pharmacology, Biochemistry and Behavior, 20*, 639–642.

Marczinski, C. A., Harrison, E. L. R., & Fillmore, M. T. (2008). Effects of alcohol on simulated driving and perceived driving impairment in binge drinkers. *Alcoholism: Clinical and Experimental Research, 32*, 1329–1337.

Maylor, F. A., & Rabbit, P. M. A. (1987). Effect of alcohol on rate of forgetting. *Psychopharmacology, 91*, 230–235.

Maylor, E. A., & Rabbitt, P. M. (1993). Alcohol, reaction time and memory: A meta-analysis. *British Journal of Psychology, 84*, 301–317.

Mello, N. K. (1973). Short-term memory function in alcohol addicts during intoxication. In M. M. Gross (Ed.), *Alcohol intoxication and withdrawal: Experimental studies* (pp. 333–344). New York: Plenum.

Mintzer, M. Z. (2007). The acute effects of alcohol on memory: A review of laboratory studies in healthy adults. *International Journal on Disability and Human Development, 6*, 397–403.

Mohler-Kuo, M., Dowdall, G. W., Koss, M. P., & Wechsler, H. (2004). Correlates of rape while intoxicated in a national sample of college women. *Journal of Studies on Alcohol, 65*, 37–45.

Molnár, M., Boha, R., Czigler, B., & Gaál, Z. A. (2010). The acute effect of alcohol on various memory processes. *Journal of Psychophysiology, 24*, 249–252.

Moulton, P. L., Petros, T. V., Apostal, K. J., Park, R. V., II, Ronning, E. A., King, B. M., & Penland, J. G. (2005). Alcohol-induced impairment and enhancement of memory: A test of the interference theory. *Physiology & Behavior, 85*, 240–245.

National Institute of Justice [NIJ], Police Executive Research Reform, Office of Justice Programs, U.S. Department of Justice (2013). *A national survey of eyewitness identification procedures in law enforcement agencies.* NIJ Publication No. 2010-IJ-CX0032. Retrieved from www.ncjrs.gov/pdffiles1/nij/grants/242617.pdf

Nordby, K., Watten, R. G., Raanaas, R. K., & Magnussen, S. (1999). Effects of moderate doses of alcohol on immediate recall of numbers: Some implications for information technology. *Journal of Studies on Alcohol, 60*, 873–878.

Palmer, F. T., Flowe, H. D., Takarangi, M. K. T., & Humphries, J. E. (2013). Intoxicated witnesses and suspects: An archival analysis of their involvement in criminal case processing. *Law and Human Behavior, 37*, 54–59.

Parker, E. S., Birnbaum, I. M., & Noble, E. P. (1976). Alcohol and memory: Storage and state dependency. *Journal of Verbal Learning & Verbal Behavior, 15*, 691–702.

Perry, P. J., Argo, T. R., Barnett, M. J., Liesveld, J. L., Liskow, B., Hernan, J. M., . . . Brabson, M. A. (2006). The association of alcohol-induced blackouts and grayouts to blood alcohol concentrations. *Journal of Forensic Sciences, 51*, 896–899.

Rape, Abuse, and Incest National Network [RAINN] (2016). *Reporting Results.* Retrieved from https://rainn.org/get-information/statistics/reporting-rates

Ray, S., Bates, M. E., & Ely, B. M. (2004). Alcohol's dissociation of implicit and explicit memory processes: Implications of a parallel distributed processing model of semantic priming. *Experimental and Clinical Psychopharmacology, 12*, 118–125.

Read, J. D., Yuille, J. C., & Tollestrup, P. (1992). Recollections of a robbery: Effects of arousal and alcohol upon recall and person identification. *Law and Human Behavior, 16*, 425–446.

Rohsenow, D. J., & Marlatt, G. A. (1981). The balanced placebo design: Methodological considerations. *Addictive Behaviors, 6*, 107–122.

Schreiber Compo, N., Evans, J. R., Carol, R. N., Kemp, D., Villalba, D., Ham, L. S., & Rose, S. (2011). Alcohol intoxication and memory for events: A snapshot of alcohol myopia in a real-world drinking scenario. *Memory, 19*, 202–210.

Schreiber Compo, N., Evans, J. R., Carol, R. N., Villalba, D., Ham, L. S., Garcia, T., & Rose, S. (2012). Intoxicated eyewitnesses: Better than their reputation? *Law and Human Behavior, 36*, 77–86.

Schreiber Compo, N., Carol, R. N., Evans, J. R., Pimentel, P., Holness, H., Nichols-Lopez, K., . . . Furton, K. G. (2017). Witness memory and alcohol: The effects of state-dependent recall. *Law and Human Behavior, 41*, 202–215.

Söderlund, H., Parker, E. S., Schwartz, B. L., & Tulving, E. (2005). Memory encoding and retrieval on the ascending and descending limbs of the blood alcohol concentration curve. *Psychopharmacology, 182*, 305–317.

Soraci, S. A., Carlin, M. T., Read, J. D., Pogoda, T. K., Wakeford, Y., Cavanagh, S., & Shin, L. (2007). Psychological impairment, eyewitness testimony, and false memories: Individual differences. In M. P. Toglia, J. D. Read, D. F. Ross, & R. C. L. Lindsay (Eds.), *The handbook of eyewitness psychology*, Vol. 1: *Memory for events* (pp. 261–297). Mahwah, NJ: Lawrence Erlbaum Associates.

Steele, C. M., & Josephs, R. A. (1990). Alcohol myopia: Its prized and dangerous effects. *American Psychologist, 45*, 921–933.

Tamerin, J. S., Weiner, S., Poppen, R., Steinglass, P., & Mendelson, J. H. (1971). Alcohol and memory: Amnesia and short-term memory function during experimentally induced intoxication. *American Journal of Psychiatry, 127*, 1659–1664.

Testa, M., Hoffman, J. H., & Livingston, J. A. (2010). Alcohol and sexual risk behaviors as mediators of the sexual victimization-revictimization relationship. *Journal of Consulting and Clinical Psychology, 78*, 249–259.

Testa, M., & Livingston, J. A. (2009). Alcohol consumption and women's vulnerability to sexual victimization: Can reducing women's drinking prevent rape? *Substance Use & Misuse, 44*, 1349–1376.

Testa, M., Fillmore, M. T., Norris, J., Abbey, A., Curtin, J. J., Leonard, K. E., . . . Hayman, L. W., Jr. (2006). Understanding alcohol expectancy effects: Revisiting the placebo condition. *Alcoholism: Clinical and Experimental Research, 30*, 339–348.

Tracy, J. I., & Bates, M. E. (1999). The selective effects of alcohol on automatic and effortful memory processes. *Neuropsychology, 13*, 282–290.

Tyson, P. D., & Schirmuly, M. (1994). Memory enhancement after drinking ethanol: Consolidation, interference, or response bias? *Physiology & Behavior, 56*, 933–937.

Van Oorsouw, K., & Merckelbach, H. L. G. J. (2012). The effects of alcohol on crime-related memories: A field study. *Applied Cognitive Psychology, 26*, 82–90.

Van Oorsouw, K., Merckelbach, H., & Smeets, T. (2015). Alcohol intoxication impairs memory and increases suggestibility for a mock crime: a field study. *Applied Cognitive Psychology, 29*, 493–501.

Walker, D. W., & Hunter, B. E. (1978). Short-term memory impairment following chronic alcohol consumption in rats. *Neuropsychologia, 16*, 545–553.

Weissenborn, R., & Duka, T. (2000). State-dependent effects of alcohol on explicit memory: The role of semantic associations. *Psychopharmacology, 149*, 98–106. doi: 10.1007/s002139900349

Wells, G. L. (1978). Applied eyewitness-testimony research: System and estimator variables. *Journal of Personality and Social Psychology, 36*(12), 1546–1557.

Wells, G. L., & Olson, E. A. (2003). Eyewitness testimony. *Annual Review of Psychology, 54*, 277–295.

White, A. M. (2003). What happened? Alcohol, memory blackouts, and the brain. *Alcohol Research & Health, 27*, 186–196.

White, A. M., Matthews, D. B., & Best, P. J. (2000). Ethanol, memory, and hippocampal function: A review of recent findings. *Hippocampus, 10*, 88–93.

White, A. M., Signer, M. L., Kraus, C. L., & Swartzwelder, H. S. (2004). Experiential aspects of alcohol-induced blackouts among college students. *American Journal of Drug and Alcohol Abuse, 30*, 205–224.

Yuille, J. C. (1986). Meaningful research in the police context. In J. C. Yuille (Ed.), *Police selection and training: The role of psychology* (pp. 225–246). Dordrecht: Martinus Nijhoff.

Yuille, J. C., & Tollestrup, P. A. (1990). Some effects of alcohol on eyewitness memory. *Journal of Applied Psychology, 75*, 268–273.

6

FROM THE POLICE STATION TO THE HOSPITAL BED

Using the Cognitive Interview to Enhance Epidemiologic Interviewing

Alexandra E. Mosser and Jacqueline R. Evans

There is a plethora of research on investigative interviewing in criminal contexts. However, other areas in which interviewing is critical to an investigation remain unstudied. One notable context in which the outcome of the investigation hinges on the quality of an individual's report is during an epidemiological investigation. Epidemiological investigations are conducted during outbreaks of infectious diseases, foodborne illnesses, and other threats to public health. During these investigations, critical interviews are conducted to trace the origins of an outbreak or to identify other potentially infected individuals. As such, investigators need to generate the most exhaustive reports possible during the interviews. Consider an outbreak of an infectious disease: investigators will be seeking to identify the source of the infection and/or to locate all those who were exposed to the pathogen by asking infected interviewees to recall individuals they had contact with (i.e., their contacts) during the time they were contagious.

Providing information during such an interview is fundamentally a memory task. As such, the interviewee is subject to the conventional principles and fallibilities of human memory. Indeed, extensive cognitive psychology research has demonstrated that during a simple listing task, both errors of omission (i.e., forgetting) and errors of commission (i.e., false alarms) occur regularly (e.g., Anderson, Bjork & Bjork, 1994; Tulving & Osler, 1968; Tulving & Pearlstone, 1966). Even more troubling for epidemiological investigation contexts, research has demonstrated that errors of omission and commission are often committed by witnesses when recalling the people encountered over the course of a criminal event (e.g., Cohen & Faulkner, 1989; Migueles & García-Bajos, 2007; Shaw, Bjork, & Handal, 1995).

Despite its importance, surprisingly little research has examined the extent to which people can provide an exhaustive report of relevant information during an epidemiological interview. The minimal literature suggests that the fallibility of human memory is indeed evident in epidemiological interviewing (e.g., Brewer, Garrett, & Kulasingam, 1999). Because of its generalizability to many types of interviewing contexts, as well as its basis in basic psychological theory, we expect the Cognitive Interview (CI) to be beneficial across many types of epidemiologic interviewing. Below we discuss epidemiological interviewing in general and how the CI might be used to increase the efficacy of these interviews. We give particular attention to contact tracing for infectious disease interventions.

Epidemiological Interviewing

Infectious disease contact tracing interviews: Contact tracing is the chief procedure used by the Centers for Disease Control and Prevention (CDC) to control several infectious diseases and is comprised of identifying and isolating individuals who have come in contact with infectious parties. One of the most critical components of the contact tracing process is the interview, which involves asking infectious individuals to list both the people encountered and the places visited since the time of infection (Eames & Keeling, 2003). For example, imagine that a sick individual is admitted to a hospital for treatment. During questioning at intake, the medical staff learns that the individual has recently traveled from a region in which an Ebola outbreak occurred. As suspected, the individual tests positive for Ebola. In addition to providing treatment to the patient, one of the most important tasks for the medical staff becomes identifying who may have been exposed to the patient when he or she was infectious, and who may have infected the patient (and may be continuing to infect others).

To investigate the patient's contacts, a contact tracing interview (CTI) is conducted. The interview process begins by determining when the individual became contagious. This allows the interviewer (typically an epidemiologist) to pinpoint the critical timeframe during which all contacts must be established. Once the contagious period is identified, the epidemiologist asks the patient to recall every contact from the time he or she became infectious until entering the emergency room (by using anywhere from one to several open-ended prompts and follow-up questions). The listed contacts are subsequently investigated, and the relevant individuals are assessed for possible illness, quarantined if indicated, interviewed about their potential contacts, and ultimately treated if warranted.

The types of contacts requested by an epidemiologist during an interview differ depending on the disease of interest and how it is transmitted (e.g., sexual contact, droplet, airborne). For example, if a disease involves droplet transmission then an epidemiologist will request a list of everyone with whom the patient has had physical contact. However, if a disease is spread through the air an epidemiologist will request a list of everyone the patient may have been in the same room with during the time the patient was contagious.

Interestingly, there is no official standard contact tracing interviewing procedure. This is common when considering interviewing of any type of cooperative interviewee across many different disciplines. For example, there is no standard procedure for police to be trained in interviewing cooperative witnesses in the USA. The same could be said for accident investigations conducted by various transportation groups, and even questioning by medical practitioners about a patient's health practices. Nevertheless, guidelines are provided by both the World Health Organization (WHO) and the Centers for Disease Control and Prevention (CDC) about how to conduct CTIs (e.g., WHO, 2015).

The CDC and WHO acknowledge the significance of the contract tracing process (CDC, 2016), and the guidance they provide is helpful in giving a broad overview of the type of information to seek during the CTI (WHO, 2015). For example, the WHO provides a standard form to be filled out that includes key information to be gathered (e.g., relation to interviewee, date of last contact, phone number). However, there is minimal guidance on the types of questions to ask. For example, the guidance provided by the WHO and CDC for implementation and management of contact tracing in response to the recent Ebola outbreak in Africa indicated that interviewers should "ask probing questions to ascertain all of the case's activities since the onset of illness and identify everyone involved in those activities. This interview should be comprehensive, detailed, and extensive" and that interviewers should "actively listen, know how to ask probing questions, show empathy, adjust the interview based on the case's or family members' emotional state, etc." (WHO, 2015). Based on the available resources (e.g., WHO, 2015) it might be surmised that a typical CTI involves some request for a list of contacts, perhaps generated by cueing specific places visited, specific categories of people (e.g., lived with, sexual contacts), and providing a calendar. These questions would likely be followed by additional, more pointed questions that allow the interviewer to complete the standard form (e.g., address, etc.).

Contact tracing is vital to containing deadly diseases for at least three reasons. First, it helps identify infected people. These infected people will then be able to obtain treatment, and further transmission can be prevented either through counseling or, if indicated, by isolation until they are no longer infectious. Second, it allows epidemiologists to identify who may have transmitted the infection to the patient. Once this person is identified, it is critical to interview him or her to determine who else may have interacted with that individual, and may also have been infected. Third, it helps identify exposed, yet symptom-free people. Symptoms can be monitored in these people, earlier treatment can be facilitated, or in rare cases, such as an Ebola exposure, quarantine may be implemented until the incubation period has passed. Because it is imperative that every potentially exposed individual is identified (both to prevent further transmission and provide treatment), the most exhaustive list of contacts possible should be produced (e.g., Brewer et al., 2005; Eames & Keeling, 2003; Potterat, 1997).

Despite its importance to public health, there is almost no research on the efficacy of interviews used by epidemiologists, and what has been conducted is limited to contact tracing in the case of sexually transmitted infection, and injection drug users (e.g., Brewer et al., 1999). Further, there is no systematic research on what a "standard" CTI involves. However, the limited literature suggests that procedures in which attempts are made to enhance cognitive or social processes during the interview will result in enhanced recall and reduced forgetting (e.g., Brewer et al., 2005). Based on this, we expect that the well-respected, and empirically validated Cognitive Interview (CI) will be an effective method of improving interviewee recall during CTIs.

The Cognitive Interview

Originally developed by Ed Geiselman and Ronald P. Fisher for use in cooperative witness interviews, the CI implements established theories of social and cognitive psychology to increase the amount of information reported (Fisher & Geiselman, 1992). The original CI, drawing on theories of encoding specificity and reminiscence, employs four specific mnemonics or memory aids to augment retrieval: mentally reinstating the emotional and physical context of the to-be-reported stimuli, changing the order in which the targeted information is reported (reverse order), recalling the event from a different perspective (change perspective), and an instruction to report exhaustively (Geiselman, Fisher, MacKinnon, & Holland, 1986).

The original version of the CI was later modified to include important tenets of social psychology (the establishment of social dynamics and enhancement of communication between the interviewee and interviewer). This most recent version of the CI employs three general components to aid in an individual's recall: (a) establishing positive social dynamics; (b) enhancing cognitive processes; and (c) facilitating communication. The establishment of social dynamics includes the development of rapport, explicit instructions that the interviewee will do most of the talking, the use of open-ended questions, and avoiding interviewer interruptions. The cognitive processes of the interviewee are facilitated by reinstating the context (both physical and emotional) in which the event took place, asking for interviewees to repeatedly search through memory and approach the memory from different perspectives, asking non-suggestive questions, tailoring the questions to match the way the interviewee encoded the event, asking the interviewee not to guess, and instructing the interviewee to close his or her eyes during responding. Finally, communication is enhanced by employing methods to help a witness or patient more effectively convey information that may not be readily provided in a verbal form. Most notably, the sketch is recommended as a way to elicit spatially encoded information. Taken together, these tools should work to alleviate concerns regarding forgetting during a CTI (e.g., Brewer et al., 2005) by (a) alleviating general forgetting and (b) communicating to the interviewee that the interviewer wants the most exhaustive report possible (Fisher, Milne, & Bull, 2011; Fisher & Geiselman, 1992).

Theoretical Basis of the Cognitive Interview

The CI is heavily rooted in psychological theory. In fact, each of the CI's established techniques can be traced to classic psychological principles. The CI's reliance on evidence-based theory provides robust grounds for predicting an increase in contacts generated by a CI compared to a typical CTI.

Basis of social dynamics in psychological theory: The establishment of social dynamics was incorporated into the CI as a result of research suggesting that certain social techniques can optimize the amount of information gathered from witnesses. For example, in the CI, interviewers are instructed to develop rapport by person-alizing the interview (e.g., actively listening, using the interviewee's name) and communicating empathy (e.g., letting the interviewee know his or her feelings are understood) (Fisher & Geiselman, 1992). The establishment of rapport has clear support in the psychological literature (Collins, Lincoln, & Frank 2002). Positive working rapport has been noted to reduce the interviewee's anxiety at reporting, as well as establish trust between the parties. During a CTI, the interviewee may be reluctant to report because of the shame associated with having contracted the disease or a reluctance to confine friends and family to quarantine. Researchers have posited that positive rapport can increase trust and comfort at reporting (e.g., Chapple, 1999), thereby likely increasing the number of contacts a person provides.

The use of open-ended questions (e.g., "describe the robber") is another example of an empirically grounded technique, which influences not only social dynamics, but also the cognitive processes of the witness (Powell, Fisher, & Wright, 2005). The use of open-ended questioning has been touted as one of the most important recommendations for use in interviewing. In fact, an extensive body of literature suggests that interviewees tend to provide more information, and more accurate information in response to open-ended questions (Fisher, Schreiber Compo, Rivard, & Hirn, 2014). However, it is important to note that, as indicated by Fisher et al. (2014), it is difficult to compare the accuracy of closed-ended (e.g., "was the robber wearing a mask?") to open-ended questions (e.g., "describe the robber") because they often vary on other factors as well (e.g., differing levels of difficulty). Nevertheless, open-ended questions are primarily recommended to (a) encourage the interviewee to provide a lot of information (rather than just responding to a few, pointed closed-ended questions), (b) maximize metacognitive control, and (c) reduce the chance of suggestion by the interviewer.

The use of open-ended questions has clear social value as well. When the inter-viewer asks only specific, closed-ended questions, it suggests to interviewees that they should wait for each question before generating a response. It also communicates that the only valuable information to be provided is the information that the investigator wants to know (e.g., whether the robber was wearing a mask or not). As a result, interviewees are reluctant to provide additional information because it is perceived as unimportant. The instruction for interviewers not to interrupt has related implications. If an interviewer continually interrupts the interviewee, the interviewee assumes that what he or she has to say is less important than any contribution made by the interviewer.

Much research also suggests that in a free-recall (open-ended) report, interviewees are able to maximize their metacognitive control. Koriat and Goldsmith (1996) posited a model whereby individuals first use metacognitive monitoring to assess the subjective accuracy of a response (e.g., confidence, how fast it comes to mind), and if the subjective evaluation of accuracy passes the response threshold, the information is volunteered, otherwise it is withheld (metacognitive control). Research has suggested that interviewees are able to most effectively control the accuracy of their reports in a free report context (e.g., Evans & Fisher, 2011). As such, it is expected that open-ended questions lead to the most accurate reports, even as time passes and memory traces consequently weaken.

In addition to maximizing control, open-ended questions also influence cognitive processing by allowing the interviewee to search through memory in a way that is compatible with how the event was encoded. Classic psychological literature refers to this as Transfer Appropriate Processing (TAP). When closed-ended questions are used, the interviewee recalls the event in the way specified by the interviewer's questions (rather than how it was initially encoded). Thus, open-ended questions are recommended.

The use of open-ended questions is also important because it helps control the amount of information the interviewer inadvertently leaks to the interviewee. Oftentimes closed-ended questions can become leading or suggestive. Suggestive questions can lead the interviewee to report information that is inaccurate and based merely on information provided by the interviewer. The effects of post-event misinformation have been studied extensively, and the research suggests that the accuracy of interviewee reports is harmed by these intrusions (e.g., Loftus, 1975; Loftus & Zanni, 1975; Roebers & Schneider, 2000).

During the development of social dynamics interviewees are also explicitly instructed that they are the experts, know the most about the event, should not wait for questions to respond, and are in control of the interview. This is useful for multiple reasons. First, it helps to overcome some of the problems associated with an interviewee's preconceived notions about what a typical interview entails. Oftentimes an interviewee believes that the interview will be conducted much like seen on TV; the investigators will ask many skillful questions and will solve the case based on their masterful questioning technique. Disabusing them of this misconception should help increase the amount of information provided. This instruction also informs interviewees that they will be doing a great deal of the talking. As a result, the interviewee is likely to provide more information than if not provided with this instruction. Finally, this instruction puts the interviewee in control of the reporting process. Therefore, interviewees should be more comfortable providing new information spontaneously throughout the interview.

Basis of enhancing cognitive processes in psychological theory: The cognitive techniques of the CI are based largely on influencing the interviewee's retrieval processes. To aid in the fluent retrieval of the target information, Fisher and Geiselman borrowed from several well-established theories of cognitive psychology. For example, one of the major tenets of the CI is to search through memory repeatedly. Research suggests that the more retrieval attempts that are made, the more likely new information will be provided (Roediger & Payne, 1982). Indeed, much research has demonstrated that reminiscence (recalling an item at a second instance of retrieval that was not reported during the first) is common in repeated interviews (e.g., Gilbert & Fisher, 2006; Oeberst, 2012; Turtle & Yuille, 1994). For instance, in one study, every participant questioned about a mock crime made at least one reminiscent response (Oeberst, 2012). Gilbert and Fisher (2006) similarly reported that 98 percent of participants reminisced during a second retrieval attempt. In the CI, interviewees attempt retrieval multiple times, much like undergoing a second interview. These multiple attempts tend to lead to the addition of new details.

It has also been suggested that there are many different paths to retrieval (Anderson & Pichert, 1978). In line with this thinking, the CI encourages the interviewee to explore different means of retrieval. For example, interviewees may be asked to approach the memory through different perspectives. Classic research has demonstrated that when asked to adopt another person's perspective after an initial recall attempt, more information can be retrieved (Anderson & Pichert, 1978). For example, a customer who witnesses a convenience store robbery might first report the encounter from their own perspective, and then report it from the perspective of the cashier.

Yet another way in which retrieval can be aided is through providing retrieval cues to the interviewee during reporting. In the CI these cues can be provided through context reinstatement. Related directly to the idea that cues are necessary for successful retrieval (i.e., cue-dependent forgetting), is the finding that memory is best when the context at encoding matches the context at retrieval (i.e., the Encoding Specificity Principle; e.g. Tulving and Thomson, 1973). In one famous experiment (Godden & Baddeley, 1975) participants encoded a series of to-be-remembered information either on dry land (above water) or under water (scuba diving). Participants were then asked to recall the information either on dry land or under water. Results demonstrated that participants remembered the items better when they were encoded and recalled in the same context (either both under water or both on land).

In accordance with the literature regarding the Encoding Specificity Principle, Fisher and Geiselman incorporated context reinstatement into the CI as a tool to make the context at retrieval as close as possible to that during encoding. During context reinstatement the interviewee is asked to mentally recreate the psychological, emotional, and/or physiological context of encoding (Fisher & Geiselman, 1992). By matching (as close to possible) the context at encoding to the context at retrieval, the cues present at encoding of the event should also be present at retrieval. As a result, more information should be elicited from the interviewee than if context reinstatement is not used.

The CI's instruction for interviewees to close their eyes during reporting is also based on classic theories of human cognition. The process of retrieval, especially as it pertains to the CI, is rather effortful. Interviewees are asked to extensively search their memories, requiring substantial concentration. As a result, the interviewer should facilitate concentration in any way possible. Instructing the interviewee to close his or her eyes is one of the CI's proposed methods to enhance concentration. Closing of the eyes allows the interviewee to block out any external distractors and also allows for a more vivid mental image to be formed during retrieval (specifically during context reinstatement) (e.g., Vredeveldt et al., 2015; Vredeveldt, Baddeley & Hitch, 2014; Vredeveldt & Sauer, 2015).

Basis of facilitating communication in psychological theory: The CI also aims to facilitate communication by providing ways for the interviewee to express information that might not be amenable to verbal form. The best example of facilitating communication in the CI is perhaps the sketch. Oftentimes interviewees struggle to verbalize certain aspects of an event. For example, it may be difficult to portray where certain parties were positioned, or how they moved about the space. In this instance the CI recommends the interviewee sketch the event or scene and narrate while sketching. Not only does the sketch itself provide more information about the event, but the act of narrating while sketching also serves as another retrieval attempt, resulting in the addition of new details.

Laboratory and Field Success of the Cognitive Interview

Years of field and laboratory studies have comprehensively examined the efficacy of the CI under numerous conditions (for reviews see Fisher, Ross, & Cahill, 2010; Griffiths & Milne, 2010; for meta-analyses see Köhnken, Milne, Memon, & Bull, 1999 and Memon, Meissner, & Fraser, 2010). In a typical CI study, participants (college students) are asked to encode some to-be-remembered event (a live or videotaped event) that is criminal (e.g., bank robbery) or neutral (e.g., conversation between professor and student) in nature. After encoding the event, participants are interviewed by someone trained in either the CI or a Standard Interview commonly used in the field (e.g., Federal Law Enforcement's Five-Step Interview). Transcripts of the interviews are subsequently analyzed to assess differences in the amount and accuracy of the information gathered by the contrasting interviews. Hundreds of laboratory and field experiments have been conducted across the world and have explored many different variables including the type of witness (e.g., children, intellectually disabled, police officers), type of event (e.g., crime, accident, terrorist meeting), and delay between event and interview (e.g., immediately after, weeks after, 35 years after the event).

Research has overwhelmingly demonstrated that the CI substantially increases the amount of information gathered during an interview (e.g., Fisher, Geiselman & Amador, 1989; Fisher et al., 2011; Köhnken et al., 1999). In fact, across all published studies the CI tended to increase the amount of information gathered by anywhere from 25 percent to 50 percent compared to a Standard Interview (Memon et al., 2010). In one field study alone, detectives trained on the CI gathered 63 percent more information than untrained detectives (Fisher et al., 1989).

Two notable meta-analyses have analyzed the combined effects of the CI across all available research. In an early meta-analysis of 36 studies conducted on the CI, researchers reported a large effect size for the increase in accurate information obtained by a CI, with a slight increase in inaccurate information gathered. Nevertheless, the overall accuracy rates (i.e., the proportion of inaccurate to accurate information) did not differ between the CI and Standard Interview (Köhnken et al., 1999). In a more recent meta-analysis of 46 published studies, Memon and colleagues (2010) similarly demonstrated a large increase in correct details, a small but significant effect of increase in incorrect details (but with no difference in overall accuracy rates), and no significant increase in confabulated details.

Generalizability of the Cognitive Interview Beyond Witnesses

The CI, supported by over 25 years of research, has been acknowledged as one of the most successful advances made in the field of law and psychology (Memon et al., 2010). As such, it has been applied to a wealth of contrasting areas in which individuals are interviewed for information. Furthermore, because the CI is based on general principles of memory and cognition (e.g., Tulving & Thomson, 1973; Gilbert & Fisher, 2006), it lends itself easily to any type of interview. For example, the CI has been applied to car accident investigations (Brock, Fisher, & Cutler, 1999), epidemiological interviews about physical activity that occurred 35 years earlier (Fisher, Falkner, Trevisan, & McCauley, 2000), and food history interviews (Fisher & Quigley, 1992).

The research on foodborne illnesses is particularly relevant for predicting how the CI may work in a CTI. During investigations of foodborne illness, epidemiologists interview individuals about the food they consumed during a critical timeframe. This allows investigators to pinpoint the specific food responsible for sickening a subset of the population. For example, food histories were used in 2015 to trace various cases of E. coli and Salmonella to items from the popular Mexican fast food chain, Chipotle (Hauser, 2016). To identify the offending food, the proportion of sick individuals who had consumed a certain food is compared to the proportion of healthy individuals who had also consumed that food. The food with the largest difference between the healthy and sick individuals is deemed a likely culprit (Mann, 1981).

Research using food diaries to establish ground truth reveals that simply asking participants to report their food consumption results in errors of omission (Krall & Dwyer, 1987). Similarly, research using a monitored buffet-style meal paradigm indicated that asking participants to report what they ate resulted in errors of omission and commission (Mann, 1981). In the literature on reporting during food histories, authors have often concluded that standard procedures should be improved. Specifically, using cognitive strategies to enhance recall has been acknowledged as a promising avenue for future research (Mann, 1981).

In response to calls for improvement, Fisher and Quigley (1992) used the monitored buffet paradigm to compare the standard food history interview to a version of the CI. To compare the contrasting interview techniques, 26 participants took part in a monitored buffet-style dinner. One week later participants were interviewed using either the standard food history interview (i.e., one open-ended request for the foods consumed) or a modified version of the CI. Fisher and Quigley found that more than two times as many foods were generated using the CI compared to the standard food history (with no loss in overall accuracy). This finding has two important implications. First, if more than twice as many foods are listed using a novel technique, there are obvious flaws with the standard questioning technique. Second, using an interview designed to enhance retrieval can substantially improve outcomes. Thus, although no prior research has been conducted to examine the efficacy of CI techniques in CTIs specifically, research has tested the effects of the CI in a food history interview which is an epidemiological interview similar to infectious disease contact tracing. We therefore expect the CI to translate readily to contact tracing. In particular, the CI should work well given the additional retrieval cues in CTIs that focus on sexual and injection partners.

Sexual partner contact tracing interviews: A contact tracing interview context that has received some research attention is interviewing for sexual partners (also known as partner notification), although no research has examined the utility of the CI in this context. When a patient is diagnosed with a sexually transmitted infection, it is critical to identify his or her sexual and/or injection partners and notify the partners about their potential infection. Because patients are asked to complete this simple listing task, it is plausible that the same types of errors demonstrated when reporting food histories are made when reporting the people who were exposed to a sexually transmitted infection.

Brewer and colleagues (Brewer et al., 1999; Brewer, Garrett, & Rinaldi, 2002; Brewer & Garrett, 2001; Brewer et al., 2005) examined patients' ability to exhaustively report sexual and/or injection partners. In a typical study Brewer and his colleagues asked patients infected with sexually transmitted infections to, first, simply list their sexual and/or injection partners. They then asked the patient repeatedly for more contacts by either simply asking if there were any additional contacts he or she could list, or by using specific cues to aid in recall. For example, they cued people by listing specific places in the local community where it is likely to meet a partner, listing every letter of the alphabet and asking participants for names of any contacts that might begin with that letter, or reading back the already-remembered list of contacts to the person. Repeating requests for additional contacts and/or the additional cues caused patients to report substantially more contacts compared to what they reported initially with the first open-ended request. Alarmingly, the standard procedure (i.e., simply asking for a list of contacts) resulted in forgetting numerous partners (although accuracy could not be verified in this paradigm). In fact, Brewer et al. (1999) estimated that up to 72 percent of sexual/injection partners listed were only remembered after repeated prompting.

Brewer and colleagues (2005) concluded that omission errors during contact tracing were likely a result of both (a) the general forgetting of contacts and (b) the ignorance on the part of the patient that the interviewer wanted the most exhaustive list possible. This work has overwhelmingly demonstrated that the standard listing practice does not lead to a complete list of contacts, and that techniques designed to facilitate retrieval can increase the number of contacts reported. Furthermore, in any given contact tracing scenario, it is more important to have a very long list than to have a very accurate list. For example, if an infectious individual lists 15 potential contacts but 3 of them are false alarms, it is more advantageous than an infectious individual who lists 11 contacts, all of which are accurate but leaves one contact out. As such, the CI has the potential to be particularly effective in this context because the CI's potential increase in inaccurate details (compared to the standard interview) is not much of a concern.

Unique Cognitive and Social Demands of Contact Tracing Interviewing

Although the CI has been readily applied to various types of interviewing, features specific to contact tracing provide for unique considerations when applying the CI to this context. We argue that these considerations require tailoring some techniques of the CI to meet the demands of a CTI.

Cognitive impairment due to illness: First, and perhaps most importantly, the individuals interviewed during a CTI may be acutely ill, although this will depend on the particular illness and the stage of infection at the time of the interview. Impairment of regular cognitive function is one of many deleterious side effects of infection. Laboratory research has identified several aspects of neurocognitive functioning associated with acute infection (for a review see Smith, 2013). Because patients interviewed during a CTI may be ill, the effects of cognitive impairment on CTIs in general are worth investigating as well as the extent to which aspects of the CI may be more or less useful in this situation.

Smith (2012) evaluated the effects of acute infection on cognitive performance by first presenting participants with a series of cognitive tests to establish their baseline cognitive functioning. During a span of 90 days, a third of the participants returned to the lab after naturally developing a cold. The remaining participants never became ill and returned to the lab as the control group. Illness was associated with slower reaction times on cognitive tests, slower learning of novel information, as well as deficits (slower responses) in verbal reasoning and semantic processing compared to the healthy control group. Smith noted the failed transmission of noradrenaline (related to reaction times), choline (related to learning new information), and dopamine (related to working memory speed) as a cause of poor cognitive performance when ill. Smith (2012) also compared a group of ill and healthy individuals on a driving task. Smith found that being sick with a cold was associated with worse driving ability. Specifically, sick individuals were less likely to detect collisions and reacted more slowly to unexpected road obstacles than healthy individuals.

Along the same lines, Cvejic and colleagues (Cvejic, Lemon, Hickie, Lloyd, & Vollmer-Conna, 2014) presented a battery of neurocognitive tests to a cohort of participants infected with Epstein Barr virus, Ross River virus, or *Coxiella burnetii*. Participants were tested when ill, and again after obtaining complete recovery. Testing revealed that acute infection was related to slower matching-to-sample responses, poorer working memory capacity, mental planning, and dual attention task performance, and longer time to complete discordant Stroop trials compared to post-recovery performance. Researchers concluded that the slower responses, as well as difficulty in completing complex tasks signaled acute impairment of neurocognitive functioning (particularly as it relates to the interference of related neurotransmitters). The impairment was especially associated with higher-order executive functioning (working memory) and was noted as having potentially grave implications for completing everyday tasks when ill (e.g., remembering what you ate for lunch yesterday).

In sum, research suggests that being ill impairs the types of executive cognitive functioning critical for retrieving information during an interview (i.e., working memory). Working memory is undeniably important for both the processing and retrieval of information. As such, impairment of working memory has potentially severe consequences for performance during an interview. For example, a witness with impaired working memory may have difficulty maintaining focused attention for the length of the interview, keeping track of the questions the interviewer is asking and the names already provided during the interview, retrieving information from long-term memory, developing mental imagery, and generating internal retrieval cues, amongst many others. For any interviewing method to elicit the most extensive list possible from ill individuals, it must work for individuals with impaired working memory functioning.

Cognitive impairment and the Cognitive Interview. Little is known about the CI's effects on cognitively impaired individuals. On the one hand it is reasonable to predict that the CI will be particularly effective for the cognitively impaired. The CI employs a host of social and cognitive retrieval aids and, thus, could help mitigate impairment associated with illness. On the other hand, it is reasonable to predict that the CI will fail to improve recall in the cognitively impaired because it uses complex mnemonics and asks the participant to laboriously recall many different events in extreme detail (requiring full concentration and mental effort). Thus, the cognitively impaired may lack the resources required by the CI. Cognitive impairment might therefore lead to no increase in information gathered by the CI compared to the comparatively less demanding and less complex typical contact tracing interview.

To help predict the CI's effects on the ill, we can look to a small body of research that has examined the effects of the CI on the intellectually disabled. Much like individuals who are cognitively impaired by illness, chronically intellectually disabled (ID) adults are slower to retrieve details and provide fewer details of an event than other, non-disabled adults (Milne & Bull, 2001; Perlman, Ericson, Esses, & Isaacs, 1994). However, it should be noted that whereas sick individuals are likely only impaired at retrieval, ID adults are impaired at the encoding and storage phases of memory as well.. Testimony of ID adults is invaluable to some cases, and research has evaluated whether the CI increases the amount and accuracy of information provided by ID adults compared to a standard interview (for a review see Holliday, Brainerd, Reyna, & Humphries, 2009).

In an early study, Brown and Geiselman (1990) tested the effects of the CI versus a Standard Interview for witnesses to a to-be-remembered event who were either ID or non-disabled adults. Researchers found that ID adults provided fewer correct details, but significantly more confabulated details than the non-disabled adults. Notably, however, the CI generated more information than a Standard Interview regardless of whether participants were disabled or not.

In a second study, Milne, Clare, and Bull (1999) presented ID and non-disabled adults with a film of an accident. The next day participants were interviewed with either a CI or a structured control interview. Researchers encouragingly found that the CI led to an increase in correct details compared to the structured control interview; however, the CI also led the ID adults to generate more confabulated details (Milne & Bull, 2001).

More recent research conducted by Wright and Holliday (2007) examined the efficacy of the CI on elderly adults with dementia. Elderly adults (ages 75–96) with and without dementia viewed a short film and were subsequently interviewed using a modified CI (omitting certain difficult elements), a full CI (no elements omitted), or a control interview. As expected, the participants with dementia reported fewer correct details than the healthy adults. However, both CIs increased the amount of information recalled for participants with and without dementia compared to the control interview (and with no increase in confabulated details).

Taken together, the scant existing research suggests that the CI will increase the amount of information recalled compared to a Standard Interview for both cognitively impaired individuals and non-cognitively impaired individuals. Furthermore, the reviewed research seems to suggest that cognitive impairment at retrieval might decrease the amount of information provided compared to those who are unimpaired. Importantly, the potential presence of cognitive impairment might influence which of the CI techniques would be most effective while questioning a patient. Notably, interviewers might consider tailoring a CI based specifically on limited cognitive resources. For example, complex cognitive mnemonics that consume cognitive resources such as change-perspective (recalling the event from another perspective other than the witness's own) might not be ideal for a CI used in contact tracing contexts. In contrast, the close-eyes instruction might be important to retain, as it can help with recall when the participant is cognitively over-loaded and requires few to no resources on the part of the interviewee to implement.

Contact intimacy: A second consideration unique to epidemiological interviewing is that the amount of information provided by an interviewee is often dictated by the method of transmission (e.g., sexual versus airborne transmission) of the particular infection. The method of transmission will to some extent be related to the intimacy of the connection between the interviewee and the contact. We suspect that a CI will be especially useful for reporting during an investigation of an airborne disease, which requires no physical or intimate contact, for two reasons.

First, we suggest that the CI is most useful when the number of to-be-remembered details is high (as in airborne-transmitted diseases). In a typical CI experiment participants view some simulation of a crime and are asked to recall as many details as possible. When the to-be-remembered stimulus is rich in details, the CI works to help witnesses remember more additional details compared to the comparison interview. However, when the range of details to be remembered is restricted, the CI is likely to have less of an effect. When reporting all contacts encountered, as in the investigation of an airborne disease, the number of potential contacts to-be-reported should be high. As a result, the CI should substantially increase the number of contacts reported compared to the standard interview.

Second, the CI seems to be most effective when the retrieval task is particularly difficult. Notably, retrieval is likely more difficult when reporting airborne contacts because the patient is being asked to report contacts with whom they are likely to be unfamiliar. For example, imagine being asked to list the people who you physically touched over the past three days, as might be required for a droplet-transmitted disease like Ebola or meningococcal meningitis. Now, imagine instead being asked to list every person you were in an enclosed space with/close to in the past three days, as in an airborne disease, like measles. Providing a list of the people you physically touched is inherently easier than listing every person you may have encountered. And this is not solely because the list will be shorter. It is also likely that most of the people you physically touched are people you know well. As a result, these contacts should be remembered with more ease and in more detail than unfamiliar strangers. Because listing physical contacts over a brief period is a relatively easy task, CI mnemonics may be less able to increase the number of contacts listed. However, if the difficulty of the task were increased (e.g., a more liberal criterion for contact) the CI's efficacy will increase. Specifically, we would expect the CI to be particularly useful in an airborne context, in which many potential strangers, or non-intimate contacts need to be reported. Furthermore, we would also expect the CI to be particularly helpful in cases in which the period of contagion is especially lengthy (e.g., months/years), making remembering more difficult and the number of contacts to-be-remembered higher than during a shorter period of contagion. It is also important to note that even if the CI does not always improve recall in every instance (e.g., for an easy task), it is unlikely to *impair* recall (and worst case will result in similar performance to standard questioning).

Varied motivation: Finally, there may be unique social and motivational demands when reporting certain types of contacts, or contacts for certain illnesses (e.g., concerns about stigmatized illnesses or behaviors; e.g., Chapple, 1999). For example, during a sexually transmitted disease outbreak patients may be reluctant to admit with whom they have had intercourse or shared needles. Furthermore, in investigations of diseases such as Ebola, it is often the case that patients do not want to reveal their contacts for fear of negative retribution for those who might also be infected (e.g., will be quarantined, will be stigmatized within his or her community). As a result, special care should be used when investigating diseases in which there might be a motivation to withhold information. For example, particularly extensive rapport development, standard with the CI, might be especially beneficial in these cases. It may also be important for epidemiologists working abroad or with communities with which they have little experience to be well versed in the culture of the local community, and/or to work in conjunction with members of the local community.

An Initial Study on the Effectiveness of the Cognitive Interview in a Contact Tracing Context

Preliminary research in our lab supports the value of using the CI for a CTI. Forty-nine healthy student participants were asked to report their contacts over the past three days using either a CI or a "standard" CTI. This study is a first step in testing whether the well-established, evidence-based CI increases the number of contacts reported during a CTI compared to a more typical CTI.

Participants were assigned randomly to either a CI or a standard CTI control group and were asked to imagine that they had been feeling ill and had been diagnosed with meningococcal meningitis. Participants were then instructed that they would be listing individuals with whom they had interacted over the past three days, specifically any type of physical interaction (e.g., hug or kiss) or anyone they may have shared saliva with (e.g., shared cigarette or drink). Finally, the participants were told that they would need to provide details about the interaction, including information about the person (first name, last name, and description), the location of the interaction, and the specific type of contact. After these instructions were provided, the interviewer began the assigned protocol.

The standard CTI used was developed to be representative of a high-quality CTI, similar to that outlined in the WHO (2015) guidelines. An initial rapport phase which included a friendly exchange with the participant by asking, for example, whether the participant found parking easily at school that day was followed by a section in which the interviewer systematically asked about the participants' contacts by cuing certain levels of contact which we referred to as "circles of contacts." The circles of contacts began with the most intimate contacts (e.g., live with or significant other) and then broadened into work/school colleagues, friends, and general acquaintances (e.g., store cashier). After every contact provided, the interviewer followed up immediately with questions about where the contact took place, a description of the person, and the type of contact that had occurred. Next, participants were shown a blank calendar and were asked with whom they interacted on each of the days (e.g., Monday, Tuesday, and Wednesday). Interviewers completed each portion of the interview by asking if there were any additional contacts the participant could remember. The interviewer filled in a form throughout the duration of the interview, modeled on the form used in the 2014 Ebola outbreak (WHO, 2015), with the identified contact, descriptions of the contact, the location where the contact took place, and the type of contact (e.g., kiss, handshake).

The CI protocol was semi-structured and adhered to the following procedure. First, the interviewer established rapport by developing a connection between themselves and the participant (e.g., discussed their common issues with traffic that morning, or how they are both from the same neighborhood). Then the interviewer instructed the witness to report exhaustively and established the social dynamics of the interview by instructing the participant that he or she is the expert and to provide as much information as possible. To further demonstrate the need for a lengthy report, the interviewer provided a narration of the level of detail requested in response to a question (e.g., How did you get to work today?) in which a very detailed description of an event and the people encountered was provided (e.g., described in great detail how the interviewer arrived at school that morning). The interviewer then asked for a first recall of everything the participant did and everyone with whom they had contact over the past three days (going through each day separately). During the first recall participants were presented with the blank calendar as a reference to the critical days. Throughout all free recalls, interviewers were instructed not to interrupt the participant and to make a note of any follow-up questions related to each contact for the end of the interview. After the first recall, participants went through a second free recall. During the second recall participants were asked to close their eyes (to aid in concentration) and instead of thinking about *what* they were doing on each day (as they did in the first recall), to think about all of the *places* they had been and all of the people whom they encountered (varied retrieval). But instead of listing those places in chronological order, in this second recall participants were asked to list them in reverse order for each respective day (varied retrieval). Participants were then asked to close their eyes again and were prompted to develop a rich mental image (context reinstatement) about one particular instance, which the interviewer deemed important to readdress (e.g., a time when a lot of people were present, like a family dinner). Once participants felt as if a rich mental image was developed, they were prompted to provide a detailed narrative response about everything that happened. Participants then narrated while drawing a sketch of a scene in which many contacts were present (if possible a scene other than the one for which the context reinstatement was completed). The interviewer then requested for participants to go through their circles of contacts. Finally, the interviewer completed the same form used in the Standard Interview by asking specific follow-up questions about each of the contacts listed in their notes (e.g., What is her last name? What type of contact did you have?). Throughout the interview the interviewer was encouraged to ask "anything else," or "anyone else" to probe for additional contacts.

Note, reporting a circle of contacts is not typically part of a CI. The CI is meant to improve upon a Standard Interview by using techniques appropriate for that particular interviewee or subject matter. In practice, a specific method used to gather critical information for that particular subject matter (like the circle of contacts for CTIs) might be incorporated into the CI.

In this preliminary study the main dependent variable of interest was the quantity of contacts provided. Quantity was scored by extracting all names listed in the interviews and classifying those names as either constituting a droplet-transmitted contact or not (i.e., an airborne-transmitted contact). Each of the "total contacts" identified was subsequently categorized as either a contact for a droplet-transmitted disease specifically (the targeted contact type), or not a contact for a droplet-transmitted disease based on the *type* of interaction (e.g., hug, kiss, shared a drink or utensil) and/or whether the contact and participant lived together (Pickering, Baker, Kimberlin, & Long, 2012).

Results suggested that the CI generated significantly more total contacts ($M = 16.91$, $SD = 6.90$, 95% CI[13.93, 19.90]) than the standard interview ($M = 11.88$, $SD = 6.02$, 95% CI[9.33, 14.42]), $t(45) = 2.67$, $p = 0.011$, $d = 0.78$. When examining droplet-transmitted contacts only, there was no significant difference in the number of contacts generated by the CI ($M = 10.96$, $SD = 6.09$, 95% CI[8.32, 13.59]) compared to the standard interview ($M = 9.50$, $SD = 6.60$, 95% CI[6.71, 12.29]), $t(45) = 0.79$, $p = 0.437$, $d = 0.23$. Thus, our hypothesis that the CI would increase the number of contacts listed compared to the Standard Interview, was supported for the total contacts listed, but not for the droplet-transmitted contacts listed. We suspect that, as hypothesized above, because the droplet-transmitted contacts were easier to remember, the CI was less helpful when this subset of contacts was isolated.

The results from our initial research, as hypothesized, indicated a substantial increase in the number of total contacts reported compared to a standard

CTI. Almost 35 percent more contacts were provided by the CI compared to the Standard Interview (approximately 5 more contacts). When examining the droplet-transmitted contacts only, the CI produced a statistically non-significant 14 percent increase in droplet-transmitted contacts listed compared to the Standard Interview (approximately 1.5 more contacts). Although statistically non-significant, one could argue that in this context a single additional contact is important. For instance, in some diseases contacts have a high probability of becoming dangerously ill and infecting others. When this is the case, the identification of an additional contact may mean the difference between whether or not many people receive treatment, infect others, or succumb to the disease. Indeed, as noted by CDC "Even one missed contact can keep the outbreak going" (CDC, 2016).

Discussion

Applying the CI to this novel context provides an excellent opportunity to extend years of research on interviewing and memory to the vital contact tracing process. Encouragingly, there seem to be many practical applications of this research to various diseases, including those transmitted via air, droplet, or sexual contact. Of particular relevance now, the CI may also be useful in investigating the outbreak of mosquito-borne illnesses such as Zika and Yellow Fever. In fact, recent research suggests that combining an interview about the places a person has visited with the targeted spraying of insecticides in those places is the most effective method for controlling mosquito-borne illnesses (Vazquez-Prokopec, Montgomery, Horne, Clennon, & Ritchie, 2017).

One limitation of the initial study presented here, and much other research involving contact tracing, is that there is no way to verify whether the extra contacts generated by the CI are accurate. However, as noted previously, in a contact tracing context, it is typically more valuable to receive an exhaustive list with a small number of contacts listed in error, than to receive a more conservative (and potentially incomplete) list with no inaccurate contacts. We hope that future research will be able to creatively test the differences between the CI and the standard CTI in a paradigm in which accuracy can be assessed, while also considering ecological validity.

One potential limitation of applying the CI to a contact tracing context is that there may be situations in which interviewing a patient about his or her contacts is limited by practical constraints (e.g., sick patient cannot spend an extended amount of time on the interview). When using a CI this problem may be even more pronounced. A CI is likely more difficult for an interviewer to conduct and is demonstrated to take more time than a Standard Interview. As such, it may be beneficial to develop ways to conserve resources, allow patients to complete the interview at their own pace, take breaks etc. For example, a smartphone application was developed recently to allow potentially infected individuals to systematically input the people with whom they had been in contact (Epi Info Viral Hemorrhagic Fever (VHF) application; Schafer et al., 2016). This should allow individuals, who might otherwise not take part in a CTI for practical reasons, to contribute to contact tracing efforts. In light of the results of the present studies, the completeness of a list provided to written requests from an app is likely insufficient. Helpfully, there is research suggesting that a written version of the CI (the "self-administered interview") can be useful in generating information from a witness (Gabbert, Hope, & Fisher, 2009; Gabbert, Hope, Fisher, & Jamieson, 2012; Hope, Gabbert, & Fisher, 2011). Future research should address the effectiveness of providing contacts in response to a smartphone application compared to an in-person interview and whether the superiority of the CI over a Standard Interview still holds when the responses are provided via a smartphone application.

Contact tracing is vital to the prevention, treatment, and hopefully eradication of various infectious diseases. The reported study provides preliminary support for this, and can provide insight into how to most effectively conduct CTIs. Notably, we suggest that the significant increase in total contacts, but not droplet-transmitted contacts in the reported study supports the notion that the CI is particularly helpful for airborne-transmitted diseases. As hypothesized earlier, we suspect that because the airborne-transmitted contacts are more difficult to remember, and the ceiling for the number of contacts to remember is higher in the airborne-transmitted than droplet-transmitted contacts, the CI will be particularly effective for airborne infections. Note, the CI used in the current study was a first attempt to apply the CI to the contact tracing context. Future iterations may improve its effectiveness. For example, in the reported study context reinstatement and sketch drawing were each used only one time per participant, to allow for more experimental control. However, there is no reason that these techniques cannot be used more frequently during a CI. In addition, the CI implemented in the reported study used cognitively challenging methods (e.g., reverse order); as noted earlier, this may not be ideal for acutely ill interviewees. We hope researchers will seek to develop and test CI protocols that are tailored to interviewees who are acutely ill and have limited cognitive resources. In addition, it would be appropriate to develop CI protocols for different types of transmission mechanisms and timelines. For example, the traditional CI which involves a thorough accounting of an entire event (often multiple times) cannot be easily applied to CTIs for HIV, which typically cover all sexual and injection partners over the course of a year. Similarly, a protocol developed to focus on people may not be ideal when a pathogen is transmitted via mosquito. There may also be mnemonics that are particularly effective for remembering people and places that can be incorporated (e.g., the timeline method introduced by Hope, Mullis & Gabbert, 2013). We hope that future research will explore ways in which variations of the CI can be used to increase the amount of information reported in various epidemiological interviewing contexts.

Note

Author Note: Portions of this work were presented and published in dissertation form in fulfillment of the requirements for the Ph.D. for Alexandra E. Mosser from Florida International University. The research was supported by the Department of Psychology at Florida International University.

References

Anderson, M. C., Bjork, R. A., & Bjork, E. L. (1994). Remembering can cause forgetting: Retrieval dynamics in long-term memory. *Journal of Experimental Psychology: Learning, Memory, and Cognition, 20*, 1063–1087.

Anderson, R. C., & Pichert, J. W. (1978). Recall of previously unrecallable information following a shift in perspective. *Journal of Verbal Learning and Verbal Behavior, 17*, 1–12.

Brewer, D. D., & Garrett, S. B. (2001). Evaluation of interviewing techniques to enhance recall of sexual and drug injection partners. *Sexually Transmitted Diseases, 28*, 666–677.

Brewer, D. D., Garrett, S. B., & Kulasingam, S. (1999). Forgetting as a cause of incomplete reporting of sexual and drug injection partners. *Sexually Transmitted Diseases, 26*, 166–176.

Brewer, D. D., Garrett, S. B., & Rinaldi, G. (2002). Free listed items are effective cues for eliciting additional items in semantic domains. *Applied Cognitive Psychology, 16*, 343–358.

Brewer, D. D., Potterat, J. J., Muth, S. Q., Malone, P. Z., Montoya, P., Green, D. L., . . . Cox, P. A. (2005). Randomized trial of supplementary interviewing techniques to enhance recall of sexual partners in contact interviews. *Sexually Transmitted Diseases, 32*, 189–193.

Brock, P., Fisher, R. P., & Cutler, B. L. (1999). Examining the cognitive interview in a double-test paradigm. *Psychology, Crime & Law, 5*, 29–45.

Brown, C. L., & Geiselman, R. E. (1990). Eyewitness testimony of mentally retarded: Effect of the cognitive interview. *Journal of Police and Criminal Psychology, 6*, 14–22.

CDC (2016, January). What is contact tracing? Retrieved from www.cdc.gov/vhf/ebola/pdf/contact-tracing.pdf

Chapple, A. (1999). The use of telephone interviewing for qualitative research. *Nurse Researcher, 6*, 85–93.

Cohen, G., & Faulkner, D. (1989). Age differences in source forgetting: Effects on reality monitoring and on eyewitness testimony. *Psychology and Aging, 4*, 10–17.

Collins, R., Lincoln, R., & Frank, M. G. (2002). The effects of rapport in forensic interviewing. *Psychiatry, Psychology and Law, 91*, 69–78.

Cvejic, E., Lemon, J., Hickie, I. B., Lloyd, A. R., & Vollmer-Conna, U. (2014). Neurocognitive disturbances associated with acute infectious mononucleosis, Ross River fever and Q fever: A preliminary investigation of inflammatory and genetic correlates. *Brain, Behavior, and Immunity, 36*, 207–214.

Eames, K. T., & Keeling, M. J. (2003). Contact tracing and disease control. *Proceedings of the Royal Society of London, Series B: Biological Sciences, 270*, 2565–2571.

Evans, J. R., & Fisher, R. P. (2011). Eyewitness memory: Balancing the accuracy, precision and quantity of information through metacognitive monitoring and control. *Applied Cognitive Psychology, 25*, 501–508.

Fisher, R. P., & Geiselman, R. E. (1992). *Memory enhancing techniques for investigative interviewing: The cognitive interview.* Springfield, IL: Charles C. Thomas.

Fisher, R. P., & Quigley, K. L. (1992). Applying cognitive theory in public health investigations: Enhancing food recall with the cognitive interview. In J. M. Tanur (Ed.), *Questions about questions: Inquiries into the cognitive bases of surveys* (pp. 154–169). New York: Russell Sage Foundation.

Fisher, R. P., Geiselman, R. E., & Amador, M. (1989). Field test of the cognitive interview: Enhancing the recollection of actual victims and witnesses of crime. *Journal of Applied Psychology, 74,* 722–727.

Fisher, R. P., Falkner, K. L., Trevisan, M., & McCauley, M. R. (2000). Adapting the cognitive interview to enhance long-term (35-years) recall of psychical activities. *Journal of Applied Psychology, 85,* 180–189.

Fisher, R. P., Ross, S. J., & Cahill, B. S. (2010). Interviewing witnesses and victims. In P.-A. Granhag (Ed.), *Forensic psychology in context: Nordic and international approaches* (pp. 56–74). Cullompton: Willan.

Fisher, R. P., Milne, R., & Bull, R. (2011). Interviewing cooperative witnesses. *Current Directions in Psychological Science, 20,* 16–19.

Fisher, R. P., Schreiber Compo, N., Rivard, J., & Hirn, D. (2014). Interviewing witnesses. In T. Perfect & S. Lindsay (Eds.), *The SAGE handbook of applied memory* (pp. 559–578). Los Angeles, CA: Sage.

Gabbert, F., Hope, L., & Fisher, R. P. (2009). Protecting eyewitness evidence: Examining the efficacy of a self-administered interview tool. *Law and Human Behavior, 33,* 298–307.

Gabbert, F., Hope, L., Fisher, R. P., & Jamieson, K. (2012). Protecting against susceptibility to misinformation with the use of a self-administered interview. *Applied Cognitive Psychology, 26,* 568–575.

Geiselman, R. E., Fisher, R. P., MacKinnon, D. P., & Holland, H. L. (1986). Enhancement of eyewitness memory with the cognitive interview. *American Journal of Psychology, 99,* 385–401.

Gilbert, J. A., & Fisher, R. P. (2006). The effects of varied retrieval cues on reminiscence in eyewitness memory. *Applied Cognitive Psychology, 20,* 723–739.

Godden, D. R., & Baddeley, A. D. (1975). Context-dependent memory in two natural environments: On land and under water. *British Journal of Psychology, 66,* 325–331.

Griffiths, A., & Milne, R. (2010). The application of cognitive interview techniques as part of an investigation. In C. A. Ireland & M. J. Fisher (Eds.), *Consultancy and advising in forensic practice: Empirical and practical guidelines* (pp. 71–90). Chichester: Wiley.

Hauser, K. (2016, February 1). C.D.C. ends Chipotle case with illness still a mystery. Retrieved from www.nytimes.com/2016/02/02/business/cdc-unable-to-trace-cause-of-outbreaks-at-chipotle.html?_r=0

Holliday, R. E., Brainerd, C. J., Reyna, V. F., & Humphries, J. E. (2009). The cognitive interview: Research and practice across the lifespan. In R. Bull, T. Valentine, & T. Williamson (Eds.), *Handbook of psychology of investigative interviewing: Current developments and future directions* (pp. 137–160). Chichester: Wiley.

Hope, L., Gabbert, F., & Fisher, R. P. (2011). From laboratory to the street: Capturing witness memory using the self-administered interview. *Legal and Criminological Psychology, 16,* 211–226.

Hope, L., Mullis, R., & Gabbert, F. (2013). Who? What? When? Using a timeline technique to facilitate recall of a complex event. *Journal of Applied Research in Memory and Cognition, 2,* 20–24.

Köhnken, G., Milne, R., Memon, A., & Bull, R. (1999). The cognitive interview: A meta-analysis. *Psychology, Crime & Law, 5,* 3–27.

Koriat, A., & Goldsmith, M. (1996). Monitoring and control processes in the strategic regulation of memory accuracy. *Psychological Review, 103*, 490–517.

Krall, E. A., & Dwyer, J. T. (1987). Validity of a food frequency questionnaire and a food diary in a short-term recall situations. *Journal of the American Dietetic Association, 87*, 1374–1377.

Loftus, E. F. (1975). Leading questions and the eyewitness report. *Cognitive Psychology, 7*, 560–572.

Loftus, E. F., & Zanni, G. (1975). Eyewitness testimony: The influence of the wording of a question. *Bulletin of the Psychonomic Society, 5*, 86–88.

Mann, J. A. (1981). A prospective study of response error in food history questionnaires. *American Journal of Public Health, 70*, 401–412.

Memon, A., Meissner, C. A., & Fraser, J. (2010). The cognitive interview: A meta-analytic review and study space analysis of the past 25 years. *Psychology, Public Policy, and Law, 16*, 340–372.

Migueles, M., & García-Bajos, E. (2007). Selective retrieval and induced forgetting in eyewitness memory. *Applied Cognitive Psychology, 21*, 1157–1172.

Milne, R., & Bull, R. (2001). Interviewing witnesses with learning disabilities for legal purposes. *British Journal of Learning Disabilities, 29*, 93–97.

Milne, R., Clare, I. C. H., & Bull, R. (1999). Interviewing adults with learning disability with cognitive interview. *Psychology, Crime & Law, 5*, 81–100.

Oeberst, A. (2012). If anything else comes to mind . . . better keep it to yourself? Delayed recall is discrediting—unjustifiably. *Law and Human Behavior, 36*, 266–274.

Perlman, N. B., Ericson, K. I., Esses, V. M., & Isaacs, B. J. (1994). The developmentally handicapped witness: Competency as a function of question format. *Law and Human Behavior, 18*, 171–187.

Pickering, L. K., Baker, C. J., Kimberlin, D. W., & Long S. S. (2012). Meninigococcal infections. In L. K. Pickering & S. S. Long (Eds.), *Red Book 2012* (pp. 500–509). Itasca, IL: American Academy of Pediatrics.

Potterat, J. J. (1997). Contact tracing's price is not its value. *Sexually Transmitted Diseases, 24*, 519–521.

Powell, M. B., Fisher, R. P., & Wright, R. (2005). Investigative interviewing. In N. Brewer & K. D. Williams (Eds.), *Psychology and law: An empirical perspective* (pp. 11–42). New York: Guilford Press.

Roebers, C. M., & Schneider, W. (2000). The impact of misleading questions on eyewitness memory in children and adults. *Applied Cognitive Psychology, 14*, 509–526.

Roediger, H. L., & Payne, D. G. (1982). Hypermnesia: The role of repeated testing. *Journal of Experimental Psychology: Learning, Memory, and Cognition, 8*, 66–72.

Schafer, I. J., Knudsen, E., McNamara, L. A., Agnihotri, S., Rollin, P. E., & Islam, A. (2016). The Epi Info Viral Hemorrhagic Fever (VHF) application: A resource for outbreak data management and contact tracing in the 2014–2016 West Africa Ebola epidemic. *Journal of Infectious Diseases, 3*, 122–136.

Shaw, J. S., Bjork, R. A., & Handal, A. (1995). Retrieval-induced forgetting in an eyewitness-memory paradigm. *Psychonomic Bulletin & Review, 2*, 249–253.

Smith, A. P. (2012). Effects of the common cold on mood, psychomotor performance, the encoding of new information, speed of working memory and semantic processing. *Brain, Behavior, and Immunity, 26*, 1072–1076.

Smith, A. P. (2013). Twenty-five years of research on the behavioural malaise associated with influenza and the common cold. *Psychoneuroendocrinology, 38*, 744–751.

Tulving, E., & Osler, S. (1968). Effectiveness of retrieval cues in memory for words. *Journal of Experimental Psychology, 77*, 593–601.

Tulving, E., & Pearlstone, Z. (1966). Availability versus accessibility of information in memory for words. *Journal of Verbal Learning and Verbal Behavior, 5*, 381–391.

Tulving, E., & Thomson, D. M. (1973). Encoding specificity and retrieval processes in episodic memory. *Psychological Review, 80*, 352–373.

Turtle, J. W., & Yuille, J. C. (1994). Lost but not forgotten details: Repeated eyewitness recall leads to reminiscence but not hypermnesia. *Journal of Applied Psychology, 79*, 260–271.

Vazquez-Prokopec, G. M., Montgomery, B. L., Horne, P., Clennon, J. A., & Ritchie, S. A. (2017). Combining contact tracing with targeted indoor residual spraying significantly reduces dengue transmission. *Science Advances, 3*. doi:10.1126/sciadv.1602024

Vredeveldt, A., & Sauer, J. D. (2015). Effects of eye-closure on confidence-accuracy relations in eyewitness testimony. *Journal of Applied Research in Memory and Cognition, 4*, 51–58.

Vredeveldt, A., Baddeley, A. D., & Hitch, G. J. (2014). The effectiveness of eye-closure in repeated interviews. *Legal and Criminological Psychology, 19*, 282–295.

Vredeveldt, A., Tredoux, C. G., Nortje, A., Kempen, K., Puljević, C., & Labuschagne, G. N. (2015). A field evaluation of the eye-closure interview with witnesses of serious crimes. *Law and Human Behavior, 39*, 189. doi:10.1037/lhb0000113

WHO (2015, September). Implementation and management of contact tracing for Ebola virus disease. Retrieved from www.who.int/csr/resources/publications/ebola/contact-tracing/en/

Wright, A. M., & Holliday, R. E. (2007). Interviewing cognitively impaired older adults: How useful is a cognitive interview? *Memory, 15*, 17–33.

7

THE VERIFIABILITY APPROACH

Aldert Vrij and Galit Nahari

Verbal Lie Detection

Verbal lie detection has a long history.[1] In around 900 BC a papyrus of the Vedas mentioned that a liar "does not answer questions, or gives evasive answers; he speaks nonsense" (Trovillo, 1939a, p. 849; Trovillo, 1939b). The French forensic expert Auguste Tardieu reported in the 1850s that "quantity of detail" is amongst the best indicators to distinguish truth from deception in alleged sexual abuse cases, and the American forensic medical doctor Jerome Walker noted in 1886 that "the way in which children tell their stories in their own words and the expressions they use" is indicative for truth and deceit in alleged sexual abuse cases (see Lamers-Winkelman, 1999).

The systematic search for verbal cues to deceit has accelerated since the 1950s (DePaulo et al., 2003; Hauch, Blandón-Gitlin, Masip, & Sporer, 2015; Masip, Sporer, Garrido, & Herrero, 2005; Vrij, 2008). Sometimes verbal cues are measured in isolation (Hauch et al., 2015), but they are often examined as part of a verbal veracity assessment tool. The three verbal veracity assessment tools nowadays most frequently used by scholars or practitioners are Criteria-Based Content Analysis, Reality Monitoring, and Scientific Content Analysis. They are discussed in detail elsewhere.[2] In recent years we (together with Ronald P. Fisher) have started to work on a new verbal veracity assessment method developed by Galit Nahari: the Verifiability Approach. In this chapter we briefly introduce this approach together with the research carried out in this domain to date.

The Verifiability Approach: Rationale

The Verifiability Approach is based on different strategies truth tellers and liars employ in investigative interviews. To explain these differences, Granhag and

Hartwig (2008) refer to self-regulation theory (Fiske & Taylor, 1991). They claim that both liars (e.g., guilty suspects) and truth tellers (e.g., innocent suspects) view the upcoming interview as a threat. Both run the risk of not being believed by the investigator, a stressful experience, which can have far-reaching negative consequences. However, the threat between liars and truth tellers differs: Liars may be afraid that investigators may come to know all they know about their own activities, particularly the crime-relevant aspects, whereas truth tellers may be afraid that investigators may *not* come to know all they know about their own activities.

This different type of fear between truth tellers and liars leads to different strategies (Granhag & Hartwig, 2008). Truth tellers are inclined to be open and to tell all they remember about their activities. Since in interviews truth tellers typically do not report all they know in the initial recall, they may have to be encouraged to do so via specific prompts (Vrij, Hope, & Fisher, 2014), but their willingness to "tell it all" is, in principle, present. In contrast, liars are motivated not to tell the investigator all they know, particularly not the information they fear incriminates them. This includes crime-relevant information but also, and particularly relevant for the Verifiability Approach, information that could reveal that their alibi is false.

If liars are motivated to leave out information that could give away that their alibis are false, they will in particular leave out details investigators can check, or so-called verifiable details (e.g., "I phoned my friend Zvi at 10.30 this morning"). Liars may believe that not providing enough details sounds suspicious. The subjective belief amongst people is that stories in deceptive statements lack detail (Vrij, 2008) and the richer an account is perceived to be in detail, the more likely it is to be believed (Bell & Loftus, 1989). This may result in liars being motivated to provide details, which, to protect themselves, should be details an investigator cannot check, so-called unverifiable details (e.g., "Several people walked by when I sat there"). However, liars' main concern will be that they provide leads to investigators and they will therefore be mainly concerned with avoiding providing verifiable details.

Based on these differential considerations and strategies between truth tellers and liars, the main prediction in the Verifiability Approach is that truth tellers will report more verifiable details than liars. This distinction in reporting verifiable details can be further enhanced by asking interviewees at the beginning of the interview to provide details the investigator can check. Since truth tellers do not report all they remember without a prompt (Vrij et al., 2014), this prompt may encourage them to think about details the investigator can potentially check and to report these details. In contrast, if liars provide verifiable details about their true activities the investigator will find out that they are lying and, by definition, they cannot provide verifiable details about their fabricated activities. The main hypothesis in the Verifiability Approach is thus that *truth tellers report more verifiable details than liars, particularly if interviewees are prompted to do so.* It is more difficult to make a prediction about unverifiable details. If liars are motivated to provide much information, it may well be that they will provide more unverifiable details than truth tellers, but they may not always be motivated to provide much detail.

Thus, if we assume that truth tellers provide more verifiable details than liars and that there will be no clear difference between truth tellers and liars in reporting unverifiable details, the ratio of verifiable details (verifiable details / [verifiable + unverifiable details]) should also be diagnostic: *Truth tellers will have a higher ratio of verifiable details than liars.*

In our research we examine four types of verifiable details, but we always cluster them into one category: "verifiable details": (i) activities with identifiable or named persons who the interviewer can consult ("During the lunch break I went shopping with my colleague, Fred"; (ii) activities that have been witnessed by identifiable or named persons who the interviewer can consult ("My neighbour was cleaning his driveway when I left my house"); (iii) activities that the interviewee believes may have been captured on CCTV ("I was in the library as their CCTV footage will demonstrate"); and (iv) activities that may have been documented (e.g., the lecturer had a list of the students attending her class) or recorded through technology (other than CCTV), such as using debit cards, mobile phones, or computers.

Note that the Verifiability Approach differs in some important aspects from what investigators currently do. First, investigators check verifiable details for truthfulness, but they typically do not ask interviewees at the beginning of their free recall to include as many checkable details in their account as they possibly can. Also, it is not known whether they do this check in a systematic manner. For example, what do they consider to be verifiable details? Second, in the Verifiability Approach, the number of verifiable details reported by the interviewee serves as a veracity assessment tool, and for lie detection purposes it is not needed to actually check these verifiable details. In current investigations, investigators only make veracity assessments after they have checked the verifiable details. Third, the Verifiability Approach works from the perspective of the interviewee rather than, as typically happens, from the perspective of the investigator. An interviewee can report that he spent an hour in the library on a specific afternoon. For the investigator this is a checkable detail if the investigator is aware that the library has a CCTV camera at the entrance. However, for the Verifiability Approach this only counts as a verifiable detail if the interviewee refers to the CCTV camera in his/her statement ("And you can check the CCTV camera at the entrance"), because the interviewee may not be aware of this. The Verifiability Approach also works in the opposite way. If the interviewee believes that there is a CCTV camera and mentions it in his/her statement, we consider this to be a verifiable detail even if an investigator knows that there is no CCTV camera at that location.

The Verifiability Approach: The Findings to Date

Tables 7.1 and 7.2 provide details of the Verifiability Approach studies we are aware of. We provide a short description of each study and report whether or not the investigator asked the participants to try to include details she/he (the investigator) can check. This is labeled "IP" (Information Protocol). We then describe the findings. In Table 7.1 we report whether truth tellers included each of the three variables (verifiable details, unverifiable details, or ratio of verifiable details more (>) or less (<) in their statements than liars. A (–) sign means that there was no significant difference, and a blank column means that the variable was not investigated. We also report the effect size, d. d-values of 0.25, 0.50 and 0.80 are considered small, medium, and large effects respectively (Cohen, 1988). In Table 7.2 the accuracy rates of correct classifications of truth tellers and liars are reported. Truth accuracy refers to the correct classification of truth tellers, lie accuracy refers to the correct classification of liars, and total accuracy refers to the correct classification of truth tellers and liars combined. In all studies, these accuracy rates were calculated via a statistical analysis (discriminant analysis) except study [6] where observers made veracity judgments.

In both tables, we also distinguish between four types of setting. This is an important factor because the Verifiability Approach may be more effective in some settings than in others, which depends on the possibility for truth tellers to provide verifiable details and for liars to fool investigators.

Criminal setting: The first six studies were carried out in a criminal setting in which truth tellers told the truth about their activities and whereabouts and liars lied about them, representing nine samples. This is the most straightforward situation for the Verifiability Approach. Truth tellers will typically be able to provide verifiable details, certainly nowadays where most people have mobile phones, tablets, or laptops, which they use frequently (they leave signals and other traces that investigators can check). Liars will typically not be able to provide checkable details during the period the crime occurred because they were somewhere else during that time. The results in Table 7.1 indicate that in all but one criminal sample, truth tellers included significantly more verifiable details in their reports than liars, which supports the Verifiability Approach. The exception was study [2] in which participants reported an event after a time delay. The effect sizes related to the significant findings were large, indicating clear differences between truth tellers and liars in reporting verifiable details. In two studies the Information Protocol was manipulated (studies [2] and [4]). The IP strengthened the effect, which is also in alignment with the Verifiability Approach predictions.

Unverifiable details were examined in four out of nine samples. It showed a significant and large effect in study [2, sample 1] (truth tellers included more unverifiable details than liars), a significant and large effect in study [6] (liars included more unverifiable details than truth tellers) and no effect in study [2, sample 2] and study [3]. This suggests that the difference in unverifiable details between truth tellers and liars in criminal settings is unclear. The ratio of verifiable details was examined five times in a criminal setting (studies [1–3]) and yielded significant and large effects in the predicted direction in three studies: the ratios were significantly higher for truth tellers than for liars. To summarize the findings of Table 7.1, in criminal settings truth tellers reported more verifiable details than

TABLE 7.1 An overview of the Verifiability Approach studies: verifiable and unverifiable details reported

Description of the study	Setting	IP given	Verifiable details		Unverifiable details		Ratio of verifiable details	
			T − L	d	T − L	d	T − L	d
[1] Harvey, Vrij, Sariktas, & Nahari (2017c). Truth tellers reported their true activities during last 30 minutes, liars made up the story (N = 67). Participants gave a free recall in which they were asked to include verifiable details. Prior to that, half of the participants were asked some closed questions related to possible verifiable facts or an open question to report all they could remember.	Criminal	Yes, and closed questions	>	0.83			>	0.59
		Yes, and open question	>	1.69			>	2.05
[2] Jupe, Vrij, Leal, Nahari, & Harvey (2017b). Truth tellers reported their true activities during last 30 minutes, liars made up the story (N = 91). Participants were interviewed after a one week delay	Criminal	No	−	0.02	>	0.92	−	0.48
		Yes	>	0.81	−	0.60	−	0.34
[3] Nahari, Vrij, & Fisher (2014b). Truth tellers reported their true activities during last 30 minutes, liars made up the story (N = 38)	Criminal	No	>	1.39	−	0.23	>	0.92
[4] Nahari, Vrij, & Fisher (2014c). Truth tellers reported their true activities during last 30 minutes, liars made up the story (N = 87)	Criminal	No	>	0.70				
		Yes	>	1.17				
[5] Nahari & Vrij (2014). Pairs of truth tellers carried out a mission and reported it truthfully. Single liar carried out the same mission and pretended to have carried it out as a pair (N = 100, 50 pairs)	Criminal	Yes	>	2.05				

Study	Type							
[6] Vernham, Vrij, Leal, Mann, & Nahari (2017). Pairs of truth tellers carried out a mission and reported it truthfully. Single liar carried out the same mission and pretended to have carried it out as a pair (N = 120, 60 pairs)★	Criminal	No	>	1.37	<	−1.46		
[7] Nahari, Leal, Vrij, Warmelink, & Vernham (2014a). Truth tellers really experienced theft, loss, or damage of an item and reported it, liars made up a story about theft, loss, or damage of an item (N = 83)	Insurance	No	−	0.37				
[8] Vrij, Nahari, Isitt, & Leal (2016). Truth tellers really experienced theft, loss, or damage of an item and reported it, liars made up a story about theft, loss, or damage of an item (N = 50)	Insurance	Yes	>	1.00	<	−0.92	>	1.15
[9] Harvey, Vrij, Nahari, & Ludwig (2017a). Truth tellers really experienced theft, loss, or damage of an item and reported it, liars made up a story about theft, loss, or damage of an item (N = 80)	Insurance	No	−	0.28			−	−0.05
		Yes	>	1.17			>	1.26
[10] Harvey, Vrij, Leal, Lafferty, & Nahari (2017b). Truth tellers really experienced theft, loss, or damage of an item and reported it, liars made up a story about theft, loss, or damage of an item (N = 80)	Insurance	Yes	−	0.42	<	−1.71	>	0.71
		Yes+	>	1.22	<	−2.25	>	2.28
[11] Boskovic, Bogaard, Merckelbach, Vrij, & Hope (2017a). Participants described a typical day on which they had experienced a genuine (truth tellers) or malingered (liars) physical symptom. (N = 125, study 1, N = 105, study 2)	Malingering	No, Study 1	−	0.25	<	−0.56	>	0.46
		Yes, Study 2	−	0.13	−	0.13	−	−0.07

(continued)

TABLE 7.1 (Cont.)

Description of the study	Setting	IP given	Verifiable details		Unverifiable details		Ratio of verifiable details	
			$T-L$	d	$T-L$	d	$T-L$	d
[12] Boskovic, Tejada-Gallardo, Merckelbach, Vrij, & Hope (2917b). Truth tellers carried out an intensive physical exercise and reported their experiences. Malingerers did not carry out such an exercise but were coached (think back to time when you did carry out a similar exercise) or were not coached.	Malingering	No and not coached	–	0.41	<	–1.15	–	0.35
		No and coached	–	–0.05	<	–1.32	–	0.77
[13] Jupe, Leal, Vrij, & Nahari (2017a). Truth tellers and liars, who just finished describing their forthcoming trip, were asked what questions we could ask that would demonstrate that they were telling the truth ($N = 399$)	Airport setting	No	>	0.28			>	0.18

★ Individual and collective statements combined, checkable details (pair together) only.

Note: "T – L: >": truth tellers scored significantly higher than liars; "T – L: <": truth tellers scored significantly lower than liars; "T – L: –": no significant difference between truth tellers and liars.

A positive d-score means that truth tellers scored higher than liars, whereas a negative d-score means that truth tellers scored lower than liars.

TABLE 7.2 An overview of the Verifiability Approach studies: accuracy rates of classifying truth tellers and liars

Description of the study	Setting	IP given	Verifiable details			Ratio of verifiable details		
			Truth	Lie	Total	Truth	Lie	Total
[1] Harvey, Vrij, Sariktas, & Nahari (2017c)	Criminal	Yes, and closed questions	69	71	70	69	65	67
		Yes, and open question	59	94	79	82	88	85
[2] Jupe, Vrij, Leal, Nahari, & Harvey (2017b)	Criminal	No	ns			ni		
		Yes	44	79	59	ni		
[3] Nahari, Vrij, & Fisher (2014b)	Criminal	No	77	81	79	68	75	71
[4] Nahari, Vrij, & Fisher (2014c)	Criminal	No	68	54	61	ni		
		Yes	77	57	67	ni		
[5] Nahari & Vrij (2014)	Criminal	Yes	80	96	88	ni		
[6] Vernham, Vrij, Leal, Mann, & Nahari (2017) (N = 57 observers)★	Criminal	No	83	75	79	ni		
[7] Nahari, Leal, Vrij, Warmelink, & Vernham (2014a)	Insurance	No	nr			ni		
[8] Vrij, Nahari, Isitt, & Leal (2016)	Insurance	Yes	nr			nr		
[9] Harvey, Vrij, Nahari, & Ludwig (2017a)	Insurance	No	ns			ns		
		Yes	65	90	78	80	80	80
[10] Harvey, Vrij, Leal, Lafferty, & Nahari (2017b)	Insurance	Yes	ns			53	76	65
		Yes+	nr			81	100	90
[11] Boskovic, Bogaard, Merckelbach, Vrij, & Hope (2016)	Malingering	No, study 1	ns			nr		
		Yes, study 2	ns			ns		
[12] Boskovic, Tejada-Gallardo, Merckelbach, Vrij, & Hope (2017b)	Malingering	No and naive	ns			ns		
		No and coached	ns			ns		
[13] Jupe, Leal, Vrij, & Nahari (2017a)	Airport setting		nr			nr		

★ Unlike in all other experiments in which discriminant analyses were used, here participants read transcripts of pairs of truth tellers and pairs of liars. We only used the collective statements condition as this is the only condition in which participants relied on verifiable details.

Note: **ni**: Variable was not investigated; **nr**: Variable was investigated but the discriminant analysis was not carried out; **ns**: Variable was investigated and yielded a significant effect but the discriminant analysis was not carried out; **ns**: Variable was investigated but did not result in a significant effect, which is why the discriminant analysis was not carried out.

liars and had a higher ratio of verifiable details than liars, whereas no effect was found for unverifiable details.

In terms of accuracy rates (Table 7.2), these were high (well above the 50 percent level of chance), particularly for truth tellers with the exception of study [2, sample 2]. The accuracy rates for liars varied notably. The total accuracy rates ranged from a somewhat mediocre 59 percent to a high 88 percent. Study [6] is the only study where observers made veracity judgments based on the Verifiability Approach. These observers read the written statements of truth tellers and liars and were asked to pay attention to verifiable details, and to base their veracity judgments on the presence of such details. They were not instructed to count the verifiable details, but only to consider them. The accuracy rates were high (79 percent total) demonstrating the potential of the Verifiability Approach to be used as a lie detection tool in real-life investigations.

Studies [1] to [4] used more traditional criminal scenarios. Truth tellers described their real activities and liars reported fabricated activities, but studies [5] and [6] need perhaps some more explanation. In those studies, pairs of truth tellers and pairs of liars took part. The pairs of truth tellers carried out activities together and reported them in the interview. For the pairs of liars, Member 1 carried out the same activities as the truth tellers but alone, whereas Member 2 carried out a "criminal activity." They were instructed to report in the interview that they carried out Member 1's activities together. This is a "witness alibi" scenario in which the innocent person demonstrates the suspect's alibi, by claiming that they were together at a location other than the crime scene when the crime took place. Alibi witnesses are frequently used by defendants in court. Burke and Turtle (2003) reviewed 175 Canadian and American criminal court cases in which an alibi was presented at the trial, and found that in 86 percent of the Canadian cases and 68 percent of the American cases the alibi provided by the defendant was corroborated by a witness. Introducing a false alibi witness is likely to be common. In a survey study, it was found that 61 percent of the participants thought they could find a witness to corroborate a false alibi (Culhane, Hosch, & Kehn, 2008). Another study showed that people are willing to lie for others, especially for those with whom they have a close relationship (Hosch, Culhane, Jolly, Chavez, & Shaw, 2011). In that study 82 percent of the participants said they would lie for their romantic partner and 68 percent would lie for their oldest/best friend. Studies [5] and [6] show that the Verifiability Approach is very successful in distinguishing between true and false alibi witnesses.

Insurance setting: Studies [7] to [10] which include six samples focus on an insurance setting in which someone reported damage, loss, or theft of an object. Truth tellers reported real damage, loss, or theft, liars made up their stories. Truth tellers may have difficulty in providing verifiable details that they are telling the truth. For example, how to demonstrate that a bicycle is truly stolen? That is difficult to do unless the victim can point out that the bicycle was in an area with CCTV cover so that the CCTV footage can show the theft (this example is taken from one of our participants).

In an insurance setting a narrative of the general scene is not relevant, only the description of the incident is. Suppose someone claims the loss of a phone during a night out with friends. The scene (e.g., the description of the night out, such as where they went to, what they drank, who they met) is not likely to differ much between truth tellers and liars. Liars can describe their real experiences during a night out with friends, so this says nothing about the stolen phone. The relevant point is how the interviewee describes what happens during and following the theft and the studies carried out to date revealed that truth tellers and liars differ in this respect. Truth tellers reported that when they noticed the loss of their phone, they discussed this with their friends and started searching for their phones with their friends. In contrast, liars did not report that they discussed it with their friends. Instead, they asked bar staff or other personnel whether they have seen their phone. The stories of the truth tellers are verifiable (the investigator can consult these friends), whereas the stories of liars are unverifiable (the information given about who they asked about the phone is vague, leaving the investigator with no opportunity to consult that person).

Table 7.1 shows that truth tellers include more verifiable details in their reports than liars, but they only do this when the IP is provided. Thus, to summarize, the IP strengthens the effect in a criminal setting but is not necessary for the effect to occur (see before). In contrast, in an insurance setting the IP appears to be a necessity.

In all three samples in which it was investigated liars included significantly more unverifiable details than truth tellers and the effect size was large in each study. In five out of six samples the ratios of verifiable details were examined. In four studies truth tellers reported significantly more verifiable details than liars, and the effect sizes were large in each study. In the fifth study no difference emerged.

To summarize the findings reported in Table 7.1 regarding insurance settings, truth tellers included more verifiable details than liars when the IP was used, whereas liars included more unverifiable details than truth tellers. The ratio of verifiable details was higher for truth tellers.

Table 7.2 shows that only one sample in the insurance settings reported accuracy regarding verifiable details. Although the accuracy rates were high, no conclusions can be drawn on the basis of this single study. In three samples accuracy rates were calculated based upon the ratio of verifiable details. The detection accuracy of liars in particular was substantial. It is not surprising that unverifiable details and ratio of verifiable details yielded good results in an insurance setting. In such settings, liars realize that they must be detailed to convince the insurer that an item belonging to them was damaged, stolen, or lost. Since they cannot provide verifiable details, all that is available to them are unverifiable details. The result is that liars report more unverifiable details than truth tellers, resulting in a lower verifiable details ratio.

Malingering setting: The third setting is a malingering setting. We expect this setting to be challenging for the Verifiability Approach. In this setting medical information including doctors' notes, the use of medication, receipts of buying medication, physical symptoms that others can see or physical symptoms someone talks about with others are the verifiable details. Truth tellers may find it diffi-cult to report verifiable details if they do not take specific medication or have symptoms people can see. In addition, truth tellers often do not share all their physical symptoms, perhaps because they do not want to bother other people, feel embarrassed about it, or both. For liars, bluffing in this situation is relatively easy. For building up their case, they may intentionally inform relevant people (employers, colleagues, friends, family) about all sorts of fake symptoms and they may even go to see a doctor about them who may give them a prescription. They may also simulate symptoms other people can see.

The two studies carried out in this area so far, comprising four samples, showed no difference between truth tellers and liars in verifiable details, but three samples revealed significant medium to large effects in unverifiable details. Liars report more unverifiable details than truth tellers: perhaps in their efforts to be convin-cing they "overdo" it. In one out of four samples, truth tellers had a significantly higher ratio of verifiable details than liars, and this was a medium effect. No effect emerged in the other three samples. To summarize the malingering setting findings, verifiable details do not seem to differentiate truth tellers and liars but perhaps unverifiable details in particular do. More research is needed to validate this conclusion.

Airport setting: The airport setting (asking people at check-in about their forth-coming trip) is a new setting for testing the Verifiability Approach. We expect this setting to have potential. Truth tellers should typically be able to provide check-able details about their forthcoming trip, whereas liars may find it difficult to make these up. Providing false checkable details may not be virtually impossible for them (in that respect it differs from criminal settings), but the lies need to be sophisticated. For example, it should involve lying to their relatives, friends, and colleagues about their false activities so that these people could confirm these lies when asked, or the introduction of a false witness (someone who knows it is a lie but is willing to back up the liar).

The only study in an airport setting so far showed that truth tellers included significantly more verifiable details in their statements than liars. The effect was small, but the experimental design was not ideal to test the Verifiability Approach. In this study, participants, after being interviewed, were asked whether they could think of questions the interviewer could ask them that would demonstrate that they were telling the truth. Truth tellers asked more questions that would result in verifiable details than liars. The effect may be stronger if the interviewer asks this question at the very beginning of the interview or asks questions and counts for the number of verifiable details in the answers the interviewees provide.

Discussion

The Verifiability Approach has been tested in four different settings so far and has shown promising results. In criminal settings truth tellers included more verifiable details in their statements than liars and this effect became stronger if interviewees were encouraged to include such details into their accounts through the Information Protocol. In insurance settings truth tellers also included more verifiable details in their statements than liars, but for this effect to appear it was necessary that interviewees were asked to include such details into their accounts. In addition, liars included more unverifiable details than truth tellers and the ratio of verifiable details was higher for truth tellers. In malingering settings truth tellers and liars did not differ from each other in terms of verifiable details, but they did in terms of unverifiable details with liars including such details more into their accounts than truth tellers. Research has only just begun in an airport setting so we cannot say anything meaningful about this setting yet.

If we consider the classification rates of correctly classifying truth tellers and liars based on their inclusion of verifiable details, a positive picture emerges. In criminal and insurance settings (the only settings in which this has been investigated) the total accuracy rates of classifying truth tellers and liars based on verifiable details ranged from 59 percent to 88 percent. Two more established verbal veracity tools, Criteria-Based Content Analysis (CBCA) and Reality Monitoring (RM), obtain average accuracy rates of around 70 percent (Vrij, 2008). In the Verifiability Approach, three accuracy rates were below 70 percent and six were at or above 70 percent, which tentatively suggests that the accuracy rates of the Verifiability Approach will be at least comparable with the accuracy rates of these two other tools. The accuracy rates in another frequently used tool, Scientific Content Analysis (SCAN), are unknown due to a lack of (sound) research in that area, but the few studies in that area revealed that SCAN cannot discriminate truth tellers from liars above the level of chance (Vrij, 2015b).

These findings are promising also considering that the approach may work better in real life than in laboratory studies. One successful way for liars to fool the investigator is to start bluffing and to make up verifiable details. This is a risky approach because the bluffer runs the risk that the investigator will actually check these details. However, the lower the liar thinks the likelihood is that the investigator will check their verifiable details, the higher the chance that they will bluff. It sounds reasonable that liars think that in real life the chance is higher that the investigator will check the verifiable details than in the laboratory, which makes the chance of bluffing lower in real life. This should enhance the difference in reporting verifiable details between truth tellers and liars in real life compared to laboratory settings.

The Verifiability Approach is still in its early development but we think it has several strong features. We finish this chapter with reporting nine of them. First, the Verifiability Approach may be less sensitive to so-called countermeasures, which are attempts by interviewees who know the working of a test to counteract the test and its results. Studies carried out with the Verifiability Approach to date showed that informing examinees about the working of the Verifiability

Approach actually *improved* the ability to discriminate among truth tellers and liars. This is unique in lie detection research to date. Typically, in lie detection research it is found that informing examinees about the lie detection method impairs the efficacy of that method, because examinees will then be able to fool the examiner by employing effective countermeasures (responding in such a way that makes them appear convincing). Indeed, studies have shown that participants can fool CBCA and RM coders (give stories that are rich in CBCA and RM criteria) if they are informed about these tools (Caso, Vrij, Mann, & DeLeo, 2006; Nahari & Pazuelo, 2015; Vrij, Akehurst, Soukara, & Bull, 2002, 2004). People who can fool CBCA and RM can, in all likelihood, also fool SCAN because there is no theoretical reason as to why SCAN would be less sensitive to countermeasures than CBCA and RM.

Second, the Verifiability Approach attempts to exploit differences in truth tellers' and liars' strategies (truth tellers are more willing and able to provide verifiable details than liars) and Interview Protocols based on exploiting different strategies used by truth tellers and liars have shown good results in recent years. Prime examples are the Strategic Use of Evidence (SUE) (Hartwig, Granhag, & Luke, 2014; Granhag & Hartwig, 2015) and Cognitive Credibility Assessment research (Vrij, 2015a). The reason why such techniques are so successful is that the same interview tool encourages truth tellers and liars to react in different ways, which enlarges the differences between them. That is, for the Verifiability Approach, the prompt to include verifiable details into an account encourages truth tellers more than liars to do so and that enlarges the difference in verifiable details between them.

Third, since truth tellers provide more checkable details after been instructed to do so, the tool helps to make truth tellers sound more convincing, which may reduce the risk of a false accusation of lying. The benefits of a veracity assessment tool that makes truth tellers sound truthful should not be underestimated. In the USA when interrogators believe that a suspect who denies involvement in a crime is guilty, they are advised to submit the suspect to interrogation techniques such as "The Reid Nine Steps of Interrogation" (Inbau, Reid, Buckley, & Jayne, 2013). This is a persuasive, confrontational interrogation technique powerful enough to make suspects confess, including those who are innocent (Kassin, 2004, 2005; Kassin & Gudjonsson, 2004). Already powerful in its basic form, Kassin and his colleagues found that once innocent suspects are mistakenly identified as guilty, they run the risk of enduring an interview style that is even more grilling than the interview style guilty suspects are subjected to. That is, interrogators who do not believe the innocent suspects' denials are inclined to double their efforts to elicit a confession (Kassin, Goldstein, & Savitsky, 2003).

Fourth, investigators do not actually have to check the truthfulness of the evidence mentioned by the interviewee to form a credibility assessment but only to count the number of checkable details reported. Of course, actually checking is highly recommended because it makes the veracity assessment verdict more conclusive. However, the finding that the approach also works without these checks could help investigators in situations where they lack the opportunity to make such checks, or in situations where they want to make an initial assessment about which suspects to focus their attention on. It makes the tool time-efficient and inexpensive to use.

Fifth, the Verifiability Approach has the opportunity to be used as a within-subjects tool. Practitioners often stress the importance of "within-subjects" veracity assessment tools (Vrij, 2016). That is, they wish to make a decision about the veracity status of an interviewee by comparing different responses made by the same interviewee during a single interview. The proportion of verifiable details is an example of a within-subjects measure. The advantage of within-subjects measures is that it controls for individual differences in providing detail (Nahari & Pazuelo, 2015; Nahari & Vrij, 2015). If just "amount of detail" is considered (as happens in CBCA, RM, and SCAN), the problem arises that the amount of detail will not only be affected by veracity but also by individual differences in eloquence or preparedness (well prepared answers are typically more detailed than spontaneous answers, DePaulo et al., 2003; Sporer & Schwandt, 2006). Those additional factors play a lesser role in within-subjects comparisons. That is, it is no longer relevant how detailed an answer is (which is largely influenced by being eloquent and prepared) but it becomes relevant how many verifiable relative to unverifiable details are included (more likely to be influenced by veracity).

Sixth, the tool focuses on obtaining evidence, which is the key part of any investigation. Thus, by using the Verifiability Approach, investigators are automatically focused on the evidence and are thus involved in credibility assessment and gathering evidence at the same time. This is not the case in other lie detection tools. In those tools investigators are busy with measuring physiological responses, observing nonverbal responses, or analyzing speech without necessary gathering more evidence.

Seventh, a definite answer as to whether or not someone has been lying can rarely, if ever, be given when analyzing the outcomes of a lie detection test because none of these tests are accurate enough to do so (Vrij, 2008; Vrij & Fisher, 2016). Conclusive evidence that someone is telling the truth or lying can only be obtained by comparing actual evidence with what the examinee says about this evidence. The Verifiability Approach focuses on this crucial link between speech and evidence.

Eighth, with the exception of CBCA, credibility assessments evidence is rarely used in court (Vrij, 2008). In that respect, credibility assessments per se do not make the case for the prosecution any stronger, and efforts solely focused on credibility assessments are thus limited (Vrij & Granhag, 2012). The verifiable details provided by interviewees in the Verifiability Approach may help the prosecution's case (Vrij & Fisher, 2016).

Ninth, technology is on the side of the Verifiability Approach. In the past it would have been difficult to use the Verifiability Approach when someone uses an alibi such as "I stayed at home all night on my own and went to bed early," because truth tellers would have found it difficult to provide verifiable detail to back up this claim. Nowadays, virtually everyone has modern technology (mobile phone, tablet, computer) and uses it frequently. Activities on this technology can be traced and it can be determined where this equipment is used.

Finally, verbal coding is typically subjective and time-consuming (Vrij, 2008), but promising efforts are on their way to develop an automatic coding system (Kleinberg, Nahari, & Verschuere, 2016). That would resolve both of these issues at the same time.

Notes

1 Correspondence concerning this chapter should be addressed to Aldert Vrij, University of Portsmouth, Department of Psychology, King Henry Building, King Henry 1 Street, Portsmouth PO1 2DY, Portsmouth, United Kingdom. E-mail: aldert.vrij @port.ac.uk.
2 For more detailed information about Criteria-Based Content Analysis see Amado, Arce & Fariña (2015), Köhnken (2004), Oberlader et al. (2016), Raskin & Esplin (1991), Steller & Boychuk (1992), Vrij (2005, 2008, 2015b), and Vrij & Nahari (2017); for more detailed information about Reality Monitoring see Masip, Sporer, Garrido, & Herrero (2005), Oberlader et al. (2016); Sporer (2004), Vrij (2008, 2015b) and Vrij & Nahari (2017); for more detailed information about Scientific Content Analysis see Armistead (2011), Driscoll (1994), Nahari, Vrij, & Fisher (2012), Smith (2001), Vrij (2008, 2015b), and Vrij & Nahari (2017).

References

Amado, B. G., Arce, R., & Fariña, F. (2015). Undeutsch hypothesis and criteria based content analysis: A meta-analytic review. *European Journal of Psychology Applied to Legal Context, 7*, 3–12.

Armistead, T. W. (2011). Detecting deception in written statements: The British Home Office study of scientific content analysis (SCAN). *Policing: An International Journal of Police Strategies & Management, 34*, 588–605.

Bell, B. E., & Loftus, E. F. (1989). Trivial persuasion in the courtroom: The power of (a few) minor details. *Journal of Personality and Social Psychology, 56*, 669–679.

Boscovic, I., Boogaard, G., Merckelbach, H., Vrij, A., & Hope, L. (2017a). The verifiability approach to detection of malingered physical symptoms. *Psychology, Crime & Law, 23*, 717–729.

Boscovic, I., Tejada-Gallardo, G., Merckelbach, H., Vrij, A., & Hope, L. (2017b). Verifiability on the run: An experimental study on the Verifiability Approach to malingered symptoms. Manuscript submitted for publication.

Burke, T. M., & Turtle, J. W. (2003). Alibi evidence in criminal investigations and trials: Psychological and legal factors. *Canadian Journal of Police and Security Services, 3*, 286–294.

Caso, L., Vrij, A., Mann, S., & DeLeo, G. (2006). Deceptive responses: The impact of verbal and nonverbal countermeasures. *Legal and Criminological Psychology, 11*, 99–111.

Cohen, J. (1988). *Statistical power analysis for the behavioral sciences* (2nd ed.). Hillsdale, NJ: Lawrence Erlbaum Associates.

Culhane, S. E., Hosch, H. M., & Kehn, A. (2008). Alibi generation: Data from US Hispanics and US non-Hispanic Whites. *Journal of Ethnicity in Criminal Justice, 6,* 177–199.

DePaulo, B. M., Lindsay, J. L., Malone, B. E., Muhlenbruck, L., Charlton, K., & Cooper, H. (2003). Cues to deception. *Psychological Bulletin, 129,* 74–118.

Driscoll, L. N. (1994). A validity assessment of written statements from suspects in criminal investigations using the SCAN technique. *Police Studies, 17,* 77–88.

Fiske, S. T., & Taylor, E. T. (1991). *Social cognition.* New York: McGraw-Hill.

Granhag, P. A. & Hartwig, M. (2008). A new theoretical perspective on deception detection: On the psychology of instrumental mind-reading. *Psychology, Crime & Law, 14,* 189–200.

Granhag, P. A., & Hartwig, M. (2015). The Strategic Use of Evidence (SUE) technique: A conceptual overview. In P. A. Granhag, A. Vrij, & B. Verschuere (Eds.), *Deception detection: Current challenges and new approaches* (pp. 231–251). Chichester: Wiley Blackwell.

Hartwig, M., Granhag, P. A., & Luke, T. (2014). Strategic use of evidence during investigative interviews: The state of the science. In D. C. Raskin, C. R. Honts, & J. C. Kircher (Eds.), *Credibility assessment: Scientific research and applications* (pp. 1–36). New York: Academic Press.

Harvey, A., Vrij, A., Nahari, G,. & Ludwig, K. (2017a). Applying the Verifiability Approach to insurance claims settings: Exploring the effect of the information protocol. *Legal and Criminological Psychology, 22,* 47–59.

Harvey, A., Vrij, A., Leal, S., Lafferty, M., & Nahari, G. (2017b). Insurance based lie detection: Enhancing the Verifiability Approach with a model statement component. *Acta Psychologica, 174,* 1–8.

Harvey, A., Vrij, A., Sariktas, G., & Nahari, G. (2017c). Examining the utility of the Verifiability Approach as a function of preliminary open and closed questioning. Manuscript submitted for publication.

Hauch, V., Blandón-Gitlin, I., Masip, J., Sporer, S. L. (2015). Are computers effective lie detectors? A meta-analysis of linguistic cues to deception. *Personality and Social Psychology Review, 19,* 307–342.

Hosch, H. M, Culhane, S. E., Jolly, K. W., Chavez, R. M., & Shaw L. H. (2011). Effects of an alibi witness's relationship to the defendant on mock jurors' judgments. *Law and Human Behaviour, 35,* 127–142.

Inbau, F. E., Reid, J. E., Buckley, J. P., & Jayne, B. C. (2013). *Criminal interrogation and confessions* (5th ed.). Burlington, MA: Jones & Bartlett Learning.

Jupe, L., Leal, S., Vrij, A., & Nahari, G. (2017a). Applying the Verifiability Approach in an international airport setting. *Psychology, Crime & Law, 23,* 812–825.

Jupe, L., Vrij, A., Leal, S., Nahari, G., & Harvey, A. (2017b). Fading lies: Applying the Verifiability Approach to witness statements after a period of delay. Manuscript in preparation.

Kassin, S. M. (2004). True or false: "I'd know a false confession if I saw one." In P. A. Granhag & L. A. Strömwall (Eds.), *Deception detection in forensic contexts* (pp. 172–194). Cambridge: Cambridge University Press.

Kassin, S. M. (2005). On the psychology of confessions: Does innocence put innocents at risk? *American Psychologist, 60,* 215–228.

Kassin, S. M., & Gudjonsson, G. H. (2004). The psychology of confessions: A review of the literature and issues. *Psychological Science in the Public Interest, 5*(2), 33–67.

Kassin, S. M., Goldstein, C. J., & Savitsky, K. (2003). Behavioral confirmation in the interrogation room: On the dangers of presuming guilt. *Law and Human Behavior, 27,* 187–203.

Kleinberg, B., Nahari, G., & Verschuere, B. (2016). Using the verifiability of details as a test of deception: A conceptual framework for the automation of the verifiability approach. *Proceedings of NAACL-HLT 2016*, pp. 18–25.

Köhnken, G. (2004). Statement validity analysis and the "detection of the truth." In P. A. Granhag & L. A. Strömwall (Eds.), *Deception detection in forensic contexts* (pp. 41–63). Cambridge: Cambridge University Press.

Lamers-Winkelman, F. (1999). Statement validity analysis: Its application to a sample of Dutch children who may have been sexually abused. *Journal of Aggression, Maltreatment & Trauma, 2,* 59–81.

Masip, J., Sporer, S., Garrido, E., & Herrero, C. (2005). The detection of deception with the reality monitoring approach: A review of the empirical evidence. *Psychology, Crime & Law, 11,* 99–122.

Nahari, G., & Pazuelo, M. (2015). Telling a convincing story: Richness in detail as a function of gender and priming. *Journal of Applied Research in Memory and Cognition, 4,* 363–367.

Nahari, G., & Vrij, A. (2014). Can I borrow your alibi? The applicability of the Verifiability Approach to the case of an alibi witness. *Journal of Applied Research in Memory and Cognition, 3,* 89–94.

Nahari, G. & Vrij, A. (2015). Systematic errors (biases) in applying verbal lie detection tools: Richness in detail as a test case. *Crime Psychology Review, 1,* 98–107.

Nahari, G., Vrij, A., & Fisher, R. P. (2012). Does the truth come out in the writing? SCAN as a lie detection tool. *Law and Human Behavior, 36,* 68–76.

Nahari, G., Leal, S., Vrij, A., Warmelink, L., & Vernham, Z. (2014a). Did somebody see it? Applying the Verifiability Approach to insurance claims interviews. *Journal of Investigative Psychology and Offender Profiling, 11,* 237–243.

Nahari, G., Vrij, A., & Fisher, R. P. (2014b). Exploiting liars' verbal strategies by examining unverifiable details. *Legal and Criminological Psychology, 19,* 227–239.

Nahari, G., Vrij, A., & Fisher, R. P. (2014c). The Verifiability Approach: Countermeasures facilitate its ability to discriminate between truths and lies. *Applied Cognitive Psychology, 28,* 122–128.

Oberlader, V. A., Naefgen, C., Koppehele-Gossel, J., Quinten, L., Banse, R., & Schmidt, A. F. (2016). Validity of content-based techniques to distinguish true and fabricated statements: A meta-analysis. *Law and Human Behavior, 40*(4), 440–457.

Raskin, D. C., & Esplin, P. W. (1991). Statement validity assessment: Interview procedures and content analysis of children's statements of sexual abuse. *Behavioral Assessment, 13,* 265–291.

Smith, N. (2001). Reading between the lines: An evaluation of the scientific content analysis technique (SCAN). Police research series paper 135. London: UK Home Office, Research, Development and Statistics Directorate.

Sporer, S. L. (2004). Reality monitoring and detection of deception. In P. A. Granhag & L. A. Strömwall (Eds.), *Deception detection in forensic contexts* (pp. 64–102). Cambridge: Cambridge University Press.

Sporer, S. L., & Schwandt, B. (2006). Paraverbal indicators of deception: A meta-analytic synthesis. *Applied Cognitive Psychology, 20,* 421–446.

Steller, M., & Boychuk, T. (1992). Children as witnesses in sexual abuse cases: Investigative interview and assessment techniques. In H. Dent & R. Flin (Eds.), *Children as witnesses* (pp. 47–73). New York: Wiley.

Trovillo, P. V. (1939a). A history of lie detection, I. *Journal of Criminal Law and Criminology, 29,* 848–881.

Trovillo, P.V. (1939b). A history of lie detection, II. *Journal of Criminal Law and Criminology*, *30*, 104–119.

Vernham, Z., Vrij, A., Leal, S., Mann, S., & Nahari, G. (2017). Applying the Verifiability Approach to the detection of deception in alibi witness situations. Manuscript submitted for publication.

Vrij, A. (2005). Criteria-based content analysis: A qualitative review of the first 37 studies. *Psychology, Public Policy, and Law*, *11*, 3–41.

Vrij, A. (2008). *Detecting lies and deceit: Pitfalls and opportunities* (2nd ed.). Chichester: Wiley.

Vrij, A. (2015a). A cognitive approach to lie detection. In P. A. Granhag, A. Vrij, & B. Verschuere (Eds.), *Deception detection: Current challenges and new approaches* (pp. 205–229). Chichester: Wiley Blackwell.

Vrij, A. (2015b). Verbal lie detection tools: Statement validity analysis, reality monitoring and scientific content analysis. In P. A. Granhag, A. Vrij, & B. Verschuere (Eds.), *Detection deception: Current challenges and cognitive approaches* (pp. 3–36). Chichester: Wiley Blackwell.

Vrij, A. (2016). Baselining as a lie detection method. *Applied Cognitive Psychology*, *30*, 1112–1119.

Vrij, A., & Fisher, R. P. (2016). Which lie detection tools are ready for use in the criminal justice system? *Journal of Applied Research in Memory and Cognition*, *5*, 302–307.

Vrij, A., & Granhag, P.A. (2012). Eliciting cues to deception and truth: What matters are the questions asked. *Journal of Applied Research in Memory and Cognition*, *1*, 110–117.

Vrij, A., & Nahari, G. (2017). Verbal lie detection. In P. A. Granhag, R. Bull, A. Shaboltas, & E. Dozortseva (Eds.), *Psychology and law in Europe: When West meets East* (pp. 263–282). Boca Raton, FL: CRC Press.

Vrij, A., Akehurst, L., Soukara, S., & Bull, R. (2002). Will the truth come out? The effect of deception, age, status, coaching, and social skills on CBCA scores. *Law and Human Behaviour*, *26*, 261–283.

Vrij, A., Akehurst, L., Soukara, S., & Bull, R. (2004). Let me inform you how to tell a convincing story: CBCA and reality monitoring scores as a function of age, coaching and deception. *Canadian Journal of Behavioural Science*, *36*, 113–126.

Vrij, A., Hope, L., & Fisher, R. P. (2014). Eliciting reliable information in investigative interviews. *Policy Insights from Behavioral and Brain Sciences*, *1*, 129–136.

Vrij, A., Nahari, G., Isitt, R., & Leal, S. (2016). Using the verifiability lie detection approach in an insurance claim setting. *Journal of Investigative Psychology and Offender Profiling*, *13*, 183–197.

8

COMMONALITIES AND COMPLEMENTARITIES AMONG SCIENCE-BASED INTERVIEW METHODS

Towards a Theory of Interrogation

Susan E. Brandon and Simon Wells

Previously, we described a sequence of steps underlying an interrogation that was proposed to increase the likelihood of eliciting useful and valid information in an ethical and lawful manner (Brandon, Wells, & Seale, 2016). Those steps included Planning and Analysis, interviewing using active listening skills and rapport-building that incorporated aspects of Motivational Interviewing (Alison et al., 2013; e.g., Miller & Rollnick, 2002) and client-centered therapy (e.g., Rogers, 1959), and the Cognitive Interview (Fisher & Geiselman, 1992; Geiselman, 2012). Understanding and countering resistance was described in terms of a cylindrical model of communication behavior in crisis negotiations (Taylor, 2002; Wells, 2014; Wells et al., 2013), and categories of resistance identified in high-stakes interactions (e.g., Knowles & Linn, 2004). The Strategic Use of Evidence (SUE; Granhag & Hartwig, 2015) was offered as one method of determining the validity of the information elicited (as well of eliciting more information); other methods of detecting deception were based on a cognitive approach to this challenge (e.g., Vrij, 2015).

It should be noted here that we did not distinguish between a criminal or intelligence interview and a criminal or intelligence interrogation, contrary to what is commonly taught (e.g., Inbau, Reid, Buckley, & Jayne, 2013; [US] Army Field Manual 2–22.3, 2006). We used the term "interrogation" rather than "interview" because the term interrogation has particular meaning for US law enforcement (e.g., as part of the determination of whether to offer a Miranda warning) and the US military (which distinguishes between debriefings and interrogations). We defined "interrogation" as the lawful collection of information from a person who is presumed to have particular knowledge relevant to a criminal investigation or an intelligence requirement. In this chapter, we use the terms "interrogation" and "interview" in the same manner.

The topics described above (Planning and Analysis, active listening, Motivational Interviewing, the Cognitive Interview, sensemaking, and negotiation) are among those included when we provide instruction to various US and UK agencies and departments on science-based interrogation skills. We also have developed and helped to implement more specialized courses, each focusing on one of the models; e.g., Observing Rapport Based Interviewing Techniques (ORBIT; Alison et al., 2013), which includes components of Motivational Interviewing; sensemaking, based on the Cylindrical Model (Taylor, 2002); the Cognitive Interview (Fisher & Geiselman, 1992), the Scharff Technique (Granhag et al., 2013), detecting deception using SUE (Granhag & Hartwig, 2015), or using other, cognition-based cues (Vrij, 2015). Students – who are experienced criminal or military interrogators – have patiently and enthusiastically sat through these specialized courses as well as an overview course that begins with Planning and Analysis and ends with cognitive-based deception detection (roughly the sequence described in Brandon et al., 2016). Recently, however, the more astute students have asked how the various components fit together; when should one do a Cognitive Interview or use SUE? How do these apparently diverse models relate to each other? And how do these newer, science-based methods relate to more traditional law enforcement (e.g., Inbau et al., 2013) or military (US Army Field Manual 2–22.3, 2006) styles of debriefing and interrogating? Should the newer methods replace the old ones or complement them? Should we consider that what the science has done has been to provide additional "tools for the toolbox," or is a new approach (i.e., a new toolbox) in order?

Some of these questions might be addressed with a general theory or model of interrogation, which currently we do not have. The goal of this chapter is to describe a sequence of interactions between an interrogator and the subject of a criminal or intelligence interrogation in order to describe how these science-based methods may be incorporated and sometimes overlap. The essential components of our model are shown in Figure 8.1, which depicts these components roughly in the order in which they are described and used (while recognizing the dynamic nature of an interrogation). Questions about using the science-based methods in lieu of the older methods (e.g., the Reid method or the 19 interrogation approaches and techniques of the US Army Field Manual) have to be considered in light of both ethical issues and policy constraints, which we address (at least briefly) as well.

Analysis and Planning

Analysis and Planning occurs before the interrogator meets his subject but continues throughout the interrogation, whether that be an hour or, as is sometimes the case in military and intelligence interrogations, many days or months. The interrogation team sifts through case information to sort out what is fact and what is hearsay (HUMINT), and what inferences can be made on the basis of both.

These inferences form the basis of hypotheses, such as whether the subject will be resistant or cooperative (Hypothesis #1) and whether they are likely to focus on details of events or plans in an instrumental manner or whether they are likely to focus on their motivations and self-identity (Hypothesis #2) (*sensemaking*; Taylor, 2002). The interrogator identifies how he sees the subject's brand to uncover implicit biases that might impair decision making, such as *hindsight* (Fischhoff, 1975), *availability* (Tversky & Kahneman, 1973), and *confirmation* (Johnston, 1996) biases. The interrogation team also identifies how the subject is likely to brand the interrogator (Hypothesis #3). If possible, the interrogation team carefully prepares the room so as to encourage disclosure by *priming* openness (e.g., Chaikin & Derlega, 1976; Dawson, Hartwig, & Brimbal, 2015). Over the course of the interrogation, these hypotheses are tested, and further hypotheses are developed and tested.

Explain and Engage

The interrogation begins with an appropriately dressed interrogator – who exhibits credibility and authority by his dress and demeanor (Hovland & Weiss, 1951; Wilson & Sherrell, 1993) – describing the conditions which led to the interrogation in a manner that is frank and forthright (Alison et al., 2013). He uses terms such as "we are hoping you will be open and honest with us" to verbally prime the behavior he seeks (e.g., Davis, Soref, Villabos, & Mikulincer, 2016). Describing the goal both assuages uncertainty on the part of the subject, which reduces anxiety (e.g., Hirsh, Mar, & Peterson, 2012), and engages processes of commitment and consistency (Cialdini, Cacioppo, Bassett, & Miller, 1978; Cialdini, Trost, & Newsom, 1995; Freedman & Fraser, 1966): the subject is "agreeing" to be "open and honest" by the fact that he has not left the room. The phrase "open and honest with us" might be followed by "as others in your situation have been," to implicitly reference a normative group and persuade using *social proof* (Asch, 1955; Festinger, 1954; Cialdini, 2001). The interrogator encourages autonomy perhaps by reading the subject the Miranda warning (in the USA) or the police caution (in the UK), and/or giving him a choice of place to sit; autonomy is one component of a cluster of behaviors that underlie rapport (Alison et al., 2013).

Having described the general topic of the interrogation, the interrogator addresses any concerns or questions the subject may have, and ensures that he is comfortable and does not need food or water. The role of a secondary interrogator and/or an interpreter is explained. If the subject is exhibiting signs of stress, this stress is addressed and reduced by drawing out the concerns of the subject (Alison et al., 2013) and helping him understand what the process is. The interrogator does not engage in small talk about irrelevant subjects in the belief that this will serve to develop rapport with the subject (Ewens, Vrij, Jang, & Jo, 2014); rapport is best understood as a common understanding of the process and the goal (Kleinman 2006). To help put a subject at ease, the interrogator might subtly

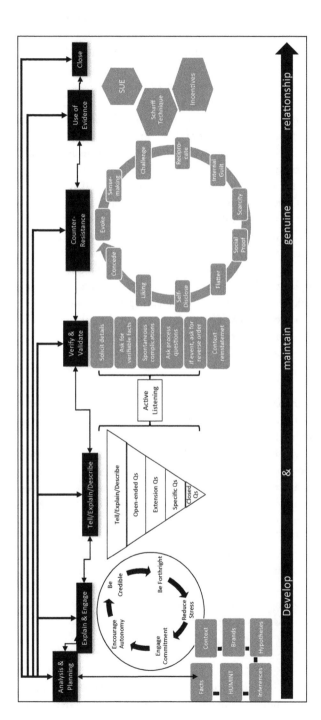

FIGURE 8.1 The components of a rapport-based, information–gathering approach to interrogations

mimic the subject's posture, words, or gestures (Shaw et al., 2015), assume a positive demeanor (this applies to all others in the room; Mann et al., 2012), and pay close attention to what the subject says and does (Tickle-Degnen & Rosenthal, 1987, 1990). The interrogator then describes to the subject that his role is to talk and the interrogator's, to listen (Fisher & Geiselman, 1992).

Obviously, the interrogator will have certain goals, objectives, or requirements he will try to meet. *We argue that a greater justice is served and/or more intelligence is gained if the overall goal of the interrogation is to accrue valid information relevant to the case.* If the subject is guilty of a crime, such information will include guilty knowledge which will incriminate the subject and may provide additional critical information or lead to additional evidence relevant to the crime. If he is innocent, or knows nothing of relevance to the intelligence operation, this provides him with the opportunity to provide information to support his claim. We recognize that confessions are powerful venues to condemn subjects with juries and prosecuting attorneys (Findley & Scott, 2006; Kassin, 2015). However, making a confession or admission the goal of an interrogation risks eliciting false confessions or admissions (Kassin, Appleby, & Torkildson-Perillo, 2010; Wrightsman & Kassin, 1993) and decreases the likelihood of uncovering unanticipated and novel information or evidence that may be critical. The internal state of the subject – to be contrite or guilt ridden – is not the purview of the justice system.[1]

Tell/Explain/Describe

While the interrogator likely has particular objectives, he does not start with direct questioning – unless the subject is assumed to have information that is critical to a life threatening situation and there is very limited time, in which case a direct question ("Do you know where the child is? If left in the woods overnight she will freeze to death") might be asked. It is our view that such situations are rare, however, and that opening an interrogation with such a direct question will increase the probability that the subject becomes wary and distrustful of both the interrogator and the process. The more effective approach is to begin with an open-ended request that the subject "Tell," "Explain," or "Describe" a context in which the critical objective sits. The funnel approach (Matsumoto, Hwang, & Sandoval, 2015), illustrated by the inverted triangle in Figure 8.1, is to start by asking a general, open-ended question, to elicit as detailed a response from the subject as possible. Details are encouraged ("Describe in as much detail as you can what you did last Saturday. Don't guess, but no details are too trivial"; Fisher & Geiselman, 1992).

Active Listening

The interrogator then engages in *active listening* (Shepherd, 2007; Rogers & Farson, 1979), which is to provide common encouragers such as nodding, saying "uh huh" to express understanding, and showing appropriate emotional responses to statements of emotion. Emotive words can be echoed, which invites the subject

and say nothing (Alison et al., 2014). It is likely that the rationale underlying such counter-interrogation behavior was that not facing the interrogator decreased the likelihood of engaging with him – because maintaining silence and refusing to respond to someone who is speaking with you is difficult. Whereas pleasantries might be easy to ignore, a mild provocation or making a claim that the subject is likely to disagree with should be harder.

Textbox 4: An exchange between a UK interrogator and his IRA subject (Brandon, personal communication, February 15, 2017).

Suspect: I need to tell you officer that I've been advised by my solicitor to go 'no comment' throughout so that's what I'll be doin'.
Detective: OK, no problem, but I'm going to need to still go through all these questions.
Suspect: OK.
Detective: Do you know Sian O'Caffrey?
Suspect: No comment.
Detective: Do you know Terry O'Flynn?
Suspect: No comment.
Detective: Do you know David O'Reilly?
Suspect: No comment.
Detective: Patrick O'Flaherty?
Suspect: Now that bastard . . . let me tell you about him! (then proceeds to do so).

There are other actions an interrogator might take with a resistant or avoidant subject, but the impact of these must be considered in light of the possibility that the subject is in fact innocent of the crime in question or has no knowledge that might incriminate him or others he may be concerned about. The interrogator's counter-resistance strategies must not lead the subject to believe that if he cooperates in a manner consistent with the apparent or actual demands of the interrogator, he will be released or that the consequences of his actions or his status will be minimized – that is, they must not make the subject compliant rather than cooperative. *Reciprocity* (Gouldner, 1960) is a powerful persuasion tactic: reciprocity can be instrumental (such as giving water or food), identity-based (such as showing honor and respect), or relational-based (such as showing empathy). In some instances, an interrogator may facilitate *internalized feelings of guilt* and accountability, and encourage the subject to take responsibility for his actions (Houston, Meissner, & Evans, 2014). The interrogator might state that there is limited time for information to be provided before either the interrogator leaves or the subject's circumstances change (in a less advantageous way) (Mittone & Savadori, 2006; Davis, Leo, & Follette, 2010); the interrogator might point out that "others in your circumstances have provided me with answers" (Cialdini, Wosinska, Barrett, Butner, & Gornik-Durose, 1999). Both *scarcity* and *social proof*, however, contain implicit incentives such that an innocent person might fabricate intelligence in order to avoid negative consequences or simply to get out of the interrogation itself, and so should be used with caution and awareness of these risks. *Flattery* (King & Snook, 2009), *self-disclosure* (Collins & Miller, 1994; Sprecher, Treger, Wondra, Hilaire, & Wallpe, 2014), and *liking* (Cialdini, 2009) should increase cooperation, as long as they can be conveyed with genuineness. Small concessions – such as not asking for an attorney – can be the basis for subsequent concessions (Freedman & Fraser, 1966); in fact, the Miranda warning or police caution can be emphasized to increase the subject's sense of autonomy; fostering a sense of autonomy in suspects has been shown to increase the likelihood of their providing critical information (Alison et al., 2013). Despite the frustrations, the interrogator should not be drawn into being demanding and rigid, parental and patronizing, over-familiar and desperate, passive and resentful, attacking and punishing, or argumentative and competitive. He might assume an attitude of "seeking guidance," in an attempt to better understand the subject's issues, but he should not be uncertain and hesitant or weak and submissive (Alison et al., 2013).

Accusatorial interrogation techniques, such as minimization and maximization (Inbau et al., 2013), increase the probability of confessions and admissions (King & Snook, 2009). The risk of such tactics is that they have also been shown to increase the likelihood of false confessions (Kassin, 1997, 2015; Kassin et al., 2010). However, a confession only has validity when embedded within new information surrounding the event; the perpetrator is, after all, the best witness to the incident. Accusatorial tactics are orthogonal to the goal of information gain: what in particular about convincing a subject that the consequences of his actions are minimal (i.e., the penalty will be small) or maximal (i.e., the penalty will be large) ensures that a guilty or knowledgeable subject won't provide false information in order to avoid self-incrimination? Or ensure that an innocent or ignorant subject might say what he thinks the interrogator wants to hear in order to be released from an interrogation that is not only inherently stressful, but additionally so because such individuals cannot provide what the interrogator is asking for? Interrogation with the goal of information collection is a game of wits, not penance.

Use of Evidence

In many instances, the interrogator will have evidence or information that connects the subject to the topic of interest. Perceptions of evidence are powerful inducements to admissions and confessions (Deslauriers-Varin, Lussier, & St-Yves, 2011). It is not uncommon, nor illegal, for American interrogators to lie about the evidence they possess (Kassin et al., 2010), although such deception is not allowed in the UK (Zander, 2013). Since such perceptions are so powerful, why shouldn't an interrogator lead a subject to believe he has convincing and damning evidence? One reason is that such a strategy may lead innocent subjects to believe they are guilty (Kassin et al., 2010). Another is that made-up evidence might in fact be contrary to the actual facts as a guilty or guilty-knowledge subject knows them: such a demonstration could convince such a subject that the interrogator knows very little and is "fishing" for admissions. In effect, the strategy risks revealing inaccurate information to a guilty subject which might impair both the interrogator's credibility and any rapport he might have with a subject. Finally, again, such a strategy provides no incentive for either a guilty or an innocent person to provide useful information; the best either can do is deny the evidence.

Evidence may be used strategically, however, to overcome resistance on the part of a subject, without the interrogator feigning false evidence (using *Strategic Use of Evidence* [SUE]; Granhag & Hartwig, 2015; Hartwig, Granhag, & Luke, 2014). The essential strategy of SUE is for the interrogator not to share what information or evidence he has until he has elicited a full narrative from the subject in such a manner that the subject will have no way to account for the evidence once it is shared. Asking the subject to provide the narrative leaves the subject uncertain of what evidence the interrogator has, since none was revealed. A guilty or guilty-knowledge subject will make the narrative as lean as possible so as not to provide any incriminating information. The interrogator then will ask for the narrative again, using a funnel approach in order to pin the subject down to the exact version he is offering.

For example, imagine a suspect denying having been close to a victim and having been at the scene of the crime. Further imagine that analysis shows blood from the victim under the suspect's sneakers. If confronted with this evidence, the suspect may state that his many friends run in and out of his flat all the time, borrowing money, food, beer, and clothes. Instead of having to disprove this, the interrogator should have exhausted this alternative explanation prior to disclosing the evidence: "Do you live alone?" "Who has access to your flat?" "Do you borrow household items, food, clothes, etc., from your friends?" "Do they borrow these things from you?" (Granhag & Hartwig, 2015, p. 242). If, after answering these questions, the interrogator then begins to disclose the evidence (e.g., by saying, "We have some evidence you were in the room where the body lay"), the suspect must deny being there, resulting in a statement that is inconsistent with the evidence. If the interrogator then makes the evidence more specific (e.g., "One of your sneakers has blood on it"), alternative accounts of how the blood might have got there have been exhausted, and the suspect can only deny or be inconsistent with what he previously claimed ("I looked into the room" after denying being in the room at all). Now the suspect might come to think that the interrogator has more evidence than he initially thought, so he adopts the counter-interrogation strategy of changing what he says to be consistent with the evidence. This leads him to be inconsistent with what he previously said. The strategy is for the interrogator to confront the suspect with these inconsistencies for several pieces of (real) evidence. This leads the suspect to think that the interrogator has more evidence than he originally thought, and increases the likelihood that he will adopt yet another counter-interrogation strategy, which is to provide information that he thinks the interrogator already has so as to appear to be forthcoming. A fortunate outcome might be that the suspect provides information the interrogator did not have.

Hanns Scharff, a World War II Luftwaffe interrogator who was renowned for his ability to collect useful information from US pilots without being abusive, hypothesized that the airmen would try to guess how much information Scharff already had – and if they perceived that he already knew the details of a particular aircraft or group, they would decide that it would do no harm to provide Scharff with that information (Granhag et al., 2013; Scharff, 1950; Toliver, 1978). So, rather than ask a series of questions, Scharff would tell the airman a story (for example) about a particular training school and the modifications to the aircraft in the latest model. He would insert a particular fact into his narrative that he wanted either confirmed or corrected; the pilot, hearing the detailed and generally accurate story, would correct Scharff and thus provide the critical bit of information. Scharff, of course, did not stop his story at this point, but continued on in order to hide the fact that a critical bit of intelligence had been elicited. If an interrogator can use what information he has so strategically, this is likely to be highly effective method. What is critical to this approach is (1) to be friendly and conversational rather than physical or coercive; (2) ask few questions and instead offer detailed narratives; (3) use the narratives to reflect back information that the interrogator already has or can reasonably speculate about, leading the subject to assume that the interrogator knows a lot already; and (4) collect new information not by asking direct questions but by using both implicit and explicit confirmation and/or disconfirmation (Granhag et al., 2013; May, Granhag, & Oleszkiewicz, 2014; May & Granhag, 2014; Oleszkiewicz, Granhag, & Montecinos, 2014a; Oleszkiewicz, Granhag, & Kleinman, 2014b). However, the method is highly risky for instances where the subject is vulnerable – for reasons of the situation, such as a lengthy interrogation (Drizin & Leo, 2004) or because he is mentally unstable (Gudjonsson, 2003), young (Redlich, 2007) and/or suggestible (Gudjonsson, 2003) – because he may adopt the narrative as his own, and even be unable at a later date to distinguish between his own (real) memories and those aspects of the story that were told to him by the interrogator (Loftus, 1997; Ofshe & Leo, 1997). But if the goal of the interrogation is information gain, and there is nothing to be gained by the subject reiterating the story (e.g., he is not going to write an incriminating statement), this method is highly effective because it makes use of the powerful influence of the subject's perception of the already-available evidence or information: if the interrogator knows this already, there should be no harm to the subject in his reiterating what is already known.

What are the options when evidence is unavailable (as may be the case in a sexual assault allegation) or cannot be shared (as may be the case in an intelligence interrogation) and the subject continues to resist? If an incentive is possible, such as suggesting that a witness protection program could be exchanged for testimony against others in a criminal case, or that a terrorist's family could be moved to a protective area in an intelligence operation, then these could be leveraged. As stated above, we do not suggest making promises that are either illegal or cannot be kept, in part because once revealed as a hoax, the subject will henceforth not trust the interrogator. It also is the case that juries tend to view testimony given in exchange for leniency or some other reward as suspicious: "he only said that because he was told he would get a reduced sentence" (Harris, 2000). If a subject is claiming innocence or ignorance, the interrogator might start by acknowledging the subject's resistance at the beginning of the encounter; "you will probably not want to explain why you think you are here. Nevertheless, now is your opportunity to tell me anything about why you are sitting in front of me." Another strategy is to ask him to explain what he can about the situation of concern: "tell me what happened that night"; "tell me what you know about the group's movements during 2014," etc. If the subject agrees to provide a narrative – and refusing to do so risks making him appear to be withholding important knowledge – then he should be encouraged to provide as many details as possible. Building a timeline on a whiteboard or Post-its on the wall, with the subject providing both the scale and the starting points (Hope et al., 2013) is one way to encourage such detail.

Close

What is the endpoint of an interrogation? If the goal is a confession or admission, an investigator might end once such is obtained. However, if the goal is the elicitation of information, a confession or admission must be followed up by further information collection: as noted, the subject is the best witness to the incident or incidents of interest; further probing via open-ended questions ("Tell," "Explain," "Describe") may lead to important facts about the case: motivations and belief systems may be revealed; others might be implicated or absolved; other witnesses might be identified; other crimes or a larger network might be identified, and so on.

Ending an interrogation session provides additional opportunities for information collection: as the interrogator summarizes what information the subject provided, the subject may correct or add to the information, assuming he has been cooperative. If he has continued to avoid providing any useful information, the interrogator by this time will have made clear what evidence he already has; explaining that the exchange is coming to an end provides the subject with one last opportunity to account for the evidence. Whether the subject has been cooperative or not, the last words should be such that reinforce a positive relationship between the subject and the interrogator – in large part because it is always possible that the subject will be questioned again by the same interrogator or others. The metaphoric "door" must be left open.

Conclusion

We acknowledge that some of the influence techniques described above can be construed as consistent with various American police manuals. In a detailed and cogent analysis of American law enforcement tactics, Davis and O'Donohue (2003, p. 963) point out that:

> Interrogation strategies are designed to overcome resistance . . . the Reid method is replete with very powerful *omega* tactics that indeed sweep away resistance, even as equally powerful *alpha* strategies provide incentives to comply and confess. Though based on common everyday tactics of influence, these strategies are particularly powerful when employed in the interrogative situation – where the target is in a relatively powerless role and an inescapable influence situation.

These authors then detail the consequences of false confessions, which have been shown to be a consequence of many of the tactics they describe (Kassin et al., 2010; Leo, 2001) and conclude that "the problem of false confessions is likely to be reduced neither through alterations in police procedures that tend to elicit them nor through lessened prejudicial impact on the prosecutors, judges and juries that react to them once elicited. Hence, it falls to the expert witness to provide context for judges ruling on admissibility and judges deciding culpability" (2003, p. 980).

It is our contention that methods of persuasion as well as methods designed to elicit full and credible narratives (as described above) can be effective for eliciting information and that false confessions will be less likely if the interrogation tactics are adjusted so that the goal of the interrogation is not a confession or an admission, but information gain. We also propose that such methods are ethical when used to promote cooperation rather than compliance (Cialdini, 2001).

Insightful as the analysis offered by Davis and O'Donohue is, they are pessimistic regarding any changes in American police interrogation practices, and suggest that there are no alternatives other than expert testimony. It is unclear whether the assumption is that all interrogations are inherently problematic (thus the need for the expert witness). We take the view that interrogations are an important and critical aspect of both law enforcement and intelligence operations. In the domain of intelligence gathering, interrogations may provide the only information

Kleinman, S. (2006). KUBARK counterintelligence interrogation review: Observations of an interrogator. Lessons learned and avenues for further research. In N. D. I. College (Ed.), *Educing information* (pp. 95–140). Washington, DC: NDIC Press.

Knowles, E. S., & Linn, J. A. (2004). *Resistance and persuasion*. Mahwah, NJ: Lawrence Erlbaum Associates.

Leins, D. A., Fisher, R. P., & Vrij, A. (2012). Drawing on liars' lack of cognitive flexibility: Detecting deception through varying report modes. *Applied Cognitive Psychology*, *26*, 601–607.

Leo, R. A. (2001). False confessions: Causes, consequences, and solutions. In S. D. Westervelt (Ed.), *Wrongly convicted: Perspectives on failed justice* (pp. 36–54). New Brunswick, NJ: Rutgers University Press.

Loftus, E. F. (1997). Creating false memories. *Scientific American*, *277*, 70–75.

Mann, S., Vrij, A., Shaw, D., Leal, S., Ewens, S., Hillman, J., ... Fisher, R. P. (2012). Two heads are better than one? How to effectively use two interviewers to elicit cues to deception. *Legal and Criminological Psychology*, *18,* 324–340.

Matsumoto, D., Hwang, H. C., & Sandoval, V. A. (2015). Interviewing tips: The funnel approach to questioning and eliciting information. *Tactics and Preparedness*, January, 7–10.

May, L., & Granhag, P. A. Techniques for eliciting human intelligence: Examining possible order effects of the Scharff tactics. *Psychiatry, Psychology and Law*, *23*, 275–287.

May, L., Granhag, P. A., & Oleszkiewicz, S. (2014). Eliciting intelligence using the Scharff-technique: Closing in on the confirmation/disconfirmation-tactic. *Journal of Investigative Psychology and Offender Profiling*, *11*, 136–150.

Miller, W. R., & Rollnick, S. (2002). *Motivational interviewing: Preparing people for change* (2nd ed.). New York: Guilford Press.

Mittone, L., & Savadori, L. (2006). The scarcity bias. *Applied Psychology: An International Review*, *58*, 453–468.

Nahari, G., Vrij, A., & Fisher, R. P. (2014a). Exploiting liars' verbal strategies by examining unverifiable details. *Legal and Criminological Psychology*, *19*, 227–239.

Nahari, G., Vrij, A., & Fisher, R. P. (2014b). The verifiability approach: Countermeasures facilitate its ability to discriminate between truths and lies. *Applied Cognitive Psychology*, *28*, 122–128.

Ofshe, R. J., & Leo, R. A. (1997). The social psychology of police interrogation: The theory and classification of true and false confessions. *Studies in Law, Politics and Society*, *16*, 189–251.

Oleszkiewicz, S., Granhag, P. A., & Kleinman, S. M. (2014a). On eliciting intelligence from human sources: Contextualizing the Scharff-technique. *Applied Cognitive Psychology*, *28*, 898–907.

Oleszkiewicz, S., Granhag, P. A., & Montecinos, S. C. (2014b). The Scharff-technique: Eliciting intelligence from human sources. *Law and Human Behavior*, *38*, 478–489.

Redlich, A. D. (2007). Double jeopardy in the interrogation room: Young age and mental illness. *American Psychologist*, *62*, 609–611.

Rivard, J. R., Fisher, R. P., Robertson, B., & Mueller, D. H. (2014). Testing the cognitive interview with professional interviewers: Enhancing recall of specific details of recurring events. *Applied Cognitive Psychology*, *28*, 926–935.

Rogers, C. (1959). A theory of therapy, personality, and interpersonal relationships as developed in the client-centered framework. In S. Koch (Ed.), *Psychology: The study of a science*, Vol. 3: *Formulations of the person and the social context* (pp. 184–256). New York: McGraw-Hill.

Rogers, C., & Farson, R. E. (1979). Active listening. In D. Kolb, I Rubin, & J. MacIntyre (Eds.), *Organizational Psychology* (3rd ed., pp. 168–180). Upper Saddle River, NJ: Prentice-Hall.

Roos af Hjelmsäter, E., Öhman, L., Granhag, P. A., & Vrij, A. (2014). 'Mapping' deception in adolescents: Eliciting cues to deceit through an unanticipated spatial drawing task. *Legal and Criminological Psychology*, *19*, 179–188.

Scharff, H. J. (1950). Without torture. *Argosy*, *39*, 87–91.

Shaw, D. J., Vrij, A., Leal, S., Mann, S., Hillman, J., Granhag, P. A., & Fisher, R. P. (2015). Mimicry and investigative interviewing: Using deliberate mimicry to elicit information and cues to deceit. *Journal of Investigative Psychology and Offender Profiling*, *12*, 217–230.

Shepherd, E. (2007). *Investigative interviewing: The conversation management approach.* Oxford: Oxford University Press.

Skerker, M. (2010). *An ethics of interrogation.* Chicago, IL: University of Chicago Press.

Sprecher, S., Treger, S., Wondra, J. D., Hilaire, N., & Wallpe, K. (2014). Taking turns: Reciprocal self-disclosure promotes liking in initial interactions. *Journal of Experimental Social Psychology*, *49*, 860–866.

Steller, M., & Köhnken, G. (1989). Criteria-based content analysis. In D. C. Raskin (Ed.), *Psychological methods in criminal investigation and evidence* (pp. 217–245). New York: Springer Verlag.

Taylor, P. J. (2002). A cylindrical model of communication behavior in crisis negotiations. *Human Communication Research*, *28*, 7–48.

Taylor, P. J., & Thomas, S. (2008). Linguistic style matching and negotiation outcome. *Negotiation and Conflict Management Research*, *1*, 263–281.

Tickle-Degnen, L., & Rosenthal, R. (1987). Group rapport and nonverbal behavior. *Review of Personality and Social Psychology*, *9*, 113–136.

Tickle-Degnen, L., & Rosenthal, R. (1990). The nature of rapport and its nonverbal correlates. *Psychological Inquiry*, *1*, 285–293.

Toliver, R. F. (1978). *The interrogator: The story of Hanns Scharff, Luftwaffe's master interrogator.* Fallbrook, CA: Aero Publishers.

Tulving, E., & Thomson, D. M. (1973). Encoding specificity and retrieval processes in episodic memory. *Psychological Review*, *80*, 352–373.

Tversky, A., & Kahneman, D. (1973). Availability: A heuristic for judging frequency and probability. *Cognitive Psychology*, *5*, 207–232.

Vrij, A. (2015). A cognitive approach to lie detection. In P. A. Granhag, A. Vrij, & B. Verschuere (Eds.), *Detecting deception: Current challenges and cognitive approaches* (pp. 205–229). Chichester: Wiley Blackwell.

Vrij, A., Mann, S., Fisher, R., Leal, S., Milne, B., & Bull, R. (2008). Increasing cognitive load to facilitate lie detection: The benefit of recalling an event in reverse order. *Law and Human Behavior*, *32*, 253–265.

Vrij, A., Leal, S., Granhag, P., Mann, S., Fisher, R., Hillman, J., & Sperry, K. (2009). Outsmarting the liars: The benefit of asking unanticipated questions. *Law and Human Behavior*, *33*, 159–166.

Warmelink, L., Vrij, A., Mann, S., Jundi, S., & Granhag, P. A. (2012). Have you been there before? The effect of experience and question expectedness on lying about intentions. *Acta Psychologica*, *141*, 178–183.

Wells, S. (2014). Negotiating in a terrorist environment. In J. Pearce (Ed.), *Terrorism case studies* (pp. 144–167). Oxford: Wiley.

Wells, S., Taylor, P., & Giebels, E. (2013). Crisis negotiation: From suicide to terrorism intervention In M. Olekalns & W. Adair (Eds.), *Handbook of research on negotiation* (pp. 473–498). Cheltenham: Edward Elgar Publishing.

Wilson, E. J., & Sherrell, D. L. (1993). Source effects in communication and persuasion research: A meta-analysis of effect size. *Journal of the Academy of Marketing Science, 21*, 101–112.

Wrightsman, L. S., & Kassin, S. (1993). *Confessions in the courtroom.* Thousand Oaks, CA: Sage.

Zander, M. (2013). *The police and criminal evidence Act 1984.* London: Sweet & Maxwell.

9

NAVIGATING THE INTERVIEW

Judgment and Decision Making in Investigative Interviewing

Drew A. Leins and Laura A. Zimmerman

Acknowledgment: Portions of this research were funded by the High-Value Detainee Interrogation Group, under Contracts JFBI-10-009, JFBI-12-198, JFBI-12-199, & DJF-15-1200-V-0009496. Other portions were funded by the Technical Support Working Group of the Combating Terrorism Technical Support Office, Contract N41756-13-C-3079. The ideas presented in this chapter are those of the authors and do not necessarily reflect the position of the US Government.

Introduction

The subject sits alone in a cell (in this chapter, we use the term "subject" to refer to human information sources, detainees, suspects, etc.). He was detained by customs agents at the airport after attempting to enter the country using a falsified passport. From another room, an interviewer observes the subject via closed circuit TV (we use the term "interviewer" to refer to human information elicitors). She watches as the subject paces in his cell. He is restless and fidgety. She notes these as cues to his internal state. She knows about the falsified passport and learns of the subject's membership on a terrorist watch list – possible cues to the subject's purpose for entering the country (to commit an attack). She also learns via intelligence reports that the subject is a new father and is struggling financially – possible cues to the subject's motivations to act badly (he needs money), and also possible leverage points to gain the subject's cooperation in an interview (he loves and wants to protect his family). She develops a plan to build rapport with him while treading lightly around threatening topics. She'll probe his financial and familial statuses to uncover details she can parlay into his cooperation. Her information requirements include determining why he tried to enter the country, his plans after entry, the identity of possible collaborators, and any impending attacks related or unrelated to his plans. Her time for gathering this information is short. Moreover, she learns that the subject speaks only Sudanese Arabic. She speaks only English and thus requires an interpreter. Now she must overcome linguistic, cultural, and other logistical barriers to connect with the subject. Thus, her plans for establishing a connection, developing rapport, and eliciting information may require revision. This all occurs before she speaks her first word to him.

Imagine now that the interview starts, but the subject will not cooperate because the interviewer is female and the subject does not recognize her authority. Consequently, she changes her tack and attempts to gain his trust and respect. To do this, she suppresses any emotional response to his protests and negotiates a deal demonstrating her authority to influence his situation: She moves him to a more comfortable setting and gives him food, tea, and cigarettes. She makes progress. He cooperates. They discuss details of his travel, but he withholds information regarding his plans. She elicits details about his family, but learns that he cares little for them. She learns he is comfortable with his financial status and with living an austere life. Family and money no longer appear to be motivators she can use to induce further cooperation. She must uncover different motivations. Moreover, he demands more concessions but her resources are limited. She must find another way to maintain his cooperation. How this interview unfolds could alone fill a book, let alone a single chapter. It illustrates the dynamic nature of many investigative interviews. Participants' motivations, internal states, and outward behaviors can change; their goals and subgoals can change; and, interviewers must remain flexible and adaptable if they are to identify and implement the right mix of approaches to satisfy their information requirements.

The above illustration highlights two general insights addressed in this chapter as key to advancing the science of investigative interviewing:

1. The interview context is complex and dynamic. With better insight into this context, researchers can develop and test interventions that aid the work of interviewers.
2. The cognitive work of interviewers is complex and demanding. With greater insight into these cognitive requirements, researchers can develop interventions compatible with how interviewers actually think or that help interviewers think differently about interviewing.

These two insights are inextricable. Interviewers' work is complex and demanding *because* the context is complex and demanding. To better understand these key components of interviewing, we began a line of research examining the context of investigative interviewing and how interviewers navigate that context. Our research incorporated interviews with practitioners, analyses of actual interviews, and controlled experiments using naturalistic stimuli. This chapter synthesizes and presents some of our findings. The following sections present an overview of our methods, a framework for understanding interviewer decision making, and descriptions of interviewer judgment and decision making across a handful of studies. Within the framework, we present qualitative data on the cognitive processes interviewers report engaging in (i.e., what they say they do) and quantitative data on some of their judgment and decision-making behaviors (i.e., what we observed them doing).

Our Approach

We began this exploration with some assumptions about what comprises the interview context and the cognitive work of interviewing. We assumed the interview context included a human source of information, a human agent and methods for eliciting information, goals for eliciting information, and a physical setting. By their nature, some of these components and how they interact are dynamic, vague, or even unknown, causing uncertainty for interviewers and leaving plenty of room to grow this line of research. To test our assumptions and expand our understanding of decision making in the interview context, we questioned professional interviewers about their practices, analyzed transcripts of real-world interviews, and conducted controlled experiments. The next few paragraphs summarize our methods for conducting these studies. Following these summaries, we present some of the results of these studies within a decision-making framework. Interested readers can find more complete descriptions of our methods in the referenced manuscripts and research reports.

Cognitive Task Analysis Interviews

To begin to understand the interview context and how interviewers navigate it, we conducted semi-structured Cognitive Task Analysis (CTA) interviews with 37 military or federal law enforcement interviewers (Zimmerman et al., 2013). CTA interviews help identify the cognitive components of work, in our case, the work of interviewing (for other examples, see Crandall, Klein, & Hoffman, 2006; Klein, 1998; Militello, 2001). The data from these interviews form the foundation of the decision-making framework discussed in this chapter.

Twenty of our participants recalled and described a challenging interview they experienced. To elicit these descriptions, we used the Critical Decision Method (CDM; see Crandall et al., 2006). Through this method, participants described a memorable and challenging interview in as much detail as possible. A researcher then recounted the narrative and asked the participant to add details. Together, they created a timeline specifying major decision and action points, and the participant added details. To elicit additional details, the researcher asked probing questions about the interview context, cue perceptions and interpretations, decision making, and action choices. Notably, the CDM is similar to the Cognitive Interview (Fisher & Geiselman, 1992), but with an added focus on decision making at the time of the critical event. These details allowed us to identify patterns of cues perceived by interviewers, methods used to assess the interview situations, and processes used to translate assessments into decisions.

Seventeen of our participants experienced a simulation interview rather than a CDM interview. These participants reviewed and commented on a recorded mock interview featuring a suspected terrorist, one federal law enforcement interviewer, and one military interviewer. The video presented different elements of an interview, including presentation of the subject's cover story, confrontation about the subject's inconsistent and implausible story details, tactical exchanges between the interviewers and the subject, and disclosure of critical information. As participants watched each segment, they described their perceptions of the interview, as well as the decisions and actions they would consider if they were conducting the mock interview. Simulation interviews allowed participants to describe their decision processes with the benefit of a richly detailed stimulus. Similar to CDM interviews, simulation interviews yielded data on interviewers' perceptions, processes for assessing and prioritizing cues, decision points, and action choices. The simulation interview also allowed novices, who lack the experience necessary for CDM interviews, to report relevant cognitive processes.

Analysis of Real-World Interviews

In a set of studies sponsored by the High-Value Detainee Interrogation Group, we accessed a set of military interviews and a set of law enforcement interviews. The set of military interviews comprised 12 sessions conducted by one interviewer with one subject and one or two interpreters at an overseas detention facility (see Leins, Zimmerman, & Cheng, 2014b).[1] The set of law enforcement (LE) interviews comprised seven interview sessions, each conducted by one or two of six different interviewers, with one of seven different subjects (see Zimmerman, Leins, Cheng, Miller, & Marcon, 2012). These LE interviews investigated five murder cases for which each suspect confessed, was adjudicated, and found guilty.

Across all interviews, we sought to identify the key verbal characteristics of interactions between interviewers and subjects to better understand the dynamics of eliciting information. To do this, we transcribed interview videos, coded each transcript, and then analyzed the coding for patterns and associations (e.g., see Glaser & Strauss, 1967). We chunked the verbal content into turns (i.e., an utterance initiated by an interviewer, followed by a response by a subject or interpreter). We coded an average of 649 turns per military interview session and 639 turns per LE interview. Within turns, we coded individual utterances – uninterrupted statements or questions made by a speaker – for the type of statement made, type of question asked, rapport-building or information elicitation tactic used, and the type of response given. The full coding scheme is available by request from either of the authors.

Observation Studies

In two controlled experiments, we tested professional interviewers' ability to judge subjects' internal states (thoughts and feelings) or veracity. In one study, 18 interviewers attempted to diagnose internal states by identifying baselines of subject behavior and evaluating departures from those baselines (the baseline study; see Leins, 2017). In the other study, 51 interviewers attempted to judge subjects' statement veracity in real-time (the deception study; see Leins, Zimmerman, & Polander, 2017b). For stimuli, both studies used naturalistic mock interviews of adult community members. All mock interviews were conducted by a professional interviewer, under only modest constraints (e.g., they conformed to practices outlined by the Army Field Manual or other commonly accepted practices). Mock interviewees included adult male community members who had either engaged in a mock act of terrorism (deception study) or applied for a job requiring a background interview (baseline study). In all interviews, subjects were generally free to respond as they wished, except deception study subjects were asked to lie about their involvement in the mock terrorism event. Across studies, these interviews generated rich stimuli, characterized by a mixture of interview techniques and respondent behavior.

In each study, participant-interviewers watched two different mock interviews and contemporaneously reported either behavioral cues and interpretations of those cues to diagnose internal states (the baseline study) or judgments of veracity (the deception study). To determine interviewers' sensitivity to cues to deception and other internal states, we compared their reports to ground truth for each relevant interview. We present some of the findings from these studies, our analyses of real-world interviews, and our CTA interviews within the following framework.

Decision-Making Framework

Understanding the Interview Context

The hypothetical example at the beginning of this chapter presents a simple schema for the interview context. During CTA interviews, practicing interviewers offered far richer illustrations of the context, including explanations of physical settings, time pressures, shifting and competing goals, missing and ambiguous information, and high levels of uncertainty. These details provide a foundation for understanding the broader context in which interviews unfold.

Time and place: The interview setting can have a significant impact on the process and outcome of an interview. Interviewers do not necessarily control where an interview occurs, but when they do, they can manipulate the setting to achieve certain goals. For example, interviewers who believe a subject will respond to acts of kindness or generosity may choose to move the subject to a more comfortable location. An upgraded location might include climate control or more comfortable chairs. Interviewers' understanding of a subject's basic cognitive needs can also guide where they conduct the interview. For example, aspects of the interview room – noise level or other distractions – may influence a subject's ability to recall critical information. An interviewer who can reduce distractions for a subject may be better able to elicit information, as focused concentration is critical to enhancing recall (Fisher & Geiselman, 1992). Our participants reported on elements of the setting they could overtly manipulate to help induce cooperation, but recent research suggests that interviewers may also be able to covertly manipulate the interview setting, for example, to prime openness and communication in subjects. A setting with features that signal openness (e.g., an open window or open book) might further induce a subject to disclose information (see Dawson, Hartwig, Brimbal, & Denisenkov, 2017).

Time may also be critical in guiding how interviewers elicit information. Time constraints can vary widely across types of investigation. Interviewers whose goals involve investigating past events or methodically identifying a rich network of individuals may enjoy looser time constraints than interviewers whose goals involve probing about possible future events or whose time may be limited by institutional or resource constraints. Extended time with a subject may be a luxury, as it allows interviewers more opportunity to build rapport and elicit comprehensive narratives; however, interviewers cannot often control how much time they have with a subject. When time is short and information goals are urgent (e.g., investigating imminent attacks), interviewer decision making becomes compressed and avenues of investigation may be relegated to "if I have time." In these cases, interviewers reported attempting to minimize time spent eliciting details that are not verifiable or that may be peripheral to the narrative or event being scrutinized. Of interest, novice interviewers we spoke to expressed concern over time constraints and their lack of control over time factors, whereas more experienced interviewers expressed confidence in their ability to manage time pressures, for example, by focusing their efforts on identifying and probing central, verifiable details. As it happens, focusing on verifiable details may also be a good strategy for judging veracity, as recent research found that liars and truth tellers report different amounts of verifiable details (Nahari, Vrij, & Fisher, 2014).

Person factors: Of course, interview subjects also add complexity to the interview context. They present with different identities, personalities, experiences, communication styles, languages, levels of cooperation, expectations of how an interview should unfold, and notions of their role versus the interviewer's role. These characteristics influence their behavior and how they interpret interviewer behavior. Thus, interviewers caution that a "one-size-fits-all" approach is generally contraindicated. Similar to subjects, interviewers present with a diversity of personal characteristics that influence how they interpret and respond to subject behavior. Over time, they may develop schemas for how an interview should unfold and how best to elicit information from a variety of subjects. Interviewers may also learn of subject-specific details that influence their approach. Schemas and idiosyncratic details can interact to profoundly influence how the interviewer and subject initially engage. For example, learning of a subject's criminal history or association with persons of interest may heighten interviewer suspicions or activate biases. In our baseline study, some interviewers commented that the ethnicity of one of the subjects primed the interviewers to interpret behavioral cues in ways that would differ if the subject were a different ethnicity. Such biases can be identified and addressed through training. However, training will remove only so much of this influence. To be faithful to real-world conditions and offer good predictions, models of interviewing should account for dynamic person factors, such as biases.

Language differences also add considerable complexity to the interview context. Eliciting information from subjects who speak languages other than the language spoken by the interviewer often requires an interpreter. Adding an interpreter can significantly change the interview context and dynamic. According to Army Field Manual 2-22.3 (United States Department of the Army, 2006), although interpreters are a valuable component of successful cross-cultural interviews, they can potentially impede the interview process and influence the quality of the information elicited (see also Berk-Seligson, 2011). Interpreters can add complexity when they move beyond interpreting and adopt the role of interviewer or subject (originating utterances on behalf of either party; e.g., see Valero Garcés, 2005). In our analysis of military interviews, we found that interpreters tended to successfully convey information between speakers, achieving accuracy rates of roughly 82 percent, but that they also committed some potentially critical interpretation errors. For example, when interpreting from Arabic to English they often substituted one phrase for another, an error they made less often when interpreting from English to Arabic. A more encouraging finding was that interpreters in our case study generally refrained from adopting the role of interrogator or subject (Leins, Zimmerman, & Marcon Zabecki, 2017a).

Within this dynamic context interviewers must attend to and process large amounts of information, decide how to act on that information, and then act. In the next section, we identify some of the processes that underlie decision making within the interview context.

A Model of Decision Making

Prior to analyzing CTA interview data, we anticipated developing an elaborate model of interviewer judgment and decision making. We expected several layers of processes to emerge. However, as we coded data, we realized that interviewers reported critical elements that fit rather neatly into the four components of an existing model called the OODA loop: Observe, Orient, Act, and Decide (Boyd, 1986; see Figure 9.1). In simple terms, Boyd observed that when making combat decisions, fighter pilots oriented to their environment, observed the evolving situation, decided a course of action, and then acted. Interviewers we spoke with

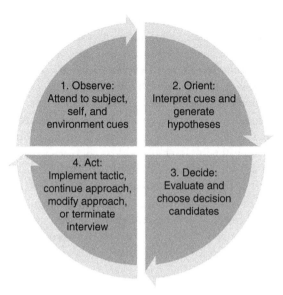

FIGURE 9.1 Interview OODA Loop

reported similar processes, by which they (1) observed and gathered information, (2) analyzed environmental cues and generated hypotheses, (3) weighed and chose candidate decisions, and (4) executed decisions. The following sections present how interviewers described these processes.

Observation: As the first component of the OODA loop indicates, decision makers first observe the environment by focusing on relevant features and then they interpret those features to generate an explanation. Unsurprisingly, interviewers reported attending to the many cues generated by subjects. These cues featured prominently in interviewers' CTA reports, as well as in reports given in the deception and baseline studies. What was surprising was the extent to which interviewers reported attending to self-generated cues, for example, their own tone of voice or body language.

Monitoring subjects: Interviewers reported benefiting from observing or monitoring subjects at multiple stages of the interview process. For example, monitoring subjects before the interview allowed interviewers to observe subjects' behavior as they anticipated the interview. Depending on how anxious or relaxed subjects appear before the interview, interviewers may adjust how they introduce themselves and how they begin building rapport. Recent research suggests the pre-interview period may also offer opportunities to assess credibility. For example, subjects who fabricate or rehearse a story prior to the interview may eschew opportunities to engage in activities unrelated to the impending interview, such as reading periodicals or other materials (Cahill, Fisher, & Rivard, 2011; see also Vrij, Mann, Leal, & Granhag, 2010).

After initiating contact with subjects, interviewers monitored subjects' verbal and nonverbal behavior. Subjects' verbal statements can contain cues to their cognitive and emotional states, their motivations, and their willingness to cooperate. For example, a subject may say things that reveal beliefs in causes that motivate or incite behavior. Interviewers can use such knowledge to select tactics that target those beliefs and potentially elicit relevant information. Interviewers can also monitor verbal content to judge the quality of the interaction and the effectiveness of their actions. For example, as subjects tell stories or answer questions, interviewers may listen for the level of detail or consistency to help judge veracity, an approach supported by empirical evidence (Vrij et al., 2009; Vrij, Leal, Mann, & Fisher, 2012). Indeed, interviewers in our baseline and deception studies reported attending to subjects' verbal cues to help them diagnose internal states and deception. Verbal cues accounted for roughly 31 percent of the cues identified as diagnostic in the deception study and roughly 23 percent of cues identified as diagnostic in the baseline study. The verbal behaviors most often cited in these studies included statement detail and consistency.

In the CTA interviews, interviewers reported that subjects' nonverbal behavior can also be diagnostic. Interviewers look for cues in body movements, eye contact, posture, breathing rate, perspiration, and grooming behaviors. For example, a common nonverbal cue identified by interviewers was a "defeated" posture – a bowed head, and shoulders slumped or rolled forward. Many interviewers perceive this posture as a cue that a previously defiant subject now has a diminished will or capacity to remain defiant. Some interviewers reported interpreting this and other nonverbal behaviors in the context of the situation rather than as absolute indicators of specific states or traits. Thus, the "defeated" posture becomes more informative if paired with other cues, for example, a verbal statement demonstrating a shift toward cooperativeness, or if it occurs after several failed attempts by a subject to contradict evidence. Interviewers reported using nonverbal cues in many instances to help make sense of subjects' reports. This often included using nonverbal cues to determine subject credibility and statement veracity, which are long-standing practices that generally lack empirical support (e.g., see Hartwig & Bond, 2011). Indeed, experienced interviewers in our baseline and deception studies were far more likely to report relying on nonverbal cues versus verbal cues to diagnose internal states and deception. Nonverbal cues accounted for just over 50 percent of all reported cues in the deception study and 44 percent of all reported cues in the baseline study. These rates are problematic, as nonverbal behavior appears not to correlate reliably with deception (DePaulo et al., 2003) and attending to nonverbal behavior to diagnose other internal states may be less efficient than attending to verbal behavior (a point we expound later in the chapter).

Monitoring self: In addition to monitoring subject behavior, interviewers reported monitoring their own behavior. They attend to their own tone of voice, style of questioning, and body language to assess how their behavior may influence their subjects. They often reported presenting a carefully crafted persona, observing how subjects received that persona, and adapting their presentation as necessary. For example, in CTA interviews, many interviewers reported first presenting themselves as a confident and competent authority figure, observing how their subject received that persona, and then manipulating their behavior to complement their perceptions of subjects' personalities and emotional states. This represents a circumscribed example of the interviewer's OODA loop: present a persona, look for cues to reception or effect (observe), interpret those cues (orient), consider whether and how to adapt the persona (decide), maintain the persona or present a changed persona (act), and repeat the loop. The emphasis interviewers placed on self-monitoring came as a surprise to us and provided insight into yet another factor that interviewers simultaneously process.

Orientation: The second step in the OODA loop involves interpreting environmental cues. At this step, interviewers synthesize incoming cues with their knowledge of a subject's culture, experiences, and background, as well as with their own experiences. A more holistic understanding of the subject in the context of the interview allows interviewers to generate explanations for a subject's behavior and to begin identifying compatible techniques for eliciting more information. Thus, interviewers continuously assemble a story throughout an interview. They receive information, interpret it, add it to the story, and then determine how best to gather more details of the story. Often, building the story is not a straightforward endeavor. Subjects can be elusive, deceptive, non-cooperative, or can impede story-building in other ways. In these cases, interviewers must determine whether and how to persuade subjects to be forthcoming. One way interviewers begin to identify candidate persuasion tactics is to determine subject motivations. By synthesizing subject cues and knowledge of a subject's background, an interviewer can hypothesize what type of message will resonate with a subject and motivate the subject to disclose information. In the example at the beginning of this chapter, the interviewer learned of the subject's financial difficulties, hypothesized that financial incentives may have induced the subject to transgress, and probed that topic only to discover that the subject was not motivated by money. This example reflects a process of hypothesis generation and testing that interviewers often reported in CTA interviews. They generally do not forgo an interview simply because they lack sufficient information to confidently construct an explanatory hypothesis. Rather, they construct a hypothesis with available information, test it, and refine it as they learn more.

When interviewers successfully compel subjects to cooperate and disclose information, they may need to determine the veracity of that information. One method interviewers use to judge veracity is to establish and evaluate baselines of subject behavior. When interviewers know some ground truth about narrative details or are confident that a line of questioning should induce a particular internal state in a subject, they take note of the subject's behavior concurrent with those details or questions. These behavioral observations serve as a baseline against which interviewers can compare future behavior. In CTA interviews, many interviewers indicated that they scrutinized subjects' "typical" verbal and nonverbal behavior so they could then detect deviations from this norm. They reported that deviations could indicate changes in subjects' cognitive and emotional states, for instance, in veracity or comfort level. Evaluating baseline behavior appears to be a particularly common method for judging veracity. In a recent survey of interviewers, 71 percent indicated relying on perceived deviations from baseline to detect deception (Russano, Narchet, Kleinman, & Meissner, 2014). The frequency with which interviewers reported relying on behavioral baselines to diagnose deception and other internal states compelled us to explore its effect in a study of deception detection and conduct a separate study focused on the practice of baselining.

In our deception study, we explored the potential for interviewers to use baseline behavior and found they gained no reliable benefit. They focused primarily on nonverbal behaviors (most frequently, gross body movements) and demonstrated no improvement in their ability to detect deception over time. Similarly, a recent study failed to find support for using baselines of behavior to detect deception (Ewens, Vrij, Jang, & Jo, 2014). That study found that gross measures of how hard subjects appeared to be thinking, and how much subjects appeared to control their hand and body movements, tended to vary naturally over the course of an interview, irrespective of veracity. Thus, the authors concluded that interviewers likely will not detect deception by relying on these behavioral baselines. However, using baselines of behavior may be a valid process for identifying respondents' internal states if those states correspond reliably with perceptible behavior and observers reliably perceive such behavior.

For our baseline study, we broadened the focus of the judgment task from detecting only deception to detecting a change in any internal state, for example, from comfortable to uncomfortable or happy to sad. The results by no means support the use of baselining as it is currently practiced, but they suggest that the approach has potential. Overall, interviewers were poor at detecting changes in subjects' internal states, achieving a hit rate of 27 percent. However, they improved from a hit rate of 20 percent in early segments, to a hit rate of 33 percent in later segments. Notably, when we examined cues identified by interviewers as diagnostic of changes in internal states, we found that interviewers were far more efficient at diagnosing changes when they attended to verbal cues versus nonverbal cues. Nearly half of all verbal cues identified as informative appeared to associate with internal state changes, compared to 39 percent of all nonverbal cues. When we expanded this analysis to include interviewers' diagnoses of subjects' normal internal states (i.e., not only departures from baseline, but baseline itself), nearly 70 percent of verbal cues associated with ground truth, compared to just over half of nonverbal cues. Thus, even though interviewers reported a preponderance of nonverbal cues as diagnostic, they were better at diagnosing internal states when they paid attention to verbal cues. This finding is supported by recent research demonstrating that observers were better at reading emotions when exposed only to a subject's voice versus when exposed to both the subject's voice and face (Kraus, 2017).

Decision making: After assessing subject behavior and forming judgments of internal states, motivations, and veracity, interviewers identify possible courses of action for advancing the interview and satisfying information requirements. In our CTA interviews, when interviewers arrived at decision points – instances when they chose (or would choose, in the case of simulation interviews) a strategy or tactic to advance the interview – they reported what they did (or would do) next, deliberation of possible actions, strategies they employed (or would employ), and the goals associated with these decisions. Interviewers' decisions tended to serve four broad categories of goals: gain cooperation, identify motivations, determine baseline, and gather information. The decisions they made to achieve these goals included selecting a rapport-building approach, selecting questioning tactics for eliciting information or cues to deception, selecting a self-presentation style, and determining when to switch methods or styles.

Rapport: Interviewers reported that building rapport is critical to gathering information and they described a variety of strategies. For some, establishing ground rules was essential to building rapport. They established ground rules by presenting clear boundaries, conveying their authority, and appealing to subjects to be mutually respectful and forthcoming. Some interviewers claimed it was critical to build on a foundation of reciprocity, and demonstrate trust as a means to gain trust. They established trust by showing empathy, demonstrating respect for subjects, promising or ensuring confidentiality, and providing comfort items (e.g., tea, cigarettes). Interviewers also suggested that finding common ground was essential for building rapport. They found common ground by illustrating how the subject and interviewer shared characteristics or identities (e.g., we are both fathers, we both reject injustice). Of interest, however, interviewers reported that to find common ground, they sometimes had to adopt personae that were incompatible with their actual attitudes. For example, to gain the respect and trust of a subject, one interviewer pretended to approve of the murder of insubordinates. This expression of approval would seem to violate a reciprocal agreement to be forthcoming, which calls into question whether sincerity is necessary to establish rapport. For many interviewers, the perception of sincerity was enough to create a working relationship. This often meant simply focusing on achieving a mutually beneficial outcome (e.g., the interviewer gains information, the subject gains some concession). Whether interviewers must be disingenuous to achieve such an outcome was often perceived as inconsequential. However, there may be consequences to presenting false personae, as creating and maintaining a false identity may increase an interviewer's cognitive load, a point on which we elaborate later in the chapter.

In practice, rapport can be defined many ways (e.g., see Meissner, Surmon-Böhr, Oleszkiewicz, & Alison, 2017). For our analyses of real-world military and LE interviews, we focused on rapport-building behaviors rather than on the phenomenon of attained rapport. We operationally defined two parts of rapport-building, one focusing on relationship and one focusing on identity. The relationship focus included behavior aimed at establishing or highlighting a relationship based on shared values, interests, or other characteristics. These behaviors include identifying common ground, highlighting similarities, and disclosing personal details. The identity focus included behaviors aimed at conveying positive affect, including the demonstration of empathy, kindness, or respect. We culled our definition from sources including Clark (2002), Clark and Brennan (1991), Norfolk, Birdi, and Walsh (2007), and Vanderhallen, Vervaeke, and Holmberg (2011).

In the military interviews we analyzed, rapport-building accounted for 7 percent of the interviewer's utterances. Roughly 75 percent of the interviewer's rapport-building behaviors involved a relationship focus. Similarly, in the LE interviews, rapport-building accounted for roughly 4 percent of the interviewers' utterances, of which 84 percent involved a relationship focus. Importantly, rapport-building may have associated with outcomes in both sets of interviews. In the military interviews, rapport-building occurred early in each session, setting up a dynamic later characterized by reciprocity in negotiations, arguments, and counterarguments. This coordinated communication has been identified as a feature of good rapport (Tickle-Degnen & Rosenthal, 1990). In the LE interviews, rapport-building behaviors tended to associate more directly with subject behavior. When interviewers highlighted common ground, demonstrated kindness, and disclosed personal information, subjects were more likely to cooperate and disclose information in response. Thus, our data support interviewers' claims that establishing rapport is critical to eliciting information. Of note, however, past research on rapport-building has revealed mixed results. For example, Beune, Giebels, and Sanders (2009) found that demonstrating kindness, in the form of active listening, tended to elicit admissions of guilt from subjects from cultures characterized by indirect communication and strong social bonds (high-context cultures). However, Beune, Giebels, and Taylor (2010) showed that interviewer kindness seemed almost as likely to elicit refusals to disclose information as it was to yield admissions. Thus, we circle back to emphasize flexibility in approaches rather than a "one-size-fits-all" approach.

Assuming interviewers are able to establish rapport, they must then maintain it. Interviewers maintain rapport by continuing the approaches described above and by carefully considering when to implement other information-gathering tactics, such as confronting a subject perceived to be deceptive. In CTA interviews, interviewers reported that confronting a subject or broaching a threatening topic at the wrong time could reduce the subject's trust in the interviewer and damage rapport. In our analyses of real-world interviews, we did not necessarily observe lost rapport. In our military interviews, the subject was uncooperative in only 5 percent of his responses and he attempted to change the topic in only 1 percent of turns. The interviewer generally stayed on topic as well, uttering unsolicited or

In the authors' jurisdictions – Australia and New Zealand – investigative interviews with sexual assault complainants are typically conducted by investigators who are specially trained in responding to sexual assault. These investigators are often detectives who are members of a criminal investigation branch (CIB) and have received evidence-based interview training.

In Australasia as well as further afield, the interviewing approach most commonly applied with adult witnesses – including complainants of sexual assault – is based on the Cognitive Interview (CI; Fisher & Geiselman, 1992; Geiselman et al., 1984). The CI incorporates scientific knowledge about human cognition, social dynamics, and communication skills. The aim of the protocol is to maximize the amount of information that witnesses provide, without compromising overall accuracy. To do this, the CI employs a variety of techniques to enhance free recall, ideally reducing the need for specific questions that might contaminate the witness's report (Geiselman & Fisher, 1988). Subsequent variations on the original CI format include the Enhanced CI (ECI; Fisher & Geiselman, 1992), which introduces several additional ways of facilitating the information-gathering process on a more personal level, and the Modified CI (MCI; Davis, McMahon, & Greenwood, 2005; Holliday, 2003), which allows for omission of specific techniques in the interests of time or witness-related factors. Empirical research shows that the CI increases the amount of correct information that witnesses provide, without a meaningful decrease in accuracy (Memon, Meissner, & Fraser, 2010); it has therefore been widely established as the 'gold standard' of adult investigative interviewing (Köhnken, Milne, Memon, & Bull, 1999; Memon et al., 2010).

In Australia and New Zealand, the nature of the investigative interview is particularly important because there is legal provision for it to be video-recorded and played as the complainant's direct evidence in any subsequent trial (Australian Law Reform Commission, 2010; Mahoney, McDonald, Optican, & Tinsley, 2007; see Criminal Justice System, 2007, for similar provisions in England and Wales). In fact, in New Zealand, interviews with sexual assault complainants are routinely recorded. This procedure stands in contrast to that of many other countries, in which the interviewer simply prepares a written statement that is endorsed by the complainant as a true record of the interview (Heaton-Armstrong & Wolchover, 1992) – an imperfect procedure about which many have expressed concern (e.g., Heaton-Armstrong & Wolchover, 1992; Köhnken, Thürer, & Zoberbier, 1994; Lamb, Orbach, Sternberg, Hershkowitz, & Horowitz, 2000; Milne & Shaw, 1999; Rock, 2001; Shepherd, 1999; Westera, Kebbell, & Milne, 2011).

Video-recorded evidence could be of considerable assistance to legal fact-finders for several reasons. First, because there are likely to be significant delays between the initial complaint and the trial (e.g., Westera et al., 2013b), pre-recorded evidence exposes fact-finders to the formal account that is the 'freshest' – that is, the least compromised by memory decay and distortion. Second, the relatively closed nature of prosecutors' questions means that they are unlikely to produce the degree of detail that can be elicited by specialist police investigators (Westera, Kebbell, & Milne, 2013a). Third, although the cross-examination process is unavoidable, presenting pre-recorded direct evidence spares the complainant from some of the stress associated with testifying – stress that can impair memory recall (see Deffenbacher, Bornstein, Penrod, & McGorty, 2004) and decrease willingness to disclose the highly personal details that are fundamental to the prosecution case (Konradi, 1999).

Indeed, there are vast differences in the degree of detail elicited from sexual assault complainants during an investigative interview versus during a trial. Westera et al. (2013b) coded transcripts of ten rape complainants' video-recorded investigative interviews, comparing their contents to the evidence that the same complainants gave on the stand. The researchers found that many of the details that went toward establishing consent (e.g., 'I told him I didn't want him near me') or described the alleged offences (e.g., 'he forced his hands down my pants') were absent from complainants' courtroom testimony. Critically, many of the missing details concerned complainants' reports of their emotions and cognitions before, during, and after the alleged offending (e.g., 'I thought that if I fought back, he would kill me') – even though these details could prove particularly helpful in offsetting fact-finders' reliance on rape myths (e.g., that a 'real' rape victim would physically resist the attacker). Westera and colleagues' (2013b) findings suggest that presenting a sexual assault complainant's video-recorded investigative interview as direct evidence in the courtroom could substantially increase the amount of relevant evidence available to fact-finders.

Yet even in countries in which video-recorded evidence is permitted in adult sexual assault cases, this provision is rarely utilized. Live evidence is still 'the norm' (Burton, Evans, & Sanders, 2006; Kingi & Jordan, 2009; Stern, 2010). In fact, in England and Wales, the law now requires prosecutors to apply for alternative modes of evidence (Home Office, 2011; McDonald & Tinsley, 2011) – a way of addressing low rates of voluntarily doing so.

Challenges

Recently, researchers have started to consider how well the various components of interview protocols like the CI align with the investigation and prosecution of sexual offences. The CI in particular was originally designed to be used in police investigations with cooperative witnesses reporting stranger-perpetrated offences (e.g., robbery; Fisher & Geiselman, 1992, 2010). Cases of alleged sexual assault, however, differ markedly to these offences in terms of the criminal context, the characteristics of the witness, and the evidence necessary for a successful prosecution (Westera, Powell, & Milne, 2017).

Fisher and Geiselman (2010) have encouraged researchers to seek ways to modify the components of the CI so that they meet the needs of specific types of crime. To do so in the case of adult sexual assault, however, it is first necessary to identify the specific challenges associated with conducting these interviews. Fortunately, a small body of research has begun to answer this question by seeking the views of those who have a vested interest in the interview process. We summarize this research below, outlining the interview-related challenges faced by the three major stakeholders in sexual assault cases: prosecutors, police investigators, and the complainants themselves.

Complainants

Much of the attrition in sexual assault cases can be accounted for by complainants withdrawing from the police process (Daly & Bouhours, 2010; Harris & Grace, 1999; Kelly, 2002; Kelly, Lovett, & Regan, 2005). When this happens, there is little else that investigators can do but discontinue the investigation (Hohl & Conway, 2017).

The most common reasons for withdrawal are remarkably similar across complainants: (1) feeling as though investigators do not believe them, (2) feeling blamed or judged for what happened, and/or (3) experiencing what is often termed 'secondary victimization' – a feeling of being assaulted all over again by the criminal justice process (Jordan, 2001; McMillan & Thomas, 2009; Patterson, 2011). When victims lose trust that their complaint will be taken seriously and investigated thoroughly, the disadvantages of reliving their experiences can outweigh the perceived advantages of doing so (Jordan, 2001; Kelly, 2002; Stanko, 1985; Temkin, 1997).

How does the investigative interviewing process contribute to complainants' experiences? Unsurprisingly, a large part of the answer to this question lies with the degree to which the investigator is sympathetic and sensitive (Jordan, 2001; Kelly et al., 2005; Temkin, 1997). Complainants measure the 'success' of their disclosure chiefly by whether or not they are provided with a space to tell their story in a non-judgmental setting in which their emotional needs are attended to (e.g., Jordan, 2001). Indeed, when complainants feel that the investigator is non-judgmental, they report being more forthcoming with detailed information during the interview (Patterson, 2011). Findings like these provide a strong directive to investigators to embrace the benefits of providing therapeutic jurisprudence to sexual assault complainants (see Fisher & Geiselman, 2010) – both from an ethical standpoint and from an evidential one.

Unfortunately, despite some evidence to suggest that police handling of these cases has improved over time (Lees & Gregory, 1993; Regan & Kelly, 2003; Temkin, 1997), problems still exist. Acceptance of rape myths is still consistently demonstrated among some police investigators, many of whom accordingly overestimate the proportion of false complainants (e.g., Hine & Murphy, 2017; see Parratt & Pina, 2017, for a recent review). Such beliefs and attitudes are likely to be evident to complainants during the interview process.

Complainants' negative feelings about the interview process do not stem solely from the interviewer's manner, however; they also stem from the structure and nature of the interview questions. In countries that have adopted narrative-based interview training for investigators, a key focus has been on maximizing detail. But although investigators' pursuit of increasingly specific detail is aimed at conducting a robust and thorough investigation, it can give rise to a number of problems that in turn can lead to attrition. When the details requested appear inconsequential or irrelevant, for example, complainants can feel disbelieved – interpreting this approach as an indication that their account is being called into question, rather than clarified. The pursuit of highly specific details that are difficult – if not impossible – to recall can also make complainants lose confidence in their memory, or feel as though their account is not 'good enough' to lead to prosecution. Clearly, being asked for highly specific details about events of a sexual nature can also be both distressing and exhausting for complainants, who report feeling burdened by the interview process (McMillan & Thomas, 2009); one complainant in Jordan's (2001, p. 692) study reported that the interview was like 'sitting there with your legs open'.

Compounding all of these problems is the fact that victims of sexual assault often suffer from a range of short- and long-term psychological and emotional difficulties as a direct result of the offending (Boyd, 2011; Kilpatrick, Resick, & Veronen, 1981; Surìs, Lind, Kashner, & Borman, 2007), and the experience of recounting a highly distressing experience is likely to bring such issues to the fore (e.g., Calhoun, Atkeson, & Resick, 1982). These difficulties are likely to exert a considerable negative impact on complainants' ability to retrieve and recount details of the event(s) in question (e.g., Moran, 2016), as well as their level of comfort and cooperation with the investigative process (e.g., Holmberg, 2004).

Police Investigators

Investigators report finding interviews with adult sexual assault complainants extremely challenging to conduct. Many have expressed the need for more guidance on how to meet evidential objectives while also ensuring that the process does not cause undue distress to the complainant (Spohn & Tellis, 2014).

Some of the challenges that investigators describe are not exclusive to sexual assault interviews. Witnesses who have mental health issues, poor cognitive functioning, or were intoxicated at the time of the witnessed event, for example (see Gentle, Zajac, Westera, & Powell, 2018), are part and parcel of police work. The prevalence of these factors, however, are likely to be amplified in sexual assault cases – both because sexual assault can lead to a host of negative psychological consequences (Dworkin, Menon, Bystrynski, & Allen, 2017; Mason & Lodrick,

acknowledgement of the degree to which questioning style can negatively affect complainants' mental state and willingness to continue with the police process (but see Fisher & Geiselman, 2010). The climate of disbelief that complainants expect – and sometimes encounter – during the interview can be expected to amplify these effects. Aside from the obvious benefits, devoting more attention to complainants' needs is something that can only be expected to improve the quality and quantity of memory evidence.

Concluding Remarks

There has been growing recognition that some aspects of investigative interviewing practice employed with sexual assault complainants could be tailored (1) to better meet the specific investigative and evidential requirements of these cases; and (2) to provide complainants with improved levels of therapeutic jurisprudence, thereby increasing satisfaction and decreasing attrition. Moreover, there appears to be widespread multidisciplinary support for modifications to current practice. The next step is to identify and refine the pertinent changes to interview protocols, using a combination of laboratory- and field-based research. Doing so will lead us toward an interview framework that promotes accurate, coherent, and evidentially relevant accounts from well-supported complainants.

Acknowledgments

We pay tribute to our co-author, Dr Nina Westera, who passed away on May 25, 2017.

References

Australian Law Reform Commission (2010). *Family violence: A national legal response.* www.alrc.gov.au/sites/default/files/pdfs/publications/ALRC114_WholeReport.pdf

Ali, M., Zajac, R., Westera, N., & Powell, M. B. (2018). Multi-disciplinary stakeholders' views on improving investigative interviews with adult sexual assault complainants. Manuscript in preparation.

Bell, B. E., & Loftus, E. F. (1989). Trivial persuasion in the courtroom: The power of (a few) minor details. *Journal of Personality and Social Psychology, 56,* 669–679.

Boyd, C. (2011). *The impacts of sexual assault on women.* ACSSA Resource Sheet No. 2. https://aifs.gov.au/sites/default/files/publication-documents/rs2.pdf

Brewer, N., & Burke, A. (2002). Effects of testimonial inconsistencies and eyewitness confidence on mock-juror judgments. *Law and Human Behavior, 26,* 353–364.

Brewer, N., Potter, R., Fisher, R. P., Bond, N., & Luszcz, M. A. (1999). Beliefs and data on the relationship between consistency and accuracy of eyewitness testimony. *Applied Cognitive Psychology, 13,* 297–313.

Bull, R. (2010). The investigative interviewing of children and other vulnerable witnesses: Psychological research and working/professional practice. *Legal and Criminological Psychology, 15,* 5–23.

Burrows, K. S., & Powell, M. B. (2014). Prosecutors' recommendations for improving child witness statements about sexual abuse. *Policing and Society, 24,* 189–207.

Burton, M., Evans, R., & Sanders, A. (2006). *Are special measures for vulnerable and intimidated witnesses working? Evidence from the criminal justice agencies.* London: Home Office.

Calhoun, K. S., Atkeson, B. M., & Resick, P. A. (1982). A longitudinal examination of fear reactions in victims of rape. *Journal of Counseling Psychology, 29,* 655–661.

Criminal Justice Joint Inspection Project (2009). *Report of a joint thematic review of victim and witness experiences in the criminal justice system.* London: Home Office.

Criminal Justice System (2007). *Achieving best evidence in criminal proceedings: Guidance in interviewing victims and witnesses, and using special measures.* London: Home Office.

Daly, K., & Bouhours, B. (2010). Rape and attrition in the legal process: A comparative analysis of five countries. *Crime and Justice: An Annual Review of Research, 39,* 565–650.

Darwinkel, E., Powell, M. B., & Sharman, S. J. (2015). Police and prosecutors' perceptions of adult sexual assault evidence associated with case authorisation and conviction. *Journal of Police and Criminal Psychology, 30,* 213–220.

Davis, M. R., McMahon, M., & Greenwood, K. M. (2005). The efficacy of mnemonic components of the cognitive interview: Towards a shortened variant for time-critical investigations. *Applied Cognitive Psychology, 19,* 75–93.

Deffenbacher, K. A., Bornstein, B. H., Penrod, S. D., & McGorty, E. K. (2004). A meta-analytic review of the effects of high stress on eyewitness memory. *Law and Human Behavior, 28,* 687–706.

Dworkin, E. R., Menon, S. V., Bystrynski, J., & Allen, N. E. (2017). Sexual assault victimization and psychopathology: A review and meta-analysis. *Clinical Psychology Review, 56,* 65–81.

Edwards, J. (2003). Medical examinations of sexual assault victims: Forensic use and relevance. *Judicial Officers' Bulletin, 15,* 65–72.

Ellison, L. (2007). Promoting effective case-building in rape cases: A comparative perspective. *Criminal Law Review, 9,* 691–708.

Ellison, L., & Munro, V. E. (2010). A stranger in the bushes or an elephant in the room? Critical reflection upon received rape myth wisdom in the context of a mock jury study. *New Criminal Law Review: An International and Interdisciplinary Journal, 13,* 781–801.

Ellsberg, M., Jansen, A. F. M., Heise, L., Watts, C. H., & Garcia-Moreno, C. (2008). Intimate partner violence and women's physical and mental health in the WHO multi-country study on women's health and domestic violence: An observational study. *The Lancet, 371,* 1165–1172.

Estrich, S. (1987). *Real rape.* Cambridge, MA: Harvard University Press.

Feltis, B. B., Powell, M. B., Snow, P. C., & Hughes-Scholes, C. H. (2010). An examination of the association between interviewer question type and story-grammar detail in child witness interviews about abuse. *Child Abuse & Neglect, 34,* 407–413.

Fileborn, B. (2011). *Sexual assault laws in Australia.* ACSSA Resource Sheet No. 1. https:// aifs.gov.au/publications/sexual-assault-laws-australia

Fisher, R. P., & Geiselman, R. E. (1992). *Memory enhancing techniques for investigative interviewing: The cognitive interview.* Springfield, IL: Charles C. Thomas.

Fisher, R. P., & Geiselman, R. E. (2010). The cognitive interview method of conducting police interviews: Eliciting extensive information and promoting therapeutic jurisprudence. *International Journal of Law and Psychiatry, 33,* 321–328.

Fisher, R. P., & Schreiber, N. (2007). Interview protocols for improving eyewitness memory. In M. P. Toglia, J. D. Read, D. R. Foss, & R. C. L. Lindsay (Eds.), *The handbook of eyewitness psychology*, vol. 1: *Memory for events* (pp. 53–80). Mahwah, NJ: Lawrence Erlbaum Associates.

Fisher, R. P., Brewer, N., & Mitchell, G. (2009). The relation between consistency and accuracy of eyewitness testimony: Legal versus cognitive explanations. In R. Bull, T. Valentine, & T. Williamson (Eds.), *Handbook of psychology of investigative interviewing: Current developments and future directions* (pp. 121–136). Chichester: Wiley.

Fitzgerald, R. J., & Price, H. L. (2015). Eyewitness identification across the life span: A meta-analysis of age differences. *Psychological Bulletin, 141,* 1228–1265.

Geiselman, R. E., & Fisher, R. P. (1988). The cognitive interview: An innovative technique for questioning witnesses of crime. *Journal of Police and Criminal Psychology, 4,* 2–5.

Geiselman, R. E., Fisher, R. P., Firstenberg, I., Hutton, L. A., Sullivan, S. J., Avetissian, I. V., & Prosk, A. L. (1984). Enhancement of eyewitness memory: An empirical evaluation of the cognitive interview. *Journal of Police Science & Administration, 12,* 74–80.

Gentle, M., Zajac, R., Westera, N., & Powell, M. B. (2018). Police officers' perceptions of the challenges associated with interviewing adult sexual assault complainants. Manuscript in preparation.

Harris, J., & Grace, S. (1999). *A question of evidence? Investigating and prosecuting rape in the 1990s.* Home Office Research Study 196. London: Home Office.

Heaton-Armstrong, A., & Wolchover, D. (1992). Recording witness statements. *Criminal Law Review.* Reprinted in A. Heaton-Armstrong, E. Shepherd, & D. Wolchover (Eds.), *Analysing witness testimony: A guide for legal practitioners & other professionals* (pp. 222–248). London: Blackstone Press, 1999.

Herman, J. L. (2005). Justice from the victim's perspective. *Violence Against Women, 11,* 571–602.

Hine, B., & Murphy, A. (2017). The impact of victim–perpetrator relationship, reputation and initial point of resistance on officers' responsibility and authenticity ratings towards hypothetical rape cases. *Journal of Criminal Justice, 49,* 1–13.

HM Crown Prosecution Service Inspectorate & HM Inspectorate of Constabulary (2007). *Without consent: A report on the joint review of the investigation and prosecution of rape cases.* London: HMCPSI and HMIC.

HMIC (2014). *Rape Monitoring Group: Adult and child rape data 2012/13.* London: HMIC.

Hohl, K., & Conway, M. A. (2017). Memory as evidence: How normal features of victim memory lead to the attrition of rape complaints. *Criminology & Criminal Justice, 17,* 248–265.

Hohl, K., & Stanko, E. A. (2015). Complaints of rape and the criminal justice system: Fresh evidence on the attrition problem in England and Wales. *European Journal of Criminology, 12,* 324–341.

Holliday, R. E. (2003). Reducing misinformation effects in children with cognitive interviews: Dissociating recollection and familiarity. *Child Development, 74,* 728–751.

Holmberg, U. (2004). Crime victims' experiences of police interviews and their inclination to provide or omit information. *International Journal of Police Science and Management, 6,* 155–170.

Home Office (2011). *The government response to the Stern Review: An independent review into how rape complaints are handled by public authorities in England and Wales.* London: Home Office.

Horney, J., & Spohn, C. (1996). The influence of blame and believability factors on the processing of simple versus aggravated rape cases. *Criminology, 34,* 135–162.

Ibabe, I., & Sporer, S. L. (2004). How you ask is what you get: On the influence of question form on accuracy and confidence. *Applied Cognitive Psychology, 18,* 711–726.

Johnson, D., Peterson, J., Sommers, I., & Baskin, D. (2012). Use of forensic science in investigating crimes of sexual violence: Contrasting its theoretical potential with empirical realities. *Violence Against Women, 18*, 193–222.

Jones, J. S., Wynn, B. N., Kroeze, B., Dunnuck, C., & Rossmann, L. (2004). Comparison of sexual assaults by strangers versus known assailants in a community-based population. *American Journal of Emergency Medicine, 22*, 454–9.

Jordan, J. (2001). Worlds apart? Women, rape and the police reporting process. *British Journal of Criminology, 41*, 679–706.

Kebbell, M. R., & Westera, N. J. (2011). Promoting pre-recorded complainant evidence in rape trials: Psychological and practice perspectives. *Criminal Law Journal, 35*, 376–385.

Kebbell, M. R., O'Kelly, C. M. E., & Gilchrist, E. L. (2007). Rape victims' experiences of giving evidence in English courts: A survey. *Psychiatry, Psychology and Law, 14*, 111–119.

Kelly, L. (2002). *Routes to (in)justice: A research review on the reporting, investigation and prosecution of rape cases.* London: HMCPSI.

Kelly, L., Lovett, J., & Regan, L. (2005). *A gap or a chasm? Attrition in reported rape cases.* London: Home Office.

Kerstetter, W. A. (1990). Gateway to justice: Police and prosecutorial response to sexual assaults against women. *Criminology, 81*, 267–313.

Kilpatrick, D. G., Resick, P. A., & Veronen, L. J. (1981). Effects of a rape experience: A longitudinal study. *Journal of Social Issues, 37*, 105–122.

Kingi, V., & Jordan, J. (2009). *Responding to sexual violence: Pathways to recovery.* Wellington, New Zealand: Ministry of Women's Affairs.

Köhnken, G., Thürer, C., & Zoberbier, D. (1994). The cognitive interview: Are the interviewers' memories enhanced, too? *Applied Cognitive Psychology, 8*, 13–24.

Köhnken, G., Milne, R., Memon, A., & Bull, R. (1999). The cognitive interview: A meta-analysis. *Psychology, Crime & Law, 5*, 3–27.

Konradi, A. (1999). "I don't have to be afraid of you": Rape survivors' emotion management in court. *Symbolic Interaction, 22*, 45–77.

Lamb, M. E., Orbach, Y., Sternberg, K. J., Hershkowitz, I., & Horowitz, D. (2000). Accuracy of investigators' verbatim notes of their forensic interviews with alleged child abuse victims. *Law and Human Behavior, 24*, 699–708.

Lees, S. (2002). *Carnal knowledge: Rape on trial* (2nd ed.). London: Women's Press.

Lees, S., & Gregory, J. (1993). *Rape and sexual assault: A study of attrition.* London: Islington Council.

Lipton, J. P. (1977). On the psychology of eyewitness testimony. *Journal of Applied Psychology, 62*, 90–95.

McDonald, E., & Tinsley, Y. (2011). *From "real rape" to real justice: Prosecuting rape in New Zealand.* Wellington, New Zealand: Victoria University Press.

McMillan, L., & Thomas, M. (2009). Police interviews of rape victims: Tensions and contradictions. In M. Horvath & J. Brown (Eds.), *Rape: Challenging contemporary thinking* (pp. 255–280). Cullompton: Willan.

Mahoney, R., McDonald, E., Optican, S., & Tinsley, Y. (2007). *The Evidence Act 2006: Act and analysis.* Wellington, New Zealand: Brookers.

Martin, E. K., Taft, C. T., & Resick, P. A. (2007). A review of marital rape. *Aggression and Violent Behavior, 12*, 329–347.

Mason, F., & Lodrick, Z. (2013). Psychological consequences of sexual assault. *Best Practice & Research Clinical Obstetrics & Gynaecology, 27*, 27–37.

Memon, A., Meissner, C. A., & Fraser, J. (2010). The cognitive interview: A meta-analytic review and study space analysis of the past 25 years. *Psychology, Public Policy and Law, 16,* 340–372.

Milne, R., & Shaw, G. (1999). Obtaining witness statements: The psychology, best practice and proposals for innovation. *Medicine, Science and the Law, 39,* 127–137.

Moran, T. P. (2016). Anxiety and working memory capacity: A meta-analysis and narrative review. *Psychological Bulletin, 142,* 831–864.

Parratt, K. A., & Pina, A. (2017). From "real rape" to real justice: A systematic review of police officers' rape myth beliefs. *Aggression and Violent Behavior, 34,* 68–83.

Patterson, D. (2011). The impact of detectives' manner of questioning on rape victims' disclosure. *Violence Against Women, 17,* 1349–1373.

Pennington, N., & Hastie, R. (1992). Explaining the evidence: Tests of the story model for juror decision making. *Journal of Personality and Social Psychology, 62,* 189–206.

Phillips, J., & Park, M. (2006). Measuring domestic violence and sexual assault against women. Canberra, Australia: Parliament of Australia. www.aph.gov.au/About_Parliament/ Parliamentary_Departments/ Parliamentary_Library/Publications_Archive/ archive/ ViolenceAgainstWomen

Planty, M., Langton, L., Krebs, C., Berzofsky, M., & Smiley-McDonald, H. (2013). *Female victims of sexual violence, 1994–2010.* Washington, DC: US Department of Justice.

Potter, R., & Brewer, N. (1999). Perceptions of witness behaviour–accuracy relationships held by police, lawyers and jurors. *Psychiatry, Psychology and Law, 6,* 97–103.

Powell, M. B., Fisher, R. P., & Wright, R. (2005). Investigative interviewing. In N. Brewer & K. D. Williams (Eds.), *Psychology and law: An empirical perspective* (pp. 11–42). New York: Guilford Press.

Powell, M. B., Garry, B., & Brewer, N. (2009). Eyewitness testimony. In I. Freckelton & H. Selby (Eds.), *Expert evidence.* North Ryde, NSW: Law Book Co.

Powell, M. B., Wright, R., & Hughes-Scholes, C. H. (2011). Contrasting the perceptions of child testimony experts, prosecutors and police officers regarding individual child abuse interviews. *Psychiatry, Psychology and Law, 18,* 33–43.

Read, J. D., & Connolly, A. (2007). The effects of delay on long-term memory for witnessed events. In M. P. Toglia, J. D. Read, D. R. Ross, & R. C. L. Lindsay (Eds.), *Handbook of eyewitness psychology,* vol. 1. *Memory for events* (pp. 117–155). New York: Lawrence Erlbaum Associates.

Regan, L., & Kelly, L. (2003). *Rape: Still a forgotten issue.* London: Child and Women Abuse Studies Unit.

Rock, F. (2001). The genesis of a witness statement. *Forensic Linguistics, 8,* 44–72.

Schuller, R. A., McKimmie, B. M., Masser, B. M., & Klippenstine, M. A. (2010). Judgments of sexual assault: The impact of complainant emotional demeanor, gender, and victim stereotypes. *New Criminal Law Review: An International and Interdisciplinary Journal, 13,* 759–780.

Shepherd, E. (1999). "Non-barking dogs and other odd species": Identifying anomaly in witness testimony. *Medicine, Science and the Law, 39,* 138–145.

Spohn, C., & Tellis, K. (2014). *Policing and prosecuting sexual assault: Inside the criminal justice system.* London: Lynne Rienner.

Stanko, E. (1985). *Intimate intrusions: Women's experience of male violence.* London: Routledge.

Stermac, L. E., Du Mont, J., & Kalemba, V. (1995). Comparison of sexual assaults by strangers and known assailants in an urban population of women. *Canadian Medical Association Journal, 153,* 1089–1094.

Stern, V. (2010). *The Stern Review*. London: Home Office.

Sternberg, K. J., Lamb, M. E., Davies, G. M., & Westcott, H. L. (2001). The Memorandum of Good Practice: Theory versus application. *Child Abuse & Neglect*, 25, 669–681.

Surìs, A., Lind, L., Kashner, T. M., & Borman, P. D. (2007). Mental health, quality of life, and health functioning in women veterans: Differential outcomes associated with military and civilian sexual assault. *Journal of Interpersonal Violence*, 22, 179–197.

Taylor, C. (2004). *Court licensed abuse*. New York: Peter Lang.

Temkin, J. (1997). Plus ça change: Reporting rape in the 1990s. *British Journal of Criminology*, 37, 507–528.

Temkin, J. (2000). Prosecuting and defending rape: Perspectives from the bar. *Journal of Law and Society*, 27, 219–248.

Temkin, J. (2002). *Rape and the legal process*. Oxford: Oxford University Press.

Temkin, J., & Krahé, B. (2008). *Sexual assault and the justice gap: A question of attitude*. Portland, OR: Hart Publishing.

Venema, R. M. (2016). Police officer schema of sexual assault reports: Real rape, ambiguous cases, and false reports. *Journal of Interpersonal Violence*, 31, 872–899.

Wells, G. L., Malpass, R. S., Lindsay, R. C. L., Fisher, R., Turtle, J. W., & Fulero, S. (2000). From the lab to the police station: A successful application of eyewitness research. *American Psychologist*, 55, 581–598.

Westera, N., Kebbell, M. R., & Milne, R. (2011). Interviewing rape complainants: Police officers' perceptions of interview format and quality of evidence. *Applied Cognitive Psychology*, 25, 917–926.

Westera, N., Kebbell, M. R., & Milne, B. (2013a). It is better, but does it look better? Prosecutor perceptions of using rape complainant investigative interviews as evidence. *Psychology, Crime & Law*, 19, 595–610.

Westera, N., Kebbell, M. R., & Milne, B. (2013b). Losing two thirds of the story: A comparison of the video recorded police interview and live evidence of rape complainants. *Criminal Law Review*, 4, 290–308.

Westera, N., Powell, M. B., & Milne, R. (2017). Lost in the detail: Prosecutors' perceptions of the utility of video recorded police interviews as rape complainant evidence. *Australian and New Zealand Journal of Criminology*, 50, 1–17.

Zydervelt, S., Zajac, R., Kaladelfos, A., & Westera, N. (2017). Lawyers' strategies for cross-examining rape complainants: Have we moved beyond the 1950s? *British Journal of Criminology*, 57, 551–569.

11

TECHNIQUES FOR INTERVIEWING RELUCTANT CHILD WITNESSES

Nicole E. Lytle, Jason J. Dickinson, and Debra A. Poole

Introduction

Child maltreatment is a seemingly intractable public health crisis. Despite tens of millions of dollars spent annually on prevention and education initiatives, each year millions of children become victims of abuse or neglect. In the USA alone, for example, child protective service agencies received an estimated 4 million referrals of child abuse and neglect in 2016 regarding over 7 million children (US Department of Health and Human Services, Administration for Children, Youth and Families, 2018). Because children are most likely to be maltreated in their first years of life (Office for Victims of Crimes, 2015), victims are not always old enough to aid the professionals who investigate these cases. But when children are able to describe their experiences, authorities rely heavily on forensic (investigative) interviews to learn what happened. When physical evidence is lacking, as in many sexual abuse cases, outcomes hinge largely on the quality and completeness of the testimony provided in these interviews.

The number of forensic interviews triggered by abuse and neglect referrals is unknown. US children's advocacy centers served over 300,000 children in 2015 and conducted more than 250,000 forensic interviews (mostly involving suspected sexual abuse; National Children's Alliance, 2016). This figure does not capture interviews conducted by child protection service workers, however, nor does it include interviews of child witnesses carried out by municipal, state, and federal law enforcement agencies. Patterns in institutional data from children's advocacy centers nevertheless speak to a major challenge of these cases: Among children served in 2015, approximately one third did not disclose abuse (National Children's Alliance, 2016). Given that some cases are triggered by mere suspicions of abuse (Lamb, Hershkowitz, Orbach, & Esplin, 2008), it is likely that nondisclosing children comprise some children who were not abused along with a sizable percentage of abused but unforthcoming victims.

Reluctance to talk about abuse is one reason why authorities consider child maltreatment one of the most difficult crimes to detect, investigate, and prosecute. Many victims are never interviewed because they have not (or will never) come forward (London, Bruck, Wright, & Ceci, 2008), including some who are unaware they are victims (Mack, 2017). Among the remaining children, disclosure is often a gradual process rather than a discrete event, and barriers to revealing abuse details are substantial (for a review see Alaggia, Collin-Vézina, & Lateef, 2017). The majority of perpetrators are familiar to their victims (Schaeffer, Leventhal, & Asnes, 2011), leading some children to conceal abuse in order to maintain the household order or to protect family members and friends (Malloy, Mugno, Rivard, Lyon, & Quas, 2016). Others have been threatened or sworn to secrecy by perpetrators, feel they lack the social support needed to come forward (Hershkowitz, Lanes, & Lamb, 2007), or fear that a full account of events will reveal details that make them seem complicit or culpable in the eyes of adults (Orbach, Shiloach, & Lamb, 2007).

Society's approach to increase the detection and disclosure of abuse can be distilled into four types of efforts: legislative, public outreach, research-based, and organizational. An important legislative response involved laws requiring adults to report reasonable suspicions of abuse to authorities (i.e., mandated reporting laws; Brown & Gallagher, 2013; Matthews, Lee, & Norman, 2016). At the same time, other legislative and statutory reforms sought to increase children's direct participation in legal proceedings by relaxing evidentiary standards (Bottoms & Goodman, 1996). Although legislative reforms were increasing awareness of child abuse among professionals, child advocates launched public awareness campaigns to distribute information about signs of maltreatment, increase children's personal protective behaviors, and encourage victimized children to come forward (e.g., safersmarterkids.org). The increased publicity about abuse, along with media coverage of problematic investigations, prompted more scientists to study the strengths and limitations of children's testimony, resulting in findings that were translated into best-practice standards for investigating cases and interviewing children (e.g., American Professional Society on the Abuse of Children, 2012; Newlin et al., 2015; Lamb, Brown, Hershkowitz, Orbach, & Esplin, in press). Finally, many jurisdictions created child advocacy centers (Connell, 2009a) and embraced a multidisciplinary team model for investigations (Graham, 2014). Both of these organizational developments helped professionalize forensic interviewing and cement its status as a specialized skill in the child protection community.

Despite these efforts, it remains challenging to discriminate reluctant victims from children who have not been victimized. The most obvious strategy for obtaining a disclosure is to establish the normalcy of talking about sensitive issues, followed by direct questions that ask whether children have experienced the matters under investigation. This straightforward approach came under criticism

3. **Third, the interviewer should tell the child what will happen next** (e.g., "Now I am going to show you what I call photo #1. I want you to look at this photo and tell me everything that you can about it. Tell me when you are ready"). (2016, slide 33)

HSI argues that the witness's gradual exposure to the evidence reflects the fact that disclosure is often a process rather than a discrete event, and children are more likely to disclose if they are given some control in that process (see also Summit, 1983; Hershkowitz et al., 2007). HSI also argues that giving the witness time to think about the evidence and privately form a response (e.g., "Tell me when you are ready to talk") may elicit details that the child might otherwise not have provided. Though the Prepare and Predict technique appears to be a thoughtful advance in how sensitive evidence is presented to children, questions remain. There are currently no data on the rate at which presenting physical evidence elicits disclosures, let alone whether the technique elicits more disclosures or corroborating details than other approaches. There are also no data that speak to the differential impact a child's age may have on the disclosure process or what types of evidence are appropriate for different ages. (None of the professional guidelines we reviewed contained age-related recommendations.) Finally, research has yet to explore the effect that presenting physical evidence might have on the psychological well-being of witnesses.

Introducing physical evidence is potentially a powerful tool for eliciting disclosures from reluctant children, and in some circumstances this approach may be the only means for investigators to identify victims and close cases. When there is concrete evidence of abuse, the likelihood of eliciting a false allegation is reduced and investigators generally gain leeway to pursue more direct lines of questioning (Lamb, Sternberg, & Esplin, 1995). Interviewers should nevertheless exercise caution when deciding whether (and how) to introduce physical evidence. Not all evidence will conclusively link a child to a crime, and pairing specific or leading questions with even strong physical evidence runs the risk of eliciting inaccurate testimony. Although current guidelines are somewhat disparate in their recommendations, they all agree that once the evidence is presented, interviewers should follow best practices for questioning children, including delivering questions that encourage children to discuss the evidence in their own words. And due to the sensitive nature of physical evidence (e.g., depictions of nudity, issues involving chain of custody), interviewers should consult with local law enforcement and defer to jurisdictional policies. Even with these precautions, the proliferation of digital evidence in investigations of crimes against children (Canadian Centre for Child Protection, 2016; National Center for Missing & Exploited Children, 2017) heightens the need for systematic research to better understand how physical evidence is best used to elicit disclosures from reluctant children.

The Putative Confession

A different approach to using evidence to overcome children's reluctance to disclosure has been proposed by Tom Lyon and his colleagues. The putative confession is a technique in which the interviewer implicitly confronts the child with knowledge (i.e., evidence) of an alleged transgression with an adult (e.g., sexual abuse) by stating that the suspect "told me everything that happened and s/he wants you to tell the truth" (Lyon et al., 2014, p. 1760). Much like the premise behind the Prepare and Predict technique, the logic behind the putative confession is that when a victimized child learns the interviewer is aware of the abuse the child will be more forthcoming with a disclosure. The similarities between these techniques end there, however. The putative confession is a gambit: No actual evidence is presented to the child, and in fact, Lyon and colleagues have stated that the technique can be used when the statement is entirely false and the suspect has not confessed. Regardless of whether the statement is true or not, Lyon et al. (2014) posited that the technique is sufficiently ambiguous (and nonsuggestive) that those children who have transgressed with an adult will describe their misdeed, whereas those who have not will only go on to describe their innocent interaction.

To test this hypothesis, Lyon et al. conducted several studies using a paradigm in which half of participating children appeared to accidentally break toys when playing with a confederate who, in turn, expressed concern and suggested that he and the child should keep the transgression a secret. In a recent study by Quas, Stolzenberg, and Lyon (2018), 63 percent of children (4–9 years) who heard the putative confession disclosed breaking the toy when interviewed with cued recall questions (e.g., "Tell me everything that happened when the man came in while I was gone") compared to 31 percent of children in the control condition. Quas et al. reported that the putative confession did not increase false disclosures. Rush, Stolzenberg, Quas, and Lyon (2017) reported similar findings. After children (4–7 years) heard about the putative confession, they were significantly more likely to make accurate disclosures of toy breaking in response to cued recall question (57 percent) compared to control participants (35 percent). The researchers further reported that the technique did not decrease accuracy, nor did it increase false disclosures, even among children who were interviewed after they were exposed to suggestive questioning by their parents.

Though these initial findings seem promising, it was premature to conclude that the putative confession increases true disclosures without increasing false reports. This is because the control condition in the toy break paradigm (in which the toy does not break) failed to produce the adequate variability in rates of false reports needed to conduct a valid diagnostic evaluation of the technique. In the Quas et al. (2018) study, for example, none of the 107 children in the nontransgression condition falsely claimed they had broken the toy with the assistant. Similar results were reported by Stolzenberg, McWilliams, and Lyon (2017), who noted that due to the small number of false disclosures, they were unable to test for condition differences (out of 104 children in the no-transgression conditions, none made a false disclosure). These floor effects in rates of false disclosures have also prevented analyses of other important factors that would speak to the putative confession's overall efficacy, including the effects of age and suggestibility. For example, though Rush and her colleagues (2017) reported that the putative confession did not increase false reports after children were exposed to suggestive questioning by parents, virtually none of the children in the study made false reports of toy breaking (including those who were not exposed to suggestive questions). The low rate of false disclosures in these studies can most likely be attributed to the fact that children were interviewed immediately after participating in the toy break paradigm. To begin to examine whether the putative confession increases false disclosures, the technique should be tested with delays long enough to mimic the conditions under which children's testimony is prone to common memory distortions (e.g., intrusions, forgetting, source confusions, script-based errors).

A different limitation stems from the obvious legal, ethical, and moral concerns raised by the putative confession's use of deception. For those professionals who have reservations about using trickery to question children, or are barred from doing so, Lyon and his colleagues offer two potential work-arounds. First, Lyon et al. (2014) suggested that suspects who maintain their innocence can be asked if they have provided a full and truthful account to authorities, and if they want the child to tell the truth. If the suspect responds affirmatively to this question, then technically, the statement is not deceptive (and those who refuse to accept the proffer will have implicated themselves). Second, Stolzenberg et al. (2017) have proposed that interviewers could offer a "hypothetical" putative confession, which is technically not deceptive when framed as a conditional statement (e.g., *What if I said that* your dad told everything that happened and he says he wants you to tell the truth). Interviewers will have to decide for themselves if these strategies satisfy their concerns or simply move the needle from deceptive to disingenuous.

It is important to note that presenting physical evidence and the putative confession both parallel techniques used to elicit confessions from criminal suspects. *Direct positive confrontation* is a tactic in which police begin an interrogation by presenting the suspect with evidence of his or her guilt (Inbau, Reid, Buckley, & Jayne, 2013). This tactic is designed to overcome the suspect's resistance to confessing by entirely sidestepping the question of culpability and instead directing the conversation to specific details of the crime. Presenting evidence to a child – be it real or fabricated – is designed to overcome reluctance to disclosing in much the same way. Direct positive confrontation can be very effective at eliciting true confessions when the evidence is authentic and the suspect is guilty. On the other hand, presenting false evidence to suspects is a tactic long associated with eliciting false confessions (Kassin & Kiechel, 1996), particularly when suspects have age-related vulnerabilities (e.g., susceptibility to suggestion, acquiescence to demands of authority figures) (Gudjonsson, Sigurdsson, & Sigfusdottir, 2009; Kassin et al., 2010; Meyer & Reppucci, 2007).

Though the putative confession appears to be a promising approach for overcoming reluctance among children who have participated in transgressions with an adult, existing research does not support claims that it does not increase false disclosures. This issue notwithstanding, the use of deception to question children would mark a radical departure from the ethical boundaries of contemporary interviewing practices, and it therefore seems unlikely that child protection professionals would endorse (or tolerate) a technique that leverages deceit to elicit disclosures from children – even when there is a strong suspicion of victimization.

Extended Forensic Interview Protocols

One of the most problematic features of the highly publicized daycare abuse cases in the 1980s and 1990s was the practice of conducting multiple interviews that subjected some children to repeated suggestive questioning over protracted periods of time (Ceci & Bruck, 1995; Schreiber et al., 2006). In response to this problem, many policy changes were implemented to reduce the need for multiple interviews, including the creation of multidisciplinary response teams (MacLeod, 2016), the adoption of forensic interview protocols (Lamb et al., in press), greater attention to interviewer training (Benson & Powell, 2015; Stewart, Katz, & La Rooy, 2011), and procedures for recording and documenting interviews (Vandervort, 2006). Today, most practice guidelines are designed to elicit eyewitness reports in a single-session forensic interview, which reduces children's exposure to repeated questions, eliminates contaminating influences between interviews, and prevents memory errors from compounding across interviews.

Although single-session interviewing is an integral component of child witness cases worldwide, scientists and practitioners alike have argued that one interview is not always sufficient for eliciting disclosures. Due to the impact of trauma or other mechanisms on memory, cooperative witnesses may lack access to needed information during early investigative efforts. (For an example, see Orbach, Lamb, La Rooy, & Pipe, 2012.) In such cases, attempts to re-interview children can produce that information (for reviews, see Brubacher, Peterson, La Rooy, Dickinson, & Poole, 2018; La Rooy, Katz, Malloy, & Lamb, 2010). Other times witnesses withhold information for emotional reasons, such as to protect themselves from perceived or actual threats, or to protect perpetrators (Lyon & Ahern, 2011), but these barriers may erode over time or in supportive environments, fostering disclosures in a subsequent interview.

To aid children who may be unable or unwilling to disclose abuse in a single interview session, a number of training organizations have developed protocols for conducting multiple interviews that are designed to identify and address some common developmental and emotional barriers to disclosure (e.g., National

Children's Advocacy Center's Extended Forensic Interview; CornerHouse©
MultiSession; ChildFirst© Expanded Forensic Interview Process). These protocols
are collectively referred to as *extended* or *multi-session* forensic interviews.

In general, extended interviewing protocols spread the phases of a single-session
forensic interview into a series of interviews conducted over a period of days or
weeks. Protocol developers stress that these interview sessions are nonduplicative,
meaning that each session has a distinct purpose (i.e., rapport building), which
helps prevent substantive questions from being repeated across interview sessions
(L. Cordisco Steele, personal communication, April 24, 2017). To maintain forensic
integrity, training programs encourage interviewers to follow best practices as they
would for single-session interviews (Newlin et al., 2015), including recording all
interview sessions, avoiding suggestive and leading questions, and exploring plausible alternative explanations for children's statements.

Contemporary extended interview protocols originated from Extended
Forensic Evaluation (EFE), a clinical model of assessment developed by the
National Children's Advocacy Center (NCAC). The EFE, which combined
therapeutic and forensic techniques to question children about suspected abuse,
provided a framework for mental health professionals to further interview and
evaluate children who failed to disclose during an initial forensic interview
(Carnes, Nelson-Gardell, Wilson, & Orgassa, 2001; Carnes, Wilson, & Nelson-
Gardell, 1999). In early writings, Carnes and colleagues (1999, 2001) described the
EFE as a five-stage model that unfolded over a predetermined number of sessions
(ranging from 4 to 12), depending on the evaluator's perception of the child's
developmental and emotional needs. The stages were (1) an initial interview with
the non-offending caregiver, (2) a social and behavioral assessment of the child,
(3) abuse-specific questioning that began with a body-parts inventory, (4) a discussion of touch experiences, and (5) body-safety education and closure.

Field studies that examined the effectiveness of EFE and similar extended
assessment models found that increasing numbers of children disclosed abuse as the
number of interview sessions increased, but the accuracy of children's disclosures
could not be established (Carnes et al., 1999, 2001; Faller & Nelson-Gardell, 2010).
For example, Faller and Nelson-Gardell (2010) reported that compared to a four-
session extended evaluation, children who underwent an eight-session evaluation
were more likely to be classified as having made a "credible disclosure" (29 percent
vs. 57 percent, respectively) and that 95 percent of new disclosures occurred by
the sixth interview. However, the research team did not specify how cases were
initially selected for extended evaluation, and disclosure accuracy could not be
verified. Given the subjective nature of abuse determinations in cases of clinical
evaluation, and the interviewer's dual role as clinician and interviewer, concerns
were raised over the ability of the EFE to elicit unbiased disclosures of abuse (for
a review see Connell, 2009b).

In response to these concerns, most training programs have minimized
or eliminated the use of therapeutic techniques and currently emphasize the

fact-finding nature of an investigation (L. Cordisco Steele, personal communication, April 24, 2017). For example, NCAC's Extended Forensic Interview (EFI), arguably the most popular extended interview protocol, was designed for children who have difficulty disclosing abuse, including inhibited children and those with cognitive deficits and/or a history of severe trauma. The EFI provides a general framework for interviewing children over multiple sessions (though NCAC recommends that multidisciplinary teams set the interview standards based on the needs of individual children). For example, the EFI allows for a flexible number of interviews (ranging from two to five sessions) but maintains that interviewers should use the minimum number of sessions necessary to determine a child's abuse status. The time between sessions should be as short as possible, with most extended interviews completed within two weeks.

Prior to conducting the substantive sessions of the EFI, the NCAC model encourages interviewers to review police and child protective services reports as well as prior interviews with the child. Interviewers may choose to meet with the non-offending caregiver to ask about the child's history, developmental abilities and limitations, and family structure. NCAC notes that any meeting with the child's primary caregiver should not address issues related to the investigation. Next, the interviewer conducts one to two foundational sessions to establish rapport with the child, introduce ground rules, and gauge the child's communicative abilities and limitations. Although the purpose of these foundational sessions is not to elicit a disclosure or discuss allegations, the interviewer will follow the child's lead if he or she transitions into talking about topics of concern. If the child does not disclose during foundational sessions, the interviewer prompts the child in a non-leading manner during a subsequent allegation-focused session, explores details reported by the child, and, if needed, conducts a second allegation-focused session to gather additional information. Finally, the interviewer may choose to conduct a closure session to address the child's remaining questions or concerns.

In sum, extended interview protocols offer an alternate format for talking with children who are deemed unlikely or unwilling to disclose during a single-session interview. Proponents of the extended interview model argue that when best practices are followed, the risks associated with repeated interviewing are minimized and reluctant children have additional opportunities to disclose (Newlin et al., 2015). Proponents point to research demonstrating that repeated interviews often generate additional information from children, much of which is accurate (see La Rooy et al., 2010). But although interviewing across multiple sessions likely facilitates disclosures from reluctant children, research is needed to better understand the investigative decision-making that surrounds the extended interview process. For example, though NCAC has an established extended interviewing procedure, other protocols are not publicly available (e.g., the ChildFirst© Expanded Forensic Interview Process), and there are currently no best-practice standards for deciding which case features merit an extended interview, how many interview sessions should be conducted, or when extended interviews should be terminated. Moreover, it is unknown how different jurisdictions attempt to mitigate the unique risks associated with conducting multiple-session interviews, including the perceived pressure some children might feel to provide certain types of information and the risk of exposure to misinformation between sessions through allegation-focused discussions with non-offending caregivers or other victims.

Socially Supportive Interviewing

Daycare cases such as McMartin and Kelly Michaels motivated research to distinguish the types of social influence that spawn false reports from forensically-defensible ways of creating an emotionally supportive interview. Today, there is broad consensus that interviewers should not create a "let's have fun" atmosphere (Schreiber et al., 2006 p. 38), encourage pretend or speculation, praise children or express disapproval for certain types of disclosures, or influence the content of disclosures by embedding new information in questions or by asking numerous specific questions and then following up only when children provide desired answers (Garven, Wood, Malpass, & Shaw, 1998). Unlike these suggestive behaviors, social support includes a host of content-neutral strategies that help children feel safe and cared for, such as smiling and generally acting warmly by using children's names, making frequent eye contact, and adopting an open and relaxed body posture.

A review and meta-analysis of studies that compared socially supportive to neutral or nonsupportive interviewing, including 13 experimental designs, found that children with supportive interviewers made fewer incorrect responses to nonsuggestive questions and were more accurate even in the face of suggestive questions (Saywitz, Wells, Larson, & Hobbs, 2016). Together with evidence that social support lowers anxiety levels, these results convinced interviewing experts that helping children relax decreases, rather than increases, compliance to authority figures. That adults can be warm and responsive without being suggestive was good news for the professionals charged with helping reluctant victims discuss sensitive information.

Because transcript analyses found that many interviewers lacked productive strategies for dealing with children's reluctance (Hershkowitz, Orbach, Lamb, Sternberg, & Horowitz, 2006), Michael Lamb and his colleagues built social support into the fabric of the NICHD interview protocol to explore the impact of enhanced support on children's responsiveness. The Revised NICHD protocol maintained an emphasis on free-recall prompts but included changes designed to improve rapport and cooperation between children and interviewers. In one version, for instance, interviewers incorporated welcoming greetings at the start of interviews and showed more interest in children's well-being (e.g., "I'm interested in getting to know you"), conducted the rapport-building phase before the ground rules phase, responded directly to emotional behavior and reluctance, and delivered various encouragements for effort ("You are being very clear") (Blasbalg, Hershkowitz, Lamb, Karni-Visel, & Ahern, 2018b).

A series of studies found that the Revised NICHD protocol, when delivered by well-trained interviewers, provides tools that help interviewers respond more supportively to children's reluctance (Hershkowitz et al., 2017). Moreover, this behavior is associated with increased responsiveness from children (Ahern, Hershkowitz, Lamb, Blasbalg, & Winstanley, 2014; Hershkowitz, Lamb, Katz, & Malloy, 2013) and a corresponding increase in the amount of forensically-relevant information obtained (Blasbalg, Hershkowitz, Karni-Visel, & Lamb, 2018a; Karni-Visel, Hershkowitz, Blasbalg, & Lamb, 2018; Blasbalg et al., 2018b; see Hershkowitz, Lamb, & Katz, 2014, for evidence of increased disclosures of independently verified abuse). Also important is that interviewers using the Revised NICHD protocol resort less frequently to specific, rather than open, question forms (Blasbalg et al., 2018b). Although Revised NICHD interviews were conducted after practice shifts, making results correlational, the lack of undesirable outcomes in field and analog studies cements the belief that children are more forthcoming when trained interviewers, using an evidence-based protocol, nonsuggestively provide an atmosphere of social support during interviews.

Promoting Honesty

Other approaches to increasing disclosures have centered on appealing to children's moral obligation to be honest and forthcoming, particularly in cases where children's denials may be the product of deception or coaching. These techniques are an outgrowth of statutory requirements to secure a commitment of honesty (i.e., an "oath") from children prior to providing courtroom testimony. (In some jurisdictions, children are also required to demonstrate competency, which includes understanding the difference between a truth and lie; Klemfuss & Ceci, 2012; Lyon, 2011.)

Techniques designed to promote honesty have enjoyed mixed success. Eliciting an affirmation from children that they will tell the truth in the initial phases of an interview has been found to modestly increase disclosures of laboratory facilitated transgressions across a wide age range (3 to 16 years old; see Evans & Lee, 2010; Lyon & Dorado, 2008; Lyon, Malloy, Quas, & Talwar, 2008; Talwar, Lee, Bala, & Lindsay, 2002). However, engaging children in more conceptual dialog about honesty and deception (i.e., truth–lie discussions) has not been consistently successful: In two studies, children who participated in truth–lie discussions were more forthcoming about a transgression (Huffman, Warren, & Larson, 1999; London & Nunez, 2002); in another study, promising to tell the truth was effective, but discussing the morality of honesty was not (Evans & Lee, 2010).

In sum, asking children to affirm that they will tell the truth does not guarantee that a child's disclosure (or denial) will be truthful or accurate (even candid testimony is subject to memory errors) but can promote truth-telling among some children. Moreover, a commitment to tell the truth has not been found to increase false reports. For these reasons, most major training organizations currently promote appeals to honesty as a best practice (see Newlin et al., 2015), and a number of major interviewing protocols have integrated the technique into their interview instructions (e.g., ChildFirst Forensic Interview Protocol: Gundersen National Child Protection Training Center, 2016b; State of Michigan Governor's Task Force on Children's Justice and Department of Human Services, 2017).

Conclusion

Eliciting disclosures from reluctant children remains a formidable challenge for child protection professionals. As outlined in this chapter, current efforts to surmount children's reluctance include a wide range of approaches that are backed by varying levels of empirical support. Collectively, these techniques illustrate how researchers and practice professionals are increasingly drawing inspiration from disciplines not traditionally associated with children's eyewitness testimony. Given that the study of child maltreatment is increasingly translational and interdisciplinary, it would not be surprising if the next best approach to overcoming children's reluctance to disclose originated from an allied discipline. But regardless of the origin of an innovative technique, the heart of establishing evidence-based practice will always involve careful consideration of how best to balance the need to elicit disclosures from reluctant victims with the risks of eliciting false reports.

References

Ahern, E. C., Hershkowitz, I., Lamb, M. E., Blasbalg, U., & Winstanley, A. (2014). Support and reluctance in the pre-substantive phase of alleged child abuse victim investigative interviews: Revised versus Standard NICHD Protocols. *Behavioral Sciences & the Law, 32,* 762–774.

Alaggia, R., Collin-Vézina, D., & Lateef, R. (2017). Facilitators and barriers to child sexual abuse (CSA) disclosures: A research update (2000–2016). *Trauma, Violence, & Abuse.* doi:10.1177/1524838017697312

American Professional Society on the Abuse of Children (2012). *Practice guidelines: Investigative interviewing in cases of alleged sexual abuse.* www.apsac.org

Anderson, J. N. (2013). The CornerHouse Forensic Interview Protocol: An evolution in practice for almost 25 years. *APSAC Advisor, 4,* 2–7.

Anderson, J., Ellefson, J., Lashley, J., Miller, A. L., Olinger, S., Russell, A., . . . Weigman, J. (2010). The CornerHouse Forensic Interview Protocol: RATAC. *Thomas M. Cooley Journal of Practical and Clinical Law, 12,* 193–331.

Benson, M. S., & Powell, M. B. (2015). Evaluation of a comprehensive interactive training system for investigative interviewers of children. *Psychology, Public Policy, and Law, 21,* 309–322.

Blasbalg, U., Hershkowitz, I., Karni-Visel, Y., & Lamb, M. E. (2018a, March). The associations among interviewer support, child reluctance, and informativeness in forensic interviews with alleged victims of intra-familial abuse. Paper presented at the annual meeting of the American Psychology-Law Association, Memphis, Tennessee.

Blasbalg, U., Hershkowitz, I., Lamb, M. E., Karni-Visel, Y., & Ahern, E. C. (2018b). Does interviewer support promote the forensic informativeness of alleged child abuse victims? Manuscript submitted for publication.

Boat, B. W., & Everson, M. D. (1996). Concerning practices of interviewers when using anatomical dolls in child protective services investigations. *Child Maltreatment, 1,* 96–104.

Bottoms, B. L, & Goodman, G. S. (Eds.). (1996). *International perspectives on child abuse and children's testimony: Psychological research and law.* Thousand Oaks, CA: Sage.

Brown, D. A., Pipe, M., Lewis, C., Lamb, M. E., & Orbach, Y. (2007). Supportive or suggestive: Do human figure drawings help 5- to 7-year-old children to report touch? *Journal of Consulting and Clinical Psychology, 75,* 33–42.

Brown, D., Pipe, M., Lewis, C., Lamb, M. E., & Orbach, Y. (2012). How do body diagrams affect the accuracy and consistency of children's reports of bodily touch across repeated interviews? *Applied Cognitive Psychology, 26,* 174–181.

Brown, L. G., & Gallagher, K. (2013). Mandatory reporting of abuse: A historical perspective on the evolution of states' current mandatory reporting laws with a review of the laws in the Commonwealth of Pennsylvania. *Villanova Law Review Online: Tolle Lege, 59,* 37–80.

Brubacher, S. P., Peterson, C., La Rooy, D., Dickinson, J. J., & Poole, D. A. (2018). How children talk about events: Implications for eliciting and analyzing eyewitness reports. Manuscript under review.

Bruck, M. (2009). Human figure drawings and children's recall of touching. *Journal of Experimental Psychology: Applied, 15,* 361–374.

Bruck, M., Ceci, S. J., & Francoeur, E. (2000). Children's use of anatomically detailed dolls to report genital touching in a medical examination: Developmental and gender comparisons. *Journal of Experimental Psychology: Applied, 6,* 74–83.

Bruck, M., Kelley, K., & Poole, D. A. (2016). Children's reports of body touching in medical examinations: The benefits and risks of using body diagrams. *Psychology, Public Policy, and Law, 22,* 1–11.

Canadian Centre for Child Protection (2016). *Child sexual abuse images on the internet: A Cybertip.ca analysis.* www.cybertip.ca/pdfs/CTIP_ CSAResearchReport_2016_en.pdf

Carnes, C. N., Wilson, C., & Nelson-Gardell, D. (1999). Extended forensic evaluation when sexual abuse is suspected: A model and preliminary data. *Child Maltreatment, 4,* 242–254.

Carnes, C. N., Nelson-Gardell, D., Wilson, C., & Orgassa, U. C. (2001). Extended forensic evaluation when sexual abuse is suspected: A multisite field study. *Child Maltreatment, 6,* 230–242.

Ceci, S. J., & Bruck, M. (1995). *Jeopardy in the courtroom: A scientific analysis of children's testimony.* Washington, DC: American Psychological Association.

Connell, M. (2009a). The child advocacy center model. In K. Kuehnle & M. Connell (Eds.), *The evaluation of child sexual abuse allegations: A comprehensive guide to assessment and testimony* (pp. 423–450). Hoboken, NJ: Wiley.

Connell, M. (2009b). The extended forensic evaluation. In K. Kuehnle & M. Connell (Eds.), *The evaluation of child sexual abuse allegations: A comprehensive guide to assessment and testimony* (pp. 451–487). Hoboken, NJ: Wiley.

DeLoache, J. S. (1995). Early understanding and the use of symbols. The model model. *Current Directions in Psychological Science, 4,* 109–113.

DeLoache, J. S., & Marzolf, D. P. (1995). The use of dolls to interview young children: Issues of symbolic representation. *Journal of Experimental Child Psychology, 60,* 155–173.

Dickinson, J. J., Poole, D. A., & Bruck, M. (2005). Back to the future: A comment on the use of anatomical dolls in forensic interviews. *Journal of Forensic Psychology Practice, 5,* 63–74.

Earhart, B. J., Danby, M. C., Brubacher, S. P., Sharman, S. J., & Powell, M. B. (2018). A comparison of responses to substantive transition prompts in interviews with children. *Child Maltreatment, 23,* 221–225.

Evans, A. D., & Lee, K. (2010). Promising to tell the truth makes 8- to 16-year-olds more honest. *Behavioral Sciences and the Law, 28,* 801–811.

Everson, M. D., & Boat, B. W. (1990). Sexualized doll play among young children: Implications for the use of anatomical dolls in sexual abuse evaluations. *Journal of the American Academy of Child & Adolescent Psychiatry, 29,* 736–742.

Everson, M. D., & Boat, B. W. (2002). The utility of anatomical dolls and drawings in child forensic interviews. In M. L. Eisen, J. A. Quas, & G. S. Goodman (Eds.), *Memory and suggestibility in the forensic interview* (pp. 383–408). Mahwah, NJ: Lawrence Erlbaum Associates.

Faller, K. C. (2005). Anatomical dolls: Their use in assessment of children who may have been sexually abused. *Journal of Child Sexual Abuse: Research, Treatment, & Program Innovations for Victims, Survivors, & Offenders, 14,* 1–21.

Faller, K. C. (2015). Forty years of forensic interviewing of children suspected of sexual abuse, 1974–2014: Historical benchmarks. *Social Science, 4,* 34–65.

Faller, K. C., & Nelson-Gardell, D. (2010). Extended evaluations in cases of child sexual abuse: How many sessions are sufficient? *Journal of Child Sexual Abuse, 19,* 648–668.

Foster, A. M. (2017). Contemporary use of human figure drawings and dolls: A survey of child forensic interviewers and where do we go from here? Paper presented at the National Children's Advocacy Center's 33rd International Symposium on Child Abuse, Huntsville, Alabama.

Garven, S., Wood, J. M., Malpass, R. S., & Shaw, J. (1998). More than suggestion: The effect of interviewing techniques from the McMartin preschool case. *Journal of Applied Psychology, 83,* 347–359.

Graham, B. R. (2014). *Effective child abuse investigation for the multi-disciplinary team.* Boca Raton, FL: CRC Press.

Gudjonsson, G. H., Sigurdsson, J. F., & Sigfusdottir, I. D. (2009). Interrogation and false confessions among adolescents in seven European countries. What background and psychological variables best discriminate between false confessors and non-false confessors? *Psychology, Crime & Law, 15,* 711–728.

Gundersen National Child Protection Training Center (2016a). *Anatomical dolls and diagrams.* www.gundersenhealth.org/app/files/public/3580/NCPTC-Anatomical-Dolls-and-Diagrams-position-paper.pdf

Gundersen National Child Protection Training Center (2016b). *The ChildFirst Forensic Interview Protocol.* www.gundersenhealth.org/app/files/public/2529/NCPTC-ChildFirst-Forensic-Interview-Protocol-binder.pdf

Hershkowitz, I., Orbach, Y., Lamb, M. E., Sternberg, K. J., & Horowitz, D. (2006). Dynamics of forensic interviews with suspected abuse victims who do not disclose abuse. *Child Abuse & Neglect, 30,* 753–769.

Hershkowitz, I., Lanes, O., & Lamb, M. E. (2007). Exploring the disclosure of child sexual abuse with alleged victims and their parents. *Child Abuse & Neglect, 31,* 111–123.

Hershkowitz, I., Lamb, M. E., Katz, C., & Malloy, L. C. (2013). Does enhanced rapport-building alter the dynamics of investigative interviews with suspected victims of intra-familial abuse? *Journal of Police and Criminal Psychology, 30*, 6–14.

Hershkowitz, I., Lamb, M. E., & Katz, C. (2014). Allegation rates in forensic child abuse investigations: Comparing the revised and standard NICHD protocols. *Psychology, Public Policy, and Law, 20*, 336–344.

Hershkowitz, I., Ahern, B., Lamb, M. E., Blasbalg, U., Karni-Visel, Y., & Breitman, M. (2017). Changes in interviewers' use of supportive techniques during the Revised Protocol training. *Applied Cognitive Psychology, 31*, 340–350.

Homeland Security Investigations (2016). Presenting evidence in the forensic interview: HSI's Prepare and Predict method. Training workshop presented at the 34th International Symposium on Child Abuse, Huntsville, Alabama.

Huffman, M. L., Warren, A. R., & Larson, S. M. (1999). Discussing truth and lies in interviews with children: Whether, why, and how? *Applied Developmental Science, 3*, 6–15.

Inbau, F. E., Reid, J. E., Buckley, J. P., & Jayne, B. C. (2013). *Essentials of the Reid Technique: Criminal interrogation and confessions* (2nd ed.). Burlington, MA: Jones & Bartlett.

Karni-Visel, Y., Hershkowitz, I., Blasbalg, U., & Lamb, M. E. (2018, March). The association between emotional expression and children's reports of intra-familial abuse: The facilitating role of emotional support. Paper presented at the annual meeting of the American Psychology-Law Association, Memphis, Tennessee.

Kassin, S. M., & Kiechel, K. L. (1996). The social psychology of false confessions: Compliance, internalization, and confabulation. *Psychological Science, 7*, 125–128.

Kassin, S. M., Drizin, S. A., Grisso, T., Gudjonsson, G. H., Leo, R. A., & Redlich, A. D. (2010). Police-induced confessions: Risk factors and recommendations. *Law and Human Behavior, 34*, 3–38.

Klemfuss, J. Z., & Ceci, S. J. (2012). Legal and psychological perspectives on children's competence to testify in court. *Developmental Review, 32*, 268–286.

Koocher, G. P., Goodman, G. S., White, C. S., Friedrich, W. N., Sivan, A. B., & Reynolds, C. R. (1995). Psychological science and the use of anatomically detailed dolls in child sexual-abuse assessments. *Psychological Bulletin, 118*, 199–222.

La Rooy, D., Katz, C., Malloy, L. C., & Lamb, M. E. (2010). Do we need to rethink guidance on repeated interviews? *Psychology, Public Policy, and Law, 16*, 373–392.

Lamb, M. E., Sternberg, K. J., & Esplin, P. W. (1995). Making children into competent witnesses: Reactions to the amicus brief In re Michaels. *Psychology, Public Policy, and Law, 1*, 438–449.

Lamb, M. E., Hershkowitz, I., Orbach, Y., & Esplin, P. W. (2008). *Tell me what happened: Structured investigative interviews of child victims and witnesses*. Chichester: Wiley.

Lamb, M. E., Brown, D. A., Hershkowitz, I., Orbach, Y., & Esplin, P. W. (in press). *Tell me what happened: Structured investigative interviews of child victims and witnesses* (3rd ed.). Chichester: Wiley.

London, K., & Nunez, N. (2002). Examining the efficacy of truth/lie discussions in predicting and increasing the veracity of children's reports. *Journal of Experimental Child Psychology, 83*, 131–147.

London, K., Bruck, M., Wright, D. B., & Ceci, S. J. (2008). Review of the contemporary literature on how children report sexual abuse to others: Findings, methodological issues, and implications for forensic interviewers. *Memory, 16*, 29–47.

Lyon, T. D. (2011). Assessing the competency of child witnesses: Best practice informed by psychology and law. In M. E. Lamb, D. La Rooy, C. Katz, & L. C. Malloy (Eds.),

Children's testimony: A handbook of psychological research and forensic practice (pp. 69–85). Chichester: Wiley-Blackwell.

Lyon, T. D. (2012). Twenty-five years of interviewing research and practice: Dolls, diagrams, and the dynamics of abuse disclosure. *APSAC Advisor, 24*, 14–19.

Lyon, T. D., & Ahern, E. C. (2011). Disclosure of child sexual abuse. In J. E. B. Myers (Ed.), *The APSAC handbook on child maltreatment* (3rd ed., pp. 233–252). Newbury Park, CA: Sage.

Lyon, T. D., & Dorado, J. S. (2008). Truth induction in young maltreated children: The effects of oath-taking and reassurance on true and false disclosures. *Child Abuse & Neglect, 32*, 738–748.

Lyon, T. D., Malloy, L. C., Quas, J. A., & Talwar, V. A. (2008). Coaching, truth induction, and young maltreated children's false allegations and false denials. *Child Development, 79*, 914–929.

Lyon, T. D., Wandrey, L., Ahern, E., Licht, R., Sim, M. Y., & Quas, J. A. (2014). Eliciting maltreated and nonmaltreated children's transgression disclosures: Narrative practice rapport building and a putative confession. *Child Development, 85*, 1756–1769.

Lytle, N., London, K., & Bruck, M. (2015). Young children's ability to use two-dimensional and three-dimensional symbols to show placements of body touches and hidden objects. *Journal of Experimental Child Psychology, 134*, 30–42.

Mack, J. (2017, February 20). *What We Learned in '60 Minutes' Sex Abuse Report on Former Michigan State Dr. Larry Nassar*. www.mlive.com/news/index.ssf/2017/02/60_minutes_michigan_state_nass.html

MacLeod, K. J. (2016). Working with the multidisciplinary team. In W. T. O'Donohue & M. Fanetti (Eds.), *Forensic interviews regarding child sexual abuse: A guide to evidence-based practice* (pp. 41–56). Cham, Switzerland: Springer International Publishing.

Malloy, L. C., Mugno, A. P., Rivard, J. R., Lyon, T. D., & Quas, J. A. (2016). Familial influences on recantation in substantiated child sexual abuse cases. *Child Maltreatment, 21*, 256–261.

Matthews, B., Lee, X. J., & Norman, R. E. (2016). Impact of a new mandatory reporting law on reporting and identification of child sexual abuse: A seven year time trend analysis. *Child Abuse & Neglect, 56*, 62–79.

Meyer, J. R., & Reppucci, N. D. (2007). Police practices and perceptions regarding juvenile interrogation and interrogative suggestibility. *Behavioral Sciences & the Law, 25*, 757–780.

National Center for Missing and Exploited Children (2017). *The online enticement of children: An in-depth analysis of CyberTipline reports*. www.missingkids.com/content/dam/ncmec/en_us/Online%20Enticement%20Pre-Travel.pdf

National Children's Advocacy Center (2013). *Position paper on the introduction of evidence in forensic interviews of children*. www.nationalchildrensalliance.org/sites/default/files/downloads/NCAC-position-paper-introduction-evidence-fi.pdf

National Children's Advocacy Center (2015). *Position paper on the use of human figure drawings in forensic interviews*. http://calio.org/images/position-paper-human-figure-drawings.pdf

National Children's Alliance (2016). *NCA National statistics – statistics report 2015*. www.nationalchildrensalliance.org/cac-statistics

Newlin, C., Cordisco Steele, L., Chamberlin, A., Anderson, J., Kenniston, J., Russell, A., . . . Vaughan-Eden, V. (2015). *Child forensic interview: Best practices*. US Department of Justice, Office of Juvenile Justice and Delinquency Prevention. www.ojjdp.gov/pubs/248749.pdf

Office for Victims of Crimes (2015). *Child, youth, and teen victimization*. http://victimsofcrime.org/docs/default-source/ncvrw2015/2015ncvrw_stats_children.pdf?sfvrsn=2

Orbach, Y., Shiloach, H., & Lamb, M. E. (2007). Reluctant disclosers of child sexual abuse. In M.-E. Pipe, M. E. Lamb, Y. Orbach, & A.-C. Cederborg (Eds.), *Child sexual abuse: Disclosure, delay, and denial* (pp. 115–134). Mahwah, NJ: Lawrence Erlbaum Associates.

Orbach, Y., Lamb, M. E., La Rooy, D., & Pipe, M. (2012). A case study of witness consistency and memory recovery across multiple investigative interviews. *Applied Cognitive Psychology, 26*, 118–129.

Poole, D. A., & Dickinson, J. J. (2011). Evidence supporting restrictions on uses of body diagrams in forensic interviews. *Child Abuse & Neglect, 35*, 659–669.

Poole, D. A., Dickinson, J. J., Brubacher, S. P., Liberty, A. E., & Kaake, A. M. (2014). Deficient cognitive control fuels children's exuberant false allegations. *Journal of Experimental Child Psychology, 118*, 101–109.

Poole, D. A., Brubacher, S. P., & Dickinson, J. J. (2015). Children as witnesses. In B. L. Cutler & P. A. Zapf (Eds.), *APA handbook of forensic psychology* (vol. 2, pp. 3–31). Washington, DC: American Psychological Association.

Quas, J. A., Stolzenberg, S. N., & Lyon, T. D. (2018). The effects of promising to tell the truth, the putative confession, and recall and recognition questions on maltreated and non-maltreated children's disclosure of a minor transgression. *Journal of Experimental Child Psychology, 166*, 266–279.

Rush, E. B., Stolzenberg, S. N., Quas, J. A., & Lyon, T. D. (2017). The effects of the putative confession and parent suggestion on children's disclosure of a minor transgression. *Legal and Criminological Psychology, 22*, 60–73.

Saywitz, K. J., Wells, C. R., Larson, R. P., & Hobbs, S. D. (2016). Effects of interviewer support on children's memory and suggestibility: Systematic review and meta-analyses of experimental research. *Trauma, Violence & Abuse*, 1–18. doi:10.1177/1524838016683457

Schaeffer, P., Leventhal, J. M., & Asnes, A. G. (2011). Children's disclosures of sexual abuse: Learning from direct inquiry. *Child Abuse & Neglect, 35*, 343–352.

Schreiber, N., Bellah, L. D., Martinez, Y., McLaurin, K. A., Strok, R., Garven, S., & Wood, J. M. (2006). Suggestive interviewing in the McMartin Preschool and Kelly Michaels daycare abuse cases: A case study. *Social Influence, 1*, 16–47.

State of Michigan Governor's Task Force on Children's Justice and Department of Human Services (2017). *State of Michigan Governor's Task Force on Children's Justice and Department of Human Services forensic interviewing protocol.* www.michigan.gov/documents/dhs/DHS-PUB-0779_211637_7.pdf

Steward, M. S., & Steward, D. S., with Farquhar, L., Myers, J. E. B., Reinhart, M., Welker, J., Joye, N., Driskill, J., & Morgan, J. (1996). Interviewing young children about body touch and handling. *Monograph of the Society for Research in Child Development, 61* (4–5, Serial No. 248).

Stewart, H., Katz, C., & La Rooy, D. J. (2011). Training forensic interviewers. In M. E. Lamb, D. J. La Rooy, L. C. Malloy, & C. Katz (Eds.), *Children's testimony: A handbook of psychological research and forensic practice* (pp. 199–216). Chichester: Wiley-Blackwell.

Stolzenberg, S. N., McWilliams, K., & Lyon, T. D. (2017). The effects of the hypothetical putative confession and negatively valenced yes/no questions on maltreated and nonmaltreated children's disclosure of a minor transgression. *Child Maltreatment, 22*, 167–173.

Summit, R. C. (1983). The child sexual abuse accommodation syndrome. *Child Abuse & Neglect, 7*, 177–193.

Talwar, V., Lee, K., Bala, N., & Lindsay, R. C. L. (2002). Children's conceptual knowledge of lying and its relation to their actual behaviors: Implications for court competence examinations. *Law and Human Behavior, 26*, 395–415.

US Department of Health & Human Services, Administration for Children and Families, Administration on Children, Youth and Families, Children's Bureau (2018). *Child maltreatment 2016*. www.acf.hhs.gov/sites/default/files/cb/ cm2016.pdf#page=10

Vandervort, F. E. (2006). Videotaping investigative interviews of children in cases of child sexual abuse: One community's approach. *Journal of Criminal Law and Criminology, 96*, 1353–1416.

12

INVESTIGATIVE INTERVIEWING ABOUT REPEATED EXPERIENCES

Sonja P. Brubacher and Becky Earhart

Introduction

Three case studies will illustrate concepts throughout the chapter. While elements of the accounts come from true cases, we have made numerous amalgamations across cases and altered details. Any resemblance to actual cases is therefore coincidental.

Case Study 1

For the past eight months, 15-year-old Kayla has been moved repeatedly along a major highway corridor from one dingy motel to the next. One fateful meeting with a man from an online chat room led her to this world. Each day she awakes late to receive a small meal in the form of whatever cheap or free food can be found by her captors. They give her an injection of heroin and she prepares to receive her first customer. Late afternoons sometimes involve downtime, but sometimes this is when the traffickers take their turns with the women. Beatings are relatively rare; Kayla can keep them to a minimum by being compliant. Evenings and nights bring more customers. Different men, different places, different sexual requests, but it all blends together. The routineness of her days is broken only by the disturbance of being moved to stay ahead of authorities. But these disruptions have their own patterns of repetition. The types of vehicles change and the length of drives vary considerably, but the moves always take place at night and always involve the women being split into small groups among several vehicles.

Case Study 2

It has been nearly a year since 9-year-old Asha's mother married Greg, a man who could provide the family with financial security and a permanent home for the first time in Asha's young life. Yet, Greg makes demands in exchange for his provisions. He drinks hard alcohol heavily, and Asha's mother takes the brunt of his whisky-induced anger. Asha suffers a different type of abuse from Greg. He began initiating sexual contact with her when Asha's mother started working weekends at a local restaurant. Over many months their routine has been established. When Greg pours himself an "evening drink" and tells Asha it's "our special time," she knows she will find something laid out from her mother's closet that Greg has chosen for her to wear. Sometimes Greg takes her to one of the bedrooms, or to the basement, and his desired activities change, but to Asha, it feels like it's all the same.

Case Study 3

Eric is in his twenties and works a minimum wage job at a local gas station during the day. Several evenings of the week he can be found selling cocaine. He picks up a larger quantity from one of his connections and divides it into smaller packages. Meeting spots change frequently, and occasionally so do the delivery cars and code words, but the suppliers are always one of three men he knows and trusts. Some evenings involve routine deliveries to regular customers. Other nights Eric can be found trawling bars and nightclubs cautiously looking for potential buyers. He's always watching over his shoulder for unexpected trouble, but his usual routine is consistent: pick up the product, take it home to divide, weigh, bag, deliver, and get home safely.

Memory for Repeated Events

In this chapter, we adopt the definition of *repeated events* from Theunissen, Meyer, Memon, and Weinsheimer (2017, p. 164): a series of episodes "that are conceptually linked and provide expectations about future similar encounters." Recall of episodes involves the conscious recollection and reliving of an event from the past. By definition, episodic memories include some cues about their source (e.g., when, where, how, or from whom the memory or knowledge came to be; Tulving, 1985). Memory for episodes begins during childhood, and although children start to form memories from the beginning of life, they can only retain them briefly. With age, children remember for increasingly longer periods, and most adults recall their first episodic memories from around 3.5 years (see Peterson, 2012 for a review).

When people experience repeated similar events, they develop cognitive representations that describe the typical features of the episodes. These representations are called "scripts," and they aid understanding of events, guide memory recall, and make future similar experiences predictable (Nelson, 1986; Schank & Abelson, 1977). Human knowledge is organized around memory scripts, which are acquired through direct or indirect experience. For commonplace activities, like grocery shopping and visiting the doctor, people tend to share very strong consensus regarding typical script elements, especially for the central elements (e.g., choosing the foods you want, getting in the checkout line, and paying for your groceries; Bower, Black, & Turner, 1979).

Children as young as 3 years old can provide skeletal scripts for activities they engage in routinely (Hudson, Fivush, & Kuebli, 1992). Furthermore, the ability to form scripts improves with age, such that older children can generate more comprehensive scripts after fewer experiences with a repeated event (Farrar & Goodman, 1992). Older children are more effective at mentally organizing and retrieving schematic details. Consider the following examples of restaurant scripts provided by 3-year-old Lia and 8-year-old Carlos:

Lia	Carlos
You ask for what you want	You get hungry.
And then you eat it	So then you go to the restaurant and
And get some ice cream	You pick what you want to eat.
And then it's done!	Sometimes they have a big menu and sometimes they just have a few things.
	Then you eat, like a hamburger or a sandwich.
	If you eat it all you can have some dessert.
	And sometimes there's a toy in there.
	Then you go home.

Scripts are fascinating and powerful mental structures. They have a variety of features relevant to understanding recall of routine experiences. These features are outlined next, along with illustrative examples from the restaurant script and the case studies presented at the beginning of this chapter.

Features of Scripts

1. *Scripts are temporally organized.* In contrast to schemas, which are non-temporal cognitive frameworks that represent categories of knowledge, scripts specify which actions typically or necessarily precede others (Bower et al., 1979). For example, the children's restaurant scripts are sequential: food must be chosen before it can be eaten, and dessert is typically consumed after, rather than before the meal. In Eric's drug-dealing script, there is a necessary order to picking up the drugs, dividing, weighing, bagging, and then distributing the smaller parcels.

2. *Scripts contain superordinate categories, optionals, and conditionals.* Superordinate categories are the main script components, specifying the details that are commonly a part of the event (e.g., Kayla is always housed at a highway motel; something is consumed at a restaurant). When a specific instance is recalled, various alternatives can be "slotted in" for the category (e.g., the specific motel and location; whether food is ordered from a waiter or at a

counter). Optionals refer to the categories that are changeable in the script (Nelson & Gruendel, 1986); for example, sometimes afternoons bring the only tranquil periods Kayla experiences, but other times they involve abuse at the hands of her traffickers. Conditionals are "if-then" statements, such as Carlos's advice, "If you eat it all, you can have some dessert."

3. *Scripts include generic language and can become part of one's semantic knowledge base.* Semantic knowledge refers to concepts, relations, and facts that are retrieved without source information; the original source of that knowledge may have been forgotten or is irrelevant (Tulving, 1985). For example, you probably know that Washington, DC is the capital of the USA, but are unlikely to recall where, when, or how you first learned that fact. Over time, repeated experiences are compounded into a general semantic representation of an event, containing information that is well known, but often not tied to the specific episode in which the memory was acquired. For example, Lia and Carlos know that food can be found at restaurants because this general knowledge was inferred from repeated experiences. Similarly, Asha knows what will happen when her stepdad refers to their "special time," but she no longer has a specific memory for the first time he used that term. People often recall repeated events using generic language in the timeless present tense (e.g., "You usually order something to drink with your meal"), whereas single experiences are usually recalled episodically in past tense (e.g., "I ordered a root beer with my meal"; Brubacher, Roberts & Powell, 2012).

4. *Scripts facilitate (correct and incorrect) inferences about missing elements.* People continually rely on scripts to make inferences about elements of events that are poorly remembered or were not encoded. In a classic example of how scripts are used to fill in knowledge and memory gaps, Erskine, Markham, and Howie (2002) showed 5- to 10-year-old children a slideshow of a trip to a restaurant. Critically, several central actions, such as paying for the food, were omitted. Yet, the children were highly likely to report having seen these details in response to specific questions. In the same manner, memories for specific episodes of repeated events are reconstructed using knowledge of what typically happens. Although the inferences are often correct, this reasoning process may lead to errors when part of the episode is not consistent with the script. When Asha was interviewed, she inaccurately reported that her stepfather had poured himself a drink the last time they were alone together because that was a frequently occurring part of her abuse script.

5. *Scripts allow identification of atypical details in individual episodes.* Scripts can influence attention during encoding. The schema confirmation-deployment model (Farrar & Goodman, 1992) proposes that during early experiences with an event, mental resources are devoted to determining which details are part of the script (confirmation). Once the typical details of the script have been confirmed, attention can then be devoted to how new experiences

match or modify the existing script, and which details deviate, or are atypical (deployment).

Deviations from the script have been categorized in a variety of ways. Schank and Abelson (1977) discriminated errors, obstacles, and distractions. *Errors* are unexpected substitutions, such as Asha's recollection that one evening her stepfather instructed her to choose something to wear, instead of laying it out for her on the bed. *Obstacles* are discrete types of deviations, where a condition that enables the script to proceed as usual is missing, but is overcome. For example, on his way to pick up a regular delivery of cocaine Eric's car broke down, but he called a trusted friend for a ride and was able to make the pick-up. *Distractions* are continuous deviations that temporarily or permanently alter the goal or the usual manner in which the script plays out. For example, during Kayla's interview, she recalled one very unusual night when a major ice storm closed the highway on which they were traveling. The women had to spend the night together in a single room in a motel where they had never been before. They received Danishes, yogurt, and fruit for breakfast and saw no customers that day. She remembered that the hand towels were folded like swans. Attention to routine, script-consistent elements during encoding is minimal, but the scripted representation makes atypical deviations more noticeable.

Script Recall in Interview Contexts

There are some benefits to script-based recall when describing repeated experiences. Repetition of events reinforces the script and strengthens memory for details that are often or always similar. Recalling these well-remembered aspects of a script is likely to produce accurate, if generic, information about what typically happens. In fact, such repetition minimizes age differences in the amount and accuracy of recall for frequently-occurring details. For example, Powell, Roberts, Ceci, and Hembrooke (1999) found that when children had experienced an event only once, 3- to 5-year-olds were significantly less accurate than 6- to 8-year-olds. However, when they had participated in an event multiple times, the younger children were just as accurate as the older children in recalling the details that were the same each time.

Because repetition of the script strengthens memory traces, scripted events are highly resistant to suggestion about typical details (Connolly & Lindsay, 2001; Powell et al., 1999). For example, Eric was interviewed as a cooperative suspect when one of his regular clients was found dead of an apparent drug complication. The interviewer suggested to Eric that he may have received his cocaine delivery that week from a new supplier, a man he knew in the community but had not purchased from previously. Eric resisted this suggestion because his suppliers were always the same. Although he was unable to recall which of the three suppliers he had purchased from that week, he knew that the suggestion could not be true.

Another advantage of scripted recall is that retrieving typical event features may lead to the generation of specific details that can later be followed up to elicit more information about episodes (Brubacher, Powell, & Roberts, 2014). Listening for signifiers of specific episodes embedded in a script recall could help an interviewer plan for the remainder of the interview. They give the listener an overview of the potential occurrences that should be covered, like populating a roadmap with major cities that should be visited along one's journey. For example, while recounting what *usually* happens during her evenings alone with Greg, Asha's abuse script featured mention of several key episodes: a time Mom came home early and asked why Asha was wrapped in a giant blanket (because she had no time to remove the lingerie), and the night that Greg knocked over his whisky glass in the shed and the shed smelled of booze for a week.

Recalling the script may generate information about important behavior leading up to a first offense, such as grooming (Powell, Burrows, Brubacher, & Roberts, 2017). Asha's abuse script contained details about how Greg started encouraging her to watch movies with him when Mom was working. During these sessions he began to ask if she was feeling any stress and started to massage her shoulders. The abusive relationship evolved slowly, with Greg initiating gradually more inappropriate behaviors. This information may not have been reported if Asha was focused on recalling particular episodes, rather than what usually happens, because the initial events may not have been considered abusive events worth reporting on their own.

Despite the benefits of recalling the typical pattern of events, strong scripts make it more difficult to retrieve episodic details about individual episodes. Interviewees may have difficulty generating specific episodes to talk about, and may also struggle with confusing details across different occurrences. Relying solely on script-based recall can be problematic in investigations because occurrence-specific details are often critical and may be required for legal purposes. That is, the time, place, and other contextual details specific to a particular incident may be necessary so that appropriate charges can be established, the defendant has an opportunity to generate an alibi, to assist in the identification and collection of physical evidence, or to enhance credibility. For all of these reasons, it is frequently a primary goal of an investigative interview to elicit an account about a particular episode (e.g., Guadagno, Powell, & Wright, 2006). Retrieval of individual occurrences from the script must be derived through episodic recollection (Tulving, 1985). Describing individual occurrences, however, is a challenging task for children and adults alike.

Why is it Difficult to Recall an Occurrence of a Repeated Event?

While scripts are typically recalled with ease, details that are specific to one occurrence are vulnerable to decay, contamination, and confusions (Brubacher et al., 2014). A common phenomenon following repeated experience is to confuse occurrence-specific details across occurrences (e.g., Eric reporting that he picked up from supplier A on the night one of his clients died, when it was actually supplier B). In fact, the most frequent type of error children make in analogue studies of repeated event memory is to report details that actually happened but attribute them to the wrong occurrence (Powell & Roberts, 2002; Powell et al., 1999).

Confusing details that vary across repeated occurrences reflect difficulty with source monitoring. Source monitoring refers to the process of making decisions during retrieval about the origin of memories (see Johnson, Hashtroudi, & Lindsay, 1993, for an overview). Sources are a fluid construct and can be defined in a variety of ways, depending on what is most salient to the narrator. In other words, it could be argued that source is "in the eye of the beholder." The source of information could refer to: *who* it was learned from (or with whom it was experienced), *where* it was experienced or learned, *when* (e.g., which month or year), *how* or in what modality (e.g., through reading a book, via visual observation), and so on. The way in which memory sources are categorized may depend on what qualities distinguished them at encoding, help to differentiate them from other sources in memory, or the recall cues presented during an interview. Each occurrence in a series of repeated events can be considered a source on its own, with unique source-related details that are key to the episodic nature of remembering a specific experience.

Young children have more difficulty distinguishing between the sources of their memories than do older children or adults. Developmental research shows that source monitoring develops gradually across childhood, with the largest improvements happening between age 3 and age 8. It is not until approximately age 10 that children perform as well as adults on many source-monitoring tasks (see Roberts, 2002, for a review). Although the research literature on episodic mix-ups amongst children is much larger than that for adults, adults are by no means immune to such confusions (e.g., Connolly & Price, 2013; Theunissen et al., 2017).

Several theories have attempted to explain how source confusions happen. Fuzzy-trace theory postulates that experiences are encoded as two separate representations in memory: gist and verbatim. Gist traces are vague representations of the general sense or pattern of what is being encoded, including the meaning or structure of an event. Verbatim traces represent the content of memories by preserving surface details exactly. Importantly the generic and specific representations are independent from one another, so retrieving the script does not guarantee that one can retrieve details specific to a particular occurrence (Brainerd & Reyna, 1990).

Most remembering occurs in gist form because gist representations are more accessible in memory and require less effort to retrieve (Brainerd & Reyna, 1990). In addition, verbatim traces decay more rapidly than gist traces, so it becomes more likely with the passing of time that gist traces will be retrieved because verbatim information about particular experiences may be lost. Memories become more generalized and less detailed over time. This explains why script-based recall is more accurate than memory for individual occurrences of a repeated event. The script operates at the gist level, which means it is more resistant to decay and confusions; source information related to details specific to one occurrence is verbatim information that is forgotten more quickly (Brainerd & Reyna, 1995).

The Source-Monitoring Framework highlights the reasoning processes that are used to make source-monitoring decisions (Johnson et al., 1993). Specifically, this theory describes a complex decision-making process that involves comparing the characteristics of memory traces, such as the amount of perceptual detail, in order to reason about possible sources. This account of source monitoring explains how the similarity of sources affects the decision-making process. Sources are more difficult to discriminate when they are more similar (Johnson et al., 1993) because there is more overlap between the characteristics of the sources. Individual experiences within a series of repeated events are likely to be highly similar, which leads to great difficulty differentiating which details occurred during which events.

A final explanation for confusions between events comes from the concept of feature-binding. Episodic memory requires binding the elements of an event together during encoding (Tulving, 1985). If the event features are not associated with each other from the encoding stage, it becomes more difficult to retrieve details specific to one incident. In a study of developmental differences in feature-binding, Lee, Wendelken, Bunge, and Ghetti, (2016) showed 7- to 11-year-olds and adults triplet sequences of novel objects, each presented for one second at one of three locations, sequentially (i.e., trials lasted three seconds). Memory was tested for item–space, item–time, and item–item combinations. In item–space testing blocks, participants were presented with images of three objects and had to indicate whether or not they were in their original location. In item–time testing blocks, participants had to judge whether objects were presented in their original order. In item–item blocks, participants were required to determine whether all three objects were originally co-presented or whether one had been from a different grouping. The authors observed a sharper developmental trajectory for item–time and item–item combinations than for item–space. Children reached adult levels in item–space binding by 9.5 years. Particularly relevant for repeated event memory, children only reached adult levels of item–time binding at age 11 and did not reach adult accuracy levels in item–item binding. This may explain in part why young children, in particular, confuse details from separate occurrences.

Source Monitoring in the Legal Context

Although source-monitoring decisions are difficult in everyday remembering for the reasons described, several factors specific to the legal context make reports of specific episodes even more challenging. First, legal proceedings are typically associated with lengthy delays between the event in question and the investigative interview or court proceedings. For example, historical reports of child sexual abuse often combine repeated experience with lengthy delays in reporting

(Connolly & Read, 2003). Any delay between an event and interview results in some degree of forgetting, and this is true of repeated events as well, particularly for the details that vary from one episode to another. Roberts and Powell (2007) found that 5- and 6-year-olds who experienced a single event were less accurate in recalling that event after three weeks compared to three days. However, for children who experienced a repeated event, recall for the typical details was unaffected by delay. Recall of the details that varied across events was less accurate after three weeks than at three days. The effect of delay on memory for repeated events is variable, depending on the amount of experience the interviewee has with the event, the delay between the events and the interview, and whether the details reported were consistent across occurrences. Overall, the longer delays that interviewees experience in the legal system as compared to typical lab-based research paradigms may cause even greater challenges in recalling details specific to one occurrence.

Another factor that makes remembering episodic details specific to one instance of a repeated event more difficult in the legal system is the possible traumatic nature of the events being recalled. Repeated trauma can lead to post-traumatic stress disorder or depression, which have been associated with overgeneral memory – a tendency towards recalling the gist of events rather than specific details (e.g., McNally, Litz, Prassas, Shin, & Weathers, 1994). A review of 24 studies, however, found that trauma is not the central mechanism underlying overgeneral memory; rather, associated psychopathology likely plays a role (Moore & Zoellner, 2007). Irrespective of the constellation of causes, interviewees with overgeneral memory will experience magnified difficulty in reporting details specific to individual episodes. Accessing the script may also be motivationally easier than describing specific occurrences of a repeated experience because the former does not require episodic reliving of a negative event. Regardless of the nature of the topic, interviewing people about repeated experiences should be informed by an understanding of source-monitoring challenges and empirically guided techniques to elicit the most accurate narratives possible.

Interviewing Considerations

In the remainder of the chapter, we discuss various strategies for consideration when interviewing people about repeated experiences. It is critical to note that these strategies have an empirical basis in *improving* the likelihood that interviewees can describe specific occurrences. Using these techniques, however, does not guarantee that a description of an occurrence will be accurate. Recalling an occurrence of a repeated event is an incredibly challenging task, especially for young children. Experts in children's memory for repeated events have argued that legal requirements should be relaxed when children allege repeated abuse because it is not feasible to expect them to describe specific occurrences in great detail (Woiwod & Connolly, 2017). Adult memory researchers have similarly argued that expectations of adult witnesses in the same regard may be too high (Theunissen et al., 2017). In cases when descriptions of specific episodes are needed, the following interviewing considerations may provide interviewees with the best possible chance of producing a detailed and accurate account of one occurrence.

Generating Occurrences

Depending on the purpose of the interview, it may be advantageous to encourage interviewees to generate occurrences to discuss. Ronald P. Fisher and his colleagues (Leins, Fisher, Pludwinski, Rivard, & Robertson, 2014; Willén, Granhag, Strömwall, & Fisher, 2015) have explored interviewing techniques that could assist cooperative intelligence detainees to retrieve specific occurrences of interest among many repeated events (e.g., the timing and location of a meeting where intelligence was shared).

Willén and colleagues (2015) provided insight into how adults generate occurrences by capitalizing on repeated events that people experience routinely. The authors compared reports of dental visits over the past ten years recalled by 95 adults in three interview conditions. In two of the conditions, participants were provided cues that had been derived from a pilot sample. The pilot sample was asked to recall dental visits and indicate what specifically made the visit memorable. These "derived cues" were provided to some participants as categories (e.g., "think back to *conversations* you had") and to others as quotations (e.g., "She said I had bad dental hygiene"). The third condition used cues frequently employed by police, including "the last visit," "the first visit," and "visits that stand out from the others." In general, participants in the derived cues conditions recalled more visits and more specific details about the visits, than participants in the third condition.

Recent work by Leins and colleagues (2014) provides further support for the notion that interviewees are likely better at executing memory searches for occurrences of repeated events using personally-relevant cues rather than interviewer-generated cues. The researchers asked 36 university students to generate a list of family events they had experienced in the past year (Experiment 1). They were then given a variety of mnemonics to aid them in retrieving additional occurrences. For example, they were asked to draw a family tree and think about whether there were events that involved each person in the tree, beyond what they had already reported. They were asked to think of events that made them happy or sad, or for which they bought or made a gift, and so on. With the aid of mnemonics, participants were able to generate almost as many new occurrences as they had listed previously (41 percent of all occurrences were generated after mnemonics). These events were corroborated by friends and family members at a very high rate (i.e., the participants did not just confabulate events). The implication of this work is that different kinds of cues may be helpful to aid people in generating occurrences.

The use of mnemonics to identify occurrences has not been tested with children explicitly. The most similar research was conducted by Powell and Thomson (2003), where 4- to 8-year-old children were encouraged to generate alternatives of a detail that had changed across occurrences of a laboratory repeated event (e.g., the type of sticker the child received) before deciding which of those alternatives was present in the final occurrence (Experiments 2 and 3). Powell and Thomson's work might be conceptualized as the inverse of what Leins et al. (2014) asked their participants to do. The former is akin to asking participants to list all the meals they ate at family events (or all the outfits they wore) and decide which happened on a specific occasion, while in the latter, whole occurrences were generated (e.g., family wedding, family picnic) and participants were asked about the associated content details. In general, the children in Powell and Thomson's study had difficulty generating alternatives. Just one week after the final occurrence, 4- and 5-year-olds could only report an average of 44 percent of the alternatives and 7- to 8-year olds reported an average of 68 percent.

The mnemonics and cues used in Leins and colleagues' (2014) and Willén and colleagues' (2015) studies illustrate our earlier proposal that sources are "in the eye of the beholder." For example, using the cue "events I bought a gift for" may have led to more successful memory searches (i.e., more occurrences retrieved) for some participants than the cue, "family events." There are numerous reasons why individuals may differ in the sources they use to organize their memories for repeated events, and the extent to which people actually do differ on preferred source cues is an empirical question. Research on the names, or labels, children assign to occurrences of repeated events provides some insight into the diversity of possible source cues.

Labels and Episodic Leads

Labels are the explicit names given to occurrences of repeated events (Brubacher et al., 2014). Sometimes, labels are used by interviewers to help interviewees generate occurrences (e.g., "Think of the first time this happened"). Other times, they are generated by interviewees spontaneously during recall (e.g., "He usually does it for just a couple of minutes, but *the time that Mom was at a birthday party*, he did it for longer"), or generated by interviewers based on details disclosed by the interviewee (e.g., "What else happened *the time he did it for longer?*").

Brubacher and colleagues (2014) recommend that interviewers adopt the interviewee's labels for events, or generate them using the interviewee's words. Labels may represent the sources (as conceptualized by the interviewee) of occurrences of repeated events. Labels may include temporal information (e.g., the first time), information about the location (e.g., the time in the bathroom), salient event details (e.g., the time he tried to take my clothes off), or some other contextual details (e.g., the time when Mum was at the grocery store; Brubacher,

Malloy, Lamb, & Roberts, 2013). Referring to an occurrence in the interviewee's own words could help to differentiate it from other times if the label reflects how the series of events are organized in memory.

Interviewers often seek information about the first or last occurrence of a repeated event, and there is evidence that the first and last time may be remembered better than intervening episodes. For example, Connolly and Price (2013) detail the case of a bank teller who experienced five armed robberies over a period of several years and was interviewed about these 25 years later. Her memory for the first and last robberies contained the most detail, and she was able to describe them most consistently across repeated interviews. Her memory was particularly strong for the first robbery, for which she would not have had a script at the time of encoding. She evidenced much more confusion about the details from the middle robberies.

Although the first and last times may be well remembered, there are several concerns with using temporal labels. First, they may not be helpful for younger children, who may have limited temporal knowledge (Roberts et al., 2015). In crimes that involve a grooming process (e.g., sexual abuse, domestic violence) the "first time" may be difficult to identify. Additionally, although the last time tends to be memorable because it is the most recent, it may not be a helpful cue if the last time was long before the interview (e.g., Price & Connolly, 2013). Time cues may be ineffective even for adults in certain circumstances, because they tend not to activate discrete event details (Leins & Charman, 2013). Leins and Charman found that innocent "suspects" in a lab-based study mistakenly generated false alibis in response to time cues (e.g., "Where were you last Wednesday between 1–2 p.m.?") because they reported their scripts (i.e., what they would normally be doing during that timeframe) instead of accessing the specific episodic memory in question. In this regard, temporal labels may not be helpful for eliciting episodic accounts about individual occurrences.

Sometimes interviewers ask about times that were especially memorable (i.e., "time you remember best/most/well), but research has demonstrated that children, in particular, may not have the metacognitive awareness to know which time they remember best (Danby, Brubacher, Sharman, Powell, & Roberts, 2017). In order to avoid problems associated with choosing ineffective labels as source cues, Brubacher and colleagues (2014) suggest that interviewers listen for naturally-occurring labels that arise during recall. If interviewees do not generate explicitly labeled occurrences (e.g., "the time/day when . . ."), then interviewers can listen for episodic leads – the breadcrumbs of episodic details dropped into a description of the script or of another episode.

Unique Occurrences and Unpredictable Deviations

According to the Source-Monitoring Framework, if sources are more distinct from one another they are easier to differentiate, and there is a greater chance that specific details can be correctly attributed to a source (Johnson et al., 1993). For this reason, unpredictable deviations from the typical script may be particularly memorable. Unpredictable variations comprise the errors, obstacles, and distractions described earlier in this chapter – disruptions to the script, some of which change the way the event unfolds (Schank & Abelson, 1977). These are different from predictable variations (such as a child's clothing being different each time), which are represented in the script and are unlikely to be bound to the source.

Deviations that disrupt the normal progression of the scripted activity seem to be particularly well-remembered. For example, Bower and colleagues (1979) found that adults recalled obstacles and distractions better than errors (i.e., unexpected substitutions that did not change the event trajectory). Similarly, Connolly, Gordon, Woiwod, and Price (2016) found that 6- to 8-year-old children who experienced a deviation that disrupted the script and changed the course of the event ("continuous") had better memory for a set of play activities than their peers who experienced no deviation (e.g., in the former group, a magic show was interrupted and the magician was so discombobulated that he fumbled through the rest of the show). In this experiment, a third group that experienced a discrete deviation that did not disrupt the goal of the activities did not differ from the other two groups (i.e., the show was interrupted, but carried on as normal afterwards). Since the events that are the subject of an investigative interview will have occurred before a person is interviewed, the only control an interviewer has over event distinctiveness is to help the interviewee identify atypical details that may be linked to a particularly well-remembered episode.

Specificity of Language Used in Questioning

Several studies have demonstrated that children are responsive to the specificity of language used in interviewer prompts. When interviewers use episodic prompts (e.g., "Tell me everything that *happened* at Jim's house"), children tend to respond episodically. When interviewers prompt generically (e.g., "Tell me everything that *happens* at Jim's house"), children provide script details (Brubacher, Roberts, & Powell, 2011; Schneider, Price, Roberts, & Hedrick, 2011).

Recent work has also demonstrated differential responding to general invitations that inquire about other activities or actions within an event (also referred to as breadth prompts; e.g., "What happened next?") versus cued invitations that follow up on specific details that were previously mentioned (also referred to as depth prompts; e.g., "Tell me more about the part when [disclosed detail]"; Danby, Sharman, Brubacher, Powell, & Roberts, 2017). In response to breadth prompts, children had a greater tendency to report script information or details that were consistent across occurrences than when given depth prompts. Regarding the latter type of prompts, children were more likely to provide episode-specific details. The authors speculated that the narrower depth prompts kept children's attention focused on the event in question. They are careful to point out, however, that both breadth and depth prompts are necessary during interviews. In the table below, we illustrate the findings discussed in this paragraph by applying them to Asha's interview. If the goal is to elicit a comprehensive account about a specific occurrence, using episodic language and focused depth prompts may be helpful in directing the interviewee towards providing those types of details.

Prompt specificity		
Episodic	"What happened when your Mom left that evening?"	"She left us an apple pie in the oven. She was working until closing that night. I tried to ask to go to my friend's house but he said I had too much homework."
Generic	"What happens when your Mom leaves?"	"It depends on the night or how long she's going to be, but if she has a long shift then he finds something for me to wear and then I know it's going to happen."
Prompt type		
Breadth	"What happened next?"	"I went into the bedroom, saw the nightgown thing, I put it on, sat with him in front of the TV. And then he just does it and then I go to bed."
Depth	"Tell me about the part where you sat with him."	"I just sat down and he put a blanket around me and put his arm around me, and he seemed really sleepy and I thought 'Oh, maybe he's going to leave me alone tonight.' But then he put his hand on my leg."

The Cognitive Interview

Recent advances in research on the Cognitive Interview (CI) suggest that this interview method has features that enhance reporting of specific episodes by adults. In Leins and colleagues' (2014) Experiment 2 (with a new group of participants), occurrences of family events were generated and then details of the events were elicited via the CI or a control interview. Again, mnemonics facilitated recall, yielding twice as many occurrences as originally reported. Participants who received the CI reported more than twice as many details ($M = 225$) as participants who received the control interview ($M = 94$). Overall, the use of mnemonic cues to generate occurrences was very beneficial: this strategy roughly doubled the number of occurrences participants could generate, the occurrences were "true" events that were corroborated by others, and participants were able to describe them in some specific detail, especially when interviewed with the CI.

Rivard, Fisher, Robertson, and Hirn Mueller (2014) compared the effectiveness of the Cognitive Interview to a five-step interview used by a Federal Law

Enforcement Training Center to elicit details about a specific occurrence of a repeated event (one in a set of training meetings). The interviews shared overlapping features such as rapport building and asking non-leading questions. The CI interviews, however, included primarily open-ended questions and memory strategies like mental context reinstatement and sketching of the target event. Both interviews produced very high accuracy rates (> 85 percent of details that could be corroborated were correct). After removal of details that were script in nature and thus applied to many meetings (e.g., "I usually take notes"), the CI interviews elicited almost 80 percent more episodic details about the target meeting than the comparison interview. The comparison interview elicited significantly more script details than did the CI. Although it is impossible to determine from Rivard and colleagues' study which elements of the CI are responsible for the effects, the authors do note that more than three times as much episodic information was provided in the CI as the comparison in response to the first invitation. The primary difference between the interviews at that early stage was the inclusion of ground rules in the CI (avoid guessing, report as much as possible and in detail, and actively generate information without waiting for questions).

Conclusion

Many interview topics involve events experienced multiple times. Much research has focused on children's memory for repeated events and how that understanding informs the conducting of forensic interviews about repeated abuse. More recently, there have been calls from memory experts to study adults' memories for repeated experiences.

Given the challenges associated with recalling specific episodes of repeated events, we support recent recommendations that expectations should be relaxed with regard to the specificity of interviewees' reports following repeated experience. Generic descriptions of events can be informative and may be all that is required to assess the presence of certain activities such as child sexual abuse and domestic violence. Nevertheless, there will always remain situations when securing specific details are critical, such as in Eric's case to determine whether he possessed any information about the events of the night leading to his client's overdose, or when investigators meet with high value detainees to identify critical meetings in which terror-related activities may have been discussed.

This chapter outlined the paradox of memory for repeated events. Having similar experiences multiple times leads to potent and enduring scripts that describe the usual happenings of events and make future happenings predictable. Script retrieval can also help people generate atypical information that can be useful for interviewers in directing attention to episodes. Yet, the power of scripts can lead to memory errors when an interviewee retrieves false information consistent with the script, or when true information is attributed to the wrong source. Source monitoring errors can happen during recall of any type of event, but the likelihood is higher during recall of repeated events due to an additional potential source of confusion: an episode's temporal source. Temporal information can be an ineffective retrieval cue for children in particular, but for adults as well. Lengthy delays and psychopathology associated with trauma can further compound difficulties in accurately retrieving information about specific episodes in forensic interviews and at trial.

A variety of strategies to aid interviewees in retrieving episodic detail about occurrences of repeated events were presented in this chapter. Adult interviewees may be aided with various mnemonics that lead to identification of sources. The use of such mnemonics has not been explored in detail with children. Nevertheless, research has shown that while recalling their script for a set of play activities, children were also likely to report details that varied across episodes. Features that people notice as being different from the usual happenings should be particularly salient in memory. Helping interviewees to identify unique occurrences and atypical details is key to directing to episodic recall. When children (and adults) do refer to specific episodic details, interviewers should adopt interviewees' labels for those episodes. Interviewers can also adjust their prompts depending on whether they are seeking episodic or script information. Recent research on the Cognitive Interview has shown that there are elements of the CI that assist with episodic recall, but the specific mechanisms are avenues for future exploration. Interviewing about repeated experiences can feel like trying to assemble the pieces of an IKEA entertainment unit without a picture of the finished product. The advice and strategies presented in this chapter are intended to go some way in giving interviewers a manual when talking to people about repeated experience, and will continue to improve and evolve as this research field grows.

References

Bower, G. H., Black, J. B., & Turner, T. J. (1979). Scripts in memory for text. *Cognitive Psychology, 11,* 177–220.

Brainerd, C. J. & Reyna, V. F. (1990). Gist is the grist: Fuzzy-trace theory and the new intuitionism. *Developmental Review, 47,* 1–45.

Brainerd, C. J., & Reyna, V. F. (1995). Autosuggestibility in memory development. *Cognitive Psychology, 28,* 65–101.

Brubacher, S. P., Roberts, K. P., & Powell, M. B. (2011). Effects of practicing episodic versus scripted recall on children's subsequent narratives of a repeated event. *Psychology, Public Policy, and Law, 17,* 286–314.

Brubacher, S. P., Roberts, K. P., & Powell, M. B. (2012). Retrieval of episodic versus generic information: Does the order of recall affect the amount and accuracy of details reported by children about repeated events? *Developmental Psychology, 48,* 111–122.

Brubacher, S. P., Malloy, L. C., Lamb, M. E., & Roberts, K. P. (2013). How do interviewers and children discuss individual occurrences of alleged repeated abuse in forensic interviews? *Applied Cognitive Psychology, 27,* 443–450.

Brubacher, S. P., Powell, M. B., & Roberts, K. P. (2014). Recommendations for interviewing children about repeated experiences. *Psychology, Public Policy, & Law, 20,* 325–335.

Connolly, D. A., & Lindsay, D. S. (2001). The influence of suggestions on children's reports of a unique experience versus an instance of a repeated experience. *Applied Cognitive Psychology, 15,* 205–223.

Connolly, D. A., & Price, H. L. (2013). Repeated interviews about repeated trauma from the distant past: A study of report consistency. In B. S. Cooper, D. Griesel, & M. Ternes (Eds.), *Applied issues in investigative interviewing: Eyewitness memory, and credibility assessment* (pp. 191–217). New York: Springer.

Connolly, D. A. & Read, J. D. (2003). Remembering historical child sexual abuse. *Criminal Law Quarterly, 47,* 438–480.

Connolly, D. A., Gordon, H. M., Woiwod, D. M., & Price, H. L. (2016). What children recall about a repeated event when one instance is different from the others. *Developmental Psychology, 52,* 1038–1051.

Danby, M. C., Brubacher, S. P., Sharman, S. J., Powell, M. B., & Roberts, K. P. (2017). Children's reasoning about which episode of a repeated event is best remembered. *Applied Cognitive Psychology, 31,* 99–108.

Danby, M., Sharman, S., Brubacher, S. P., Powell, M., & Roberts, K. P. (2017). Differential effects of general versus cued invitations on children's reports of a repeated event episode. *Psychology, Crime & Law. 23,* 794–811.

Erskine, A., Markham, R., & Howie, P. (2002). Children's script-based inferences: Implications for eyewitness testimony. *Cognitive Development, 16,* 871–887.

Farrar, M. J., & Goodman, G. S. (1992). Developmental changes in event memory. *Child Development, 63,* 173–187.

Guadagno, B. L., Powell, M. B., & Wright, R. (2006). Police officers and legal professionals' perceptions regarding how children are, and should be, questioned about repeated abuse. *Psychiatry, Psychology and Law, 13,* 251–260.

Hudson, J. A., Fivush, R., & Kuebli, J. (1992). Scripts and episodes: The development of event memory. *Applied Cognitive Psychology.* Special Issue: *Memory in Everyday Settings, 6,* 483–505.

Johnson, M. K., Hashtroudi, S., & Lindsay, D. S. (1993). Source monitoring. *Psychological Bulletin, 114,* 3–28.

Lee, J. K., Wendelken, C., Bunge, S. A., & Ghetti, S. (2016). A time and place for everything: Developmental differences in the building blocks of episodic memory. *Child Development, 87,* 194–210.

Leins, D. A., & Charman, S. D. (2013). Schema reliance and innocent alibi generation. *Legal and Criminological Psychology, 21,* 111–126.

Leins, D. A., Fisher, R. P., Pludwinski, L., Rivard, J., & Robertson, B. (2014). Interview protocols to facilitate human intelligence sources' recollections of meetings. *Applied Cognitive Psychology, 28,* 926–935.

McNally, R. J., Litz, B. T., Prassas, A., Shin, L. A., & Weathers, F. W. (1994). Emotional priming of autobiographical memory in post-traumatic stress disorder. *Cognition and Emotion, 8,* 351–367.

Moore, S. A., & Zoellner, L. A. (2007). Overgeneral autobiographical memory and traumatic events: An evaluative review. *Psychological Bulletin, 133,* 419–437.

Nelson, K. (Ed.). (1986). *Event knowledge: Structure and function in development.* Hillsdale, NJ: Lawrence Erlbaum Associates.

Nelson, K., & Gruendel, J. (1986). Children's scripts. In K. Nelson (Ed.), *Event knowledge: Structure and function in development* (pp. 21–46). Hillsdale, NJ: Lawrence Erlbaum Associates.

Peterson, C. (2012). Children's autobiographical memories across the years: Forensic implications of childhood amnesia and eyewitness memory for stressful events. *Developmental Review, 32*, 287–306.

Powell, M. B., & Roberts, K. P. (2002). The effect of repeated experience on children's suggestibility across two question types. *Applied Cognitive Psychology, 16*, 367–386.

Powell, M. B., & Thomson, D. M. (2003). Improving children's recall of an occurrence of a repeated event: Is it a matter of helping them to generate options? *Law and Human Behaviour, 27*, 365–384.

Powell, M. B., Roberts, K. P., Ceci, S. J., & Hembrooke, H. (1999). The effects of repeated experience on children's suggestibility. *Developmental Psychology, 35*, 1462–1477.

Powell, M. B., Burrows, K. S., Brubacher, S. P., & Roberts, K. P. (2017). Prosecutors' perceptions on questioning children about repeated abuse. *Psychiatry, Psychology and Law.* Advance online publication. doi: 10.1080/13218719.2017.1273749

Price, H. L., & Connolly, D. A. (2013). Suggestibility effects persist after one year in children who experienced a single or repeated event. *Journal of Applied Research in Memory and Cognition, 2*, 89–94.

Rivard, J. R., Fisher, R. P., Robertson, B., & Hirn Mueller, D. (2014). Testing the cognitive interview with professional interviewers: Enhancing recall of specific details of recurring events. *Applied Cognitive Psychology, 28*, 917–925.

Roberts, K. P. (2002). Children's ability to distinguish between memories from multiple sources: Implications for the quality and accuracy of eyewitness statements. *Developmental Review, 22*, 403–435.

Roberts, K. P., & Powell, M. B. (2007). The roles of prior experience and the timing of misinformation presentation on young children's event memories. *Child Development, 78*, 1137–1152.

Roberts, K. P., Brubacher, S. P., Drohan-Jennings, D. J., Glisic, U., Powell, M. B., & Friedman, W. (2015). Developmental differences in the ability to provide temporal information associated with an instance of a repeated event. *Applied Cognitive Psychology, 29*, 407–417.

Schank, R. C., & Abelson, R. P. (1977). *Scripts, plans, goals, and understanding.* Hillsdale, NJ: Lawrence Erlbaum Associates.

Schneider, L., Price, H. L., Roberts, K. P., & Hedrick, A. M. (2011). Children's episodic and generic reports of alleged abuse. *Applied Cognitive Psychology, 25*, 862–870.

Theunissen, T. P. M., Meyer, T., Memon, A., & Weinsheimer, C. C. (2017). Adult eyewitness memory for single versus repeated traumatic events. *Applied Cognitive Psychology, 31*, 164–174.

Tulving, E. (1985). Memory and consciousness. *Canadian Psychology/Psychologie canadienne, 26*, 1–12.

Willén, R. M., Granhag, P. A., Strömwall, L. A., & Fisher, R. P. (2015). Facilitating particularization of repeated similar events with context-specific cues. *Cognition and Neurosciences, 56*, 28–37.

Woiwod, D. M., & Connolly, D. A. (2017). Continuous child sexual abuse: Balancing defendants' rights and victims' capabilities to particularize individual acts of repeated abuse. *Criminal Justice Review, 42*, 206–225.

13

VIEWING THE COGNITIVE INTERVIEW THROUGH THE LENS OF SELF-DETERMINATION THEORY

Michelle R. McCauley and Angela C. Santee

Introduction

One aspect of being human is that we share experienced events with those who were not present. Typically, when we do this informally as part of daily conversation, complete accuracy is not required. However, often it is. For example, a forensic interviewer requires detailed, accurate information from witnesses to complete investigations. Similarly, in the case of infectious disease transmission it is important that the patient accurately recall and report information about the progression and timing of symptoms and all the people with whom the person had contact (see Mosser & Evans in Chapter 6 of this volume for more on this). Unlike in casual conversation, the goal in these settings is to elicit as much information from the interviewee as possible without compromising the accuracy of that information. The ways in which interviewers gather information from witnesses or patients can vary dramatically, and these differences have strong implications for the ultimate success of the interview in terms of the quantity (i.e., number of facts) and quality (i.e., accuracy) of the information obtained. At this point we have over 30 years of data on the efficacy of the Cognitive Interview (CI) to facilitate witnesses' recall (e.g., Fisher & Geiselman 1992; Geiselman, Fisher, MacKinnon, & Holland, 1986; Köhnken, Milne, Memon, & Bull, 1999; Memon, Meissner, & Fraser, 2010). This protocol has been successfully used for respondents of different ages, different cognitive abilities, and for different types of events. In most studies with children, the CI has increased the number of accurate facts recalled by 20–50 percent over traditional interviewing approaches (e.g., Akehurst, Milne, & Köhnken, 2003; Chapman & Perry, 1995; Holliday, 2003; Memon, Holley, Wark, Bull, & Köhnken, 1996; Milne & Bull, 2003; Verkampt & Ginet, 2010), with many studies finding an increase of more than 75 percent (e.g., Hayes & Delamothe, 1997; Holliday &

Albon, 2004; Larsson, Anders Granhag, & Spjut, 2003; McCauley & Fisher, 1995). The success of the CI is not surprising given how the protocol emerged from well-established, and well-tested, theories of memory, cognition, social psychology, and communication. Simply put, the CI consistently works to improve recall from witnesses across a wide range of to-be-remembered experiences. The CI is dependably effective for adults and children, when tested experimentally and in the field, for events in which witnesses participated or passively watched. Memon et al. (2010, p. 340) suggest that the CI is "one of the most successful developments in psychology ... over the last 25 years." Thus, there is little question at this point about the potential for the CI protocol to increase the amount of information witnesses recall and report about an experienced event.

However, regardless of what type of interview protocol an investigator uses, it is important that the witnesses (patients, participants, etc.) are *motivated* to engage with the interviewer and to exert the effort needed to fully recall and report their experiences. The extent to which witnesses are motivated to work with an investigator will undoubtedly predict how much they recall and report about the event in question. Although motivation is important for all interviews, we suggest that it may be especially important with the CI, particularly when interviewing children. There are three primary reasons we propose this. First, the inherent structure of the CI relies on transferring control of the flow and order of the conversation to the witness. This requires active focus and participation from both the witness and the interviewer. Second, instead of following a checklist, the CI interviewer relies on open-ended questions and prompts, which directly relate to, and follow from, the witness's narrative. Finally, the CI's use of mnemonics, including imagery and context reinstatement, are likely to require greater attention and focus (e.g., executive function) than protocols that do not ask this of witnesses. These structural components of the CI, among others, are likely to result in an interview that is more cognitively demanding than one in which the witness is allowed to passively respond by waiting for the interviewer to ask specific questions. Thus, although the CI generally increases recall, we suggest it is most helpful when witnesses are motivated to make use of the protocol by not only cooperating, but by fully engaging with this effortful task. In line with the latter point, we propose it is valuable to consider the many ways in which the structure of the CI actually supports a witness's motivation through the lens of Self-Determination Theory as outlined by Deci and Ryan (2000).

Background on Self-Determination Theory

Self-Determination Theory (SDT) is a well-established, multi-faceted, theoretical framework for understanding human motivation, engagement, and psychological well-being (Deci & Ryan, 1985, 2000, 2008). SDT is premised on the assumption that humans share an innate tendency (i.e., are motivated) to seek out novel situations and to engage in tasks that they personally find optimally-challenging (Deci

& Ryan, 2000). People integrate their personal experiences, past and current, into their understanding of the world and in doing so form a coherent sense of self. This sense of self is the basis of one's desire to engage, or not engage, in particular activities. SDT proposes that social-contextual factors (obviously important in the interview setting) either encourage or thwart people's inclination for engagement. In practice, this suggests a witness will be more likely to deeply engage with an interview protocol when the context is perceived as autonomy-supportive instead of controlling.

SDT consists of six mini-theories that together seek to explain human motivation, thriving, and well-being (Deci & Ryan, 1985, 2000, 2008, see also selfdeterminationtheory.org. 2018). One of the major underpinnings of SDT is that people perform better when they are intrinsically motivated, as opposed to extrinsically motivated, for the actions they are taking. SDT is premised on the assumption that people seek to be self-determined and the extent to which the environment supports this influences well-being and competence in the world. In doing so it emphasizes the *quality* over the *quantity* of motivation in determining engagement, performance, and well-being outcomes, favoring forms of motivation that are more autonomous (self-determined) than controlled in nature. People are said to be autonomously motivated when they are interested in an activity for its own sake or when they engage in an activity because they have identified its value to the self, even though it may not be inherently rewarding. The two foundational mini-theories most helpful for our purposes are *Organismic Integration Theory* and *Basic Psychological Needs Theory* (Deci & Ryan, 1985; Ryan & Deci, 2000). We briefly discuss each of these, albeit superficially, below as we explain why the CI may be viewed through the lens of SDT.

Organismic Integration Theory (OIT) focuses on different aspects of extrinsic, or instrumental, motivation. Realistically, if we define intrinsic motivation as something pursued for the joy of it, little of this motivation will be found within the interview setting. However, within SDT, OIT suggests that extrinsic motivation falls on a continuum of different types of motivation that are more or less internalized and, therefore, experienced by the individual as more or less autonomous (cf. controlling). The most controlling of these is external regulation followed by introjection. In both of these, a person's motivation is highly controlled by a contingency such as reward, punishment, or fear of shame. Within the interview setting, we can imagine how fear or shame may undermine any witness's, and especially a child witness's, willingness to engage in the interview process (see Lytle, Dickinson, and Poole, Chapter 11 in this volume for a discussion on techniques used to overcome such reluctance in general). On the other hand, SDT is clear that motivations may have an external source and yet, if one has internalized the extrinsic motivation via identification or integration, the person experiences the motivation as autonomous. Thus, in an interview setting, the extent to which a witness perceives the interview to be under his or her control will motivate continued engagement with the interview process. Research in OIT suggests that a person is more likely to experience internalization of motivation (an autonomous orientation towards the situations or action) when strong support for autonomy and relatedness are present.

Basic Psychological Needs Theory (BPNT) suggests that social-contextual factors that generate more active engagement and autonomous forms of motivation are those that satisfy an individual's basic psychological needs for autonomy, competence, and relatedness (Deci & Ryan, 1985; Ryan & Deci, 2000). Autonomy in this context refers to volition or the self-direction of behavior. An individual's need for autonomy is supported in situations where one has the freedom to act consistent with one's sense of self. Competence refers to efficacy or the feeling of being capable and effective in the pursuit of valued outcomes. An individual's need for competence may be supported by the provision of sufficient task-related information and the assurance that one's efforts are essential to complete a task. Finally, relatedness refers to a sense of belonging or of being connected to others. An individual's sense of relatedness may be supported in situations where others are attentive and responsive to one's needs and where one feels valued. All three needs must be met to support optimal psychological well-being and more self-determined forms of motivation. Moreover, it is not merely the presence of social-contextual factors that support autonomy, competence, and relatedness within a given situation, but also the individual's perception of those factors in his or her environment which in turn will lead to greater feelings of self-determination, engagement, and, ultimately, improved performance on a variety of tasks. When an individual's basic psychological needs are properly supported, we expect to see an increase in his or her motivation and enhanced performance on the task (in our case the interview). When needs are not supported, perhaps because the adult interviewer dominates the conversation, fails to establish strong rapport, or undermines the child's sense of competence in the interview process, the child will be less intrinsically motivated to participate in the interview.

Being well-versed in both the CI and SDT led us to notice the extent to which the CI protocol is generally supportive of the three basic psychological needs necessary to optimize witnesses' motivations. Below we detail what we see as specific links between aspects of the CI protocol and different psychological needs. Given the first author's interest in children's recall, we focus primarily on children, but we believe this lens holds for all witnesses interviewed with the CI protocol. That said, we fully acknowledge that psychological need support can be, and often is, provided in other interview protocols – specifically those tailored for child witnesses. Furthermore, we suggest that within a given protocol, much of the difference in participants' efficacy, or recall, may be based on the extent to which the person's basic needs have been supported.

As we examined this within the interview context, we reviewed the literature on psychological need support and related concepts in the context of adult–child interactions (e.g., teaching, parenting, and interviewing). In particular, it was crucial to gain an understanding of how researchers have interpreted support for each of the three psychological needs separately and how psychological need support, once measured, has been related to children's engagement, performance, and well-being. We detail this below. Additionally, we explore, albeit in a preliminary manner, whether the extent to which basic psychological needs are met within the interview correlates with recall and accuracy. In doing this we adapt findings and language from both OIT and BPNT to advance our understanding of the mechanisms for predicting successful social interactions, communication, and recall within the interview setting. First, however, we provide a discussion on research indicating that the extent to which an adult supports or thwarts a child's basic psychological needs (per SDT) is predictive of the quality of adult–child interactions, and the child's motivation for the task.

Psychological Need Support in Adult–Child Interactions

If we consider the different domains in which children and adults routinely interact, the school setting would make the top of the list. At school, an overarching goal is that children will enjoy and engage with their education and learn the material presented; we then measure their learning using assessments of objective, valid, educational outcomes. Within the SDT framework, a key to meeting this goal is the *quality* of the child's motivation for learning. This is affected by the extent to which the environment, and in this case the adult (teacher) is supportive of children's basic psychological needs and provides an autonomy-supportive environment. For example, Reeve and Jang (2006) found that teachers who demonstrated autonomy-supportive instruction in the classroom facilitated students' sense of autonomy, which increased their engagement with learning and improved their academic performance. In contrast, when teachers were overly controlling (thus thwarting students' basic need of autonomy), students reported less engagement with learning and poorer learning outcomes. Teacher behaviors that were autonomy-supportive included listening to the child, allowing the child opportunities and time to speak, encouraging students' effort, and acknowledging students' perspectives. In contrast, when teachers relied on directive statements or commands or denied students the opportunity to solve problems and answer questions themselves, students perceived the environment to be controlling (rather than autonomy-supportive) and their objective task performance was compromised. Similarly, Jang, Reeve, and Deci (2010) found that teachers who used a more autonomy-supportive, rather than controlling, instructional style engendered greater engagement in their students, in terms of both self-reported and behaviorally-exhibited engagement. In this study, students' behavioral signs of engagement included attentiveness, effort, verbal participation in the lesson, persistence in the face of difficulties, and positive emotions (all important in the interview setting). In a different context, Cleveland and Reese (2005) assessed children's reporting of experienced events based on the extent to which mothers' reminiscing styles were autonomy-supportive or not. Children provided more in-depth information around the target event when their mothers' reminiscing style supported autonomy and provided an elaborative structure compared to children whose mothers who did not. Taken together, prior research indicates that autonomy-supportive conditions contribute to a child's ability or motivation to provide extensive, detailed accounts of past events. Obviously, this is important for the forensic and medical interview settings.

It is vital that interviewers focus on how adults' behaviors shape a child's perception of having his or her basic psychological needs met (or thwarted) because this is the mechanism that either ramps up, or hinders, engagement and motivation for the task at hand. While in the interview setting this is recall of an experienced event, in the classroom it is educational outcomes and engagement. SDT researchers have clearly established that within education settings, autonomy-supportive teachers nurture their students' inner motivational resources by creating opportunities for children to approach tasks flexibly and creatively. The term *creative* here should not be limited to the artistic domain but rather considered as the ability to approach the task from multiple avenues. Second, autonomy-supportive teachers acknowledge and accept, rather than counter or try to change, students' negative emotions. Similarly, an interviewer may well need to sit with a child whose emotions are unpleasant while discussing a disturbing, painful experience. Finally, autonomy-supportive teachers use *informational* language rather than *controlling* language. In practice, this means communicating with students in a manner that is both flexible and informative, providing students with choices when possible, taking time to explain the value in fulfilling the teacher's (or interviewer's) requests, and providing clear and supportive rationale for engaging in the activity (or in our case a retrieval attempt or use of a mnemonic). Doing so shifts the child's perception of the importance of the task and correspondingly increases motivation for the task (see Jang et al., 2010; Reeve, Jang, Hardre, & Omura, 2002). These techniques mirror the CI's principles of communication for interviewing witnesses.

In addition to interpersonal dynamics and rapport quality, both education and interview environments share additional overarching structures. We propose interview outcomes will be directly related to the extent to which the interview structure supports a child's psychological needs (i.e., for autonomy, competence, and relatedness). Jang and colleagues (2010) found that students exhibited more focused attention, active effort, willingness to ask questions, tenacity to stay on task in the face of challenge, and interest when the teacher explicitly explained the structure. *Structure* in this study was operationally defined as providing clear directions, strong guidance, and instructive feedback. This structure supports a child's sense of competence insofar as she or he is clear about the teacher's expectations and how to meet them. Structure also can be used to support autonomy and relatedness. We therefore posit that it is valuable to view an adult–child interaction (instruction or interview) both from the micro level of the dyad and from a macro level of how the structure (instruction or protocol) supports the child's basic psychological needs or self-determination more broadly. We expect that child witnesses who perceive their personal autonomy to be supported by the interviewer (cf. those who feel their autonomy is thwarted) will be more engaged with the interview process, more willing to make additional retrieval attempts, and more willing to exert sustained effort to provide the small details of the experienced event.

So far we have discussed the role of autonomy support in motivation. However, competence and relatedness are also basic psychological needs within the SDT framework. Indeed, we suggest the findings from Jang and colleagues (2010) indicating a positive relation between clearly established classroom structure and positive student outcomes are premised on the fact that this structure supported students' need for competence, as defined by a sense of preparedness for the assessed educational tasks. In the interview setting, the extent to which the interviewer clearly prepares the child by articulating the goals of the interview will affect the child witness's ability to successfully navigate the process. We will return to this within the CI protocol explicitly below.

The third basic psychological need suggested by SDT is relatedness. Darner (2009) proposed that relatedness may well be the foundational need on which the other two rest. Therefore, we want to explore the concept of relatedness in depth and consider how supporting this need may relate to interview efficacy. Given different terms are often used for similar constructs, we draw not only on the SDT literature but also the research on social support when considering the connection between supporting a child witness's need for relatedness and her or his interview performance. In doing so we assert that the extent to which an adult interviewer is deemed socially supportive overlaps with the extent to which he or she is supporting the child's need for relatedness within SDT framework.

Social support is conveyed through various adult verbal and nonverbal behaviors (Almerigogna, Ost, Akehurst, & Fluck, 2008) that contribute to a child's feelings of comfort and confidence in the interview setting (Ahern, Hershkowitz, Lamb, Blasbalg, & Winstanley, 2014; Almerigogna et al., 2008; Hershkowitz, Lamb, Katz, & Malloy, 2015). A considerable amount of prior research indicates that children take cues from adults' nonverbal behaviors (e.g., smiling, mirroring, fidgeting, etc.) in determining the extent to which the interaction is supportive or not (see Almerigogna et al., 2008). Importantly, researchers have demonstrated a connection between the adults' supportive behavior (e.g., smiling) and the amount and quality of details recalled by children (Hershkowitz et al., 2017; Hershkowitz, Lamb, & Katz, 2014). These supportive behaviors appear to be particularly important in facilitating children's ability to resist misleading information (e.g., Almerigogna et al., 2008; Davis & Bottoms, 2002). We propose that expressing socially supportive behavior is, in fact, expressing behavior that supports a child's need for relatedness. Of particular importance for forensic and medical interviewers then are the above findings from Davis and Bottoms (2002) that children interviewed in a manner that provided social support (i.e., in a manner that supported relatedness) were more willing to say they *did not know* an answer when uncertain compared with those interviewed in a manner that was less socially supportive.

CI Through the Lens of SDT

There is considerable conceptual overlap between the principles of communication and social dynamics prescribed by the CI protocol and the principles of psychological need support outlined in SDT. Given prior research demonstrating a strong association between adults' behavior that supports children's self-determination and positive outcomes in education and recall, we suggest some of the value of the CI may flow from the fact that it implicitly fosters witnesses' sense of psychological need support. We believe this is true at both the dyad level (the interactions between the adult interviewer and child witness) and at the structural level given the design of the CI as a flexible toolbox. Below we describe how specific components of the CI may be viewed through the lens of SDT as support for witnesses' autonomy, competence, and relatedness.

It has always been the case that rapport development within the CI seeks to efficiently accomplish many goals. Early in translating the protocol for use with children we not only attempted to make a child comfortable through positive social support, but also to transfer control of the interview to children by instructing them to (a) tell the truth and correct the interviewer if she made a mistake, (b) say "I don't know" instead of guessing, (c) ask the interviewer to clarify a point, and (d) practice reporting an autobiographical memory in detail, (see McCauley & Fisher 1995). In hindsight, each of these serves to support the basic psychological needs described in SDT. For example, the basic goal of establishing a comfortable interaction can serve to support relatedness and autonomy insofar as the interviewer works to reduce the power differential that is inherent in any child–adult dyad. Explicitly instructing children to correct the interviewer and to say "I don't know" both support children's autonomy and competence. Similarly, having children practice giving a detailed, sequential narrative during rapport (e.g., by explaining a favorite hobby or game) increases their sense of competence in the substantive portion of the interview because they know what to expect. Because the child is asked about something personally interesting (a hobby or game), the child's autonomy is supported. This exercise also supports transferring control of the interview to the child, which in turn supports autonomy. Throughout the CI rapport development the interviewer engages in behaviors that support the child's autonomy, competence for the substantive portion of the interview task, and the need for relatedness. Ideally, this need support will continue throughout the entire interview.

Once the child witness reaches the substantive portion of the interview, the CI structure and mnemonics act to provide additional support of her or his basic psychological needs. The fact that the interview begins with an open-ended prompt provides the child witness autonomy to control the flow of information as well as to determine a personal reporting threshold. Additionally, the CI encourages the witness to play to his or her competencies by allowing the child to control which information is recalled first. The CI interviewer follows the witness's lead, and nudges the direction of conversation only as a last resort, thus demonstrating respect for the witness's autonomy. CI mnemonics facilitate the witness's sense of competence to retrieve information while the communication principles support competencies in reporting the experienced event. In sum, the CI's emphasis on open-ended prompts, coupled with its toolkit of retrieval mnemonics supports autonomy and competence while CI rapport (including consideration of communication dynamics) supports relatedness.

Need Support and Interview Outcomes

Although it may conceptually make sense that psychological need support is important to the efficacy of the CI, we believe it is nevertheless important to test whether there is a relationship between the level of psychological need support provided by the interviewer and children's recall performance. Below we discuss preliminary research that aims to address this question. We begin with the development of a valid coding scheme to assess psychological need support in the interview setting. We then describe our findings from a preliminary study assessing the relation between interviewers' use of psychological need support and witnesses' recall.

Method

Drawing on the SDT framework, we developed a coding scheme for independent observers to measure the level of autonomy, competence, and relatedness support present in adult–child interactions. These observers considered both the need-supportive behaviors of the interviewer and the child's perceptions of those behaviors. This was developed as a first step toward employing SDT to understand the mechanisms that underlie effective communication in adult-child interviews.

We began by examining 27 tapes of adult–child interviews that were conducted by McCauley, Langrock, and Allen (2007). The participants were 11 males and 16 females from various schools and childcare centers in Vermont. The children ranged in age from 3 to 8 years old ($M = 65$ months, or $5\frac{1}{2}$ years of age). In the original study, children attended an educational presentation on tarantula spiders led by two unfamiliar adults. Eight weeks later, the children were interviewed with a CI. Each interview was video recorded, transcribed, and coded for *quantity* of recall, which equaled the total number of accurate and inaccurate facts reported by the child, and the *quality* or accuracy of recall, which was calculated by dividing the number of accurate facts by the total number of facts reported by each child.

To develop the stimulus material for coding, we sampled each interview by creating two one-minute video clips. The first clip was pulled from the middle of the rapport-building section and the second was taken from the middle of the substantive recall portion (i.e., the part in which the child recalls information about the target event). The rapport-building section started at the beginning of the recording and ended prior to the interviewer introducing the goal of the interview ("I'm here today to talk to you about the day Dr. Spider came to class"). Using these points of reference, the middle of the rapport-building section was identified by dividing the total rapport duration in half. The one-minute rapport clip began 30 seconds prior to that point and ended 30 seconds after. In a similar fashion clips were identified for the substantive portion of the interview, except the reference points were the end of rapport (or the introduction of the interview's purpose) and the end of the interview.

Development of scales to assess psychological need support: Our first goal was to develop a coding framework to evaluate support for each of the three basic psychological needs, autonomy, competence, and relatedness, described by Deci and Ryan (2000, 2008) in SDT. To this aim, we developed a set of scales to assess each of the three basic psychological needs and the extent to which each need was supported, or undermined, by the actions of the interviewer. We further asked raters to assess specific need support considering the child's perspective. Using a 7-point scale, raters evaluated the extent to which an interviewer's interaction with the child was primarily undermining or supportive of the need in question (e.g., "As an outside observer, would you say the interviewer's interaction with the child was primarily autonomy-supportive or controlling?"). Raters also considered these questions from the child's perspective (e.g., "Imagine you were in the child's place, would you say the interaction in this clip was primarily autonomy-supportive or controlling?").

Our definition of autonomy was volition or the self-direction of behavior. A child's sense of autonomy is supported in situations where he/she has the opportunity to behave in self-determined ways. Because control is the commonly-accepted opposite of autonomy support in the SDT literature (see Reeve & Jang, 2006; Deci, Schwartz, Sheinman, & Ryan, 1981), we used "controlling" and "autonomy-supportive" as the anchors for this measure. Accompanying each rating scale was a brief definition of the psychological need in question as well as a table containing examples of factors that may contribute to (or undermine) the support of each basic need. Examples of interviewer behaviors supportive of children's psychological needs and children's behavioral indicators of need satisfaction were based on a search of the relevant research literature and further developed through discussions with the research team during scale development.[1] Interviewer behaviors considered autonomy-supportive include using open-ended questions, following the child's lead in conversation, allowing and encouraging the child to do the majority of the speaking, and giving the child time and opportunity to elaborate upon or change any information he or she had provided. Interviewer behaviors that directly counteract these autonomy-supportive factors (and are therefore controlling) include directing the flow of conversation, using close-ended or directive questions, not allowing the child to do the majority of the speaking, not allowing time or opportunity for elaboration or correction, and cutting the child off or moving abruptly to the next question.

We created similar instructions and scales for competence support, which was defined as the child's sense of efficacy or feeling of being capable and effective in the interview. Raters were instructed that competence was supported when interviewers provided sufficient task-relevant information to the child, along with assurances that one's efforts are essential to the completion of a task. Raters were provided examples of factors that might signal a child's competence. These included whether the child understood the purpose and procedure of the interview and seemed to feel as though her or his contributions were perceived to be important by the interviewer. Additionally raters noted the extent to which the child was confident in directing the flow of conversation and able to answer the interviewer's questions fully (or of informing the interviewer if this was not the case). Behaviors considered to not support competence included the child appearing unclear as to the purpose and procedure of the interview, expressing feelings suggesting her or his contributions were unimportant or perceived negatively, not directing the flow of conversation, and appearing unable to answer the interviewer's questions fully. In addition to taking the child's perspective, raters considered the interviewer's behaviors that facilitated the child's sense of competence. For example, did the interviewer regularly provide feedback, ensure the child directed the flow of conversation, and did the interviewer signal to the child that he or she was capable of answering questions fully? In contrast, competence-undermining interviewer behaviors included doing nothing to support the child's understanding of the interview's purpose or procedure, failing to provide feedback or providing negative feedback, or suggesting the child might not be capable of adequately answering questions. The interviewer's competence support also was rated on a 7-point scale from *competence-undermining* to *competence-supportive*.

Finally, raters assessed the extent to which the child's need for relatedness was met. The definition of relatedness in this context consisted of a demonstrated sense of belonging or of being connected to others. A child's sense of relatedness was supported in situations where others were attentive and responsive to her or his needs and where the child appeared to feel valued or the interviewer engaged in behaviors likely to facilitate this feeling. For example, if the child appeared to feel that the interviewer was attending to her or his emotional and attentional needs; the child seemed relaxed and comfortable interacting with the interviewer and felt as though her or his contributions were appreciated; and the child perceived the interaction with the interviewer as being "authentic" rather than rigid or scripted. A child who expressed feeling unimportant, uncomfortable, or unappreciated would suggest a lack of relatedness support. In line with this, raters were trained to evaluate interviewer behaviors that support relatedness such as attention to the child's emotional and attentional needs, interacting comfortably with the child, demonstrating positive regard for the child's contributions, and following the child's lead in conversation in an authentic (versus scripted) manner. In contrast, an interviewer who seems unaware of the child's emotional and attentional needs or who appears uncomfortable interacting with the child would be undermining the child's sense of relatedness. Raters indicated the extent of relatedness using a 7-point scale from relatedness-undermining behaviors to relatedness-supportive behaviors.

Interviews from a prior study were used to train research assistants to code for psychological need support in the interview setting. Once raters established reliability, they moved on to rate the target video clips for the current project. Two raters scored each clip. Raters coded each clip (segments from rapport and the substantive part of the interview) for the extent to which the segment demonstrated support for each of the three needs – autonomy, competence, and relatedness – either from the perspective of the child or by assessing the interviewer's behavior. This resulted in six measures of need support for each segment of the interview. We assigned raters randomly into working pairs for each assessment and for each tape. As such we did not have two raters always assessing the same interviews but rather varied who was rating with whom segment to segment. Furthermore, the order in which raters made their scores was counterbalanced across psychological needs and perspectives (child vs. interviewer) within each round of coding. Raters completed rating assignments in order of psychological need rather than by child to ensure that raters were coding each segment as independently as possible. All rapport clips were coded before the research team moved to coding the clips from the substantive portion of the interview. Acceptable agreement for each pair of scores was defined as being within one point on the 7-point scale. In instances where first and second raters' scores were separated by two or more points, a new set of raters (i.e., a third and fourth rater) were assigned to re-evaluate the segment for that particular psychological need support scale. The scores produced by the third and fourth raters replaced the first set of scores. Overall, percentage agreement for all need support scales was 93.12 percent for rapport clips and 95.29 percent for substantive clips.

Scores from each of the raters were averaged to create one final score for each measure of psychological need support in each portion of the interview (i.e., from the rapport and substantive interview segments). Thus, each interview yielded 12 individual need support scores, representing support for three psychological needs (autonomy, competence, relatedness) from two perspectives (child, interviewer) across two points in the interview (rapport and substantive questioning). Given the high reliability obtained in the coding process, it was determined that the study's first goal was met.

We had collected information about need support at different points in the interview (rapport and the substantive portion of the interview) and from different perspectives (what the child seemed to feel and what the interviewer was doing). We therefore created a composite score for each of the three psychological needs (autonomy, competence, or relatedness) by averaging all four scores related to each need (e.g., "average autonomy support" reflected the average of scores on child autonomy support in rapport, interviewer autonomy support in rapport, child autonomy support in substantive recall, and interviewer autonomy support in substantive recall). The three composite psychological need scores were all significantly correlated. Autonomy support correlated highly with competence support, r (27) = 0.87, p < 0.01, and with relatedness, r (27) = 0.78, p < 0.01. Furthermore, competence support correlated highly with relatedness support, r (27) = 0.89, p < 0.01. These findings suggest that interviewers who supported children's autonomy in the interview setting were also likely to support relatedness and competence (and vice versa). It also indicated that it was appropriate to simplify our preliminary analyses by collapsing across the different need support measures into one overall measure of psychological need support for rapport and one for the substantive portion of the interview.

We were also interested in whether need support declined, increased, or remained constant from rapport-building to substantive recall. A repeated-measures t-test measured the differences between rapport ratings and substantive interview ratings for total psychological need support. The level of psychological need support did not significantly differ between rapport and the substantive portion of the interview.

Psychological need support and recall performance: The coding scheme developed for the present study is only useful to the extent that it allows one to predict children's autobiographical recall performance. Thus, the second goal of this study was to assess whether observers' ratings of psychological need support related to the quantity and quality of information produced by children in recall. On average, children recalled 77 distinct facts (i.e., distinct bits of information) about the spider event (M = 77; SD = 39.45). We want to highlight here that, even after eight weeks, children's recall was generally accurate (proportion accurate 0.83, SD = 0.10). Of interest for this chapter, however, is the extent to which fulfillment of psychological needs would predict recall and accuracy. For our preliminary analyses we assessed bivariate correlations between measures of recall performance (total facts and proportion of accurate facts reported) and total basic psychological need support. Despite the fact that the correlation between global psychological need support and the *quality* of the information children recalled (i.e., proportion accurate) was not significant, there was a significant relation between the number of facts children recalled and basic psychological need support, $r(27)$ = 0.68, p < 0.01.

To evaluate this at a finer level, we assessed the relation between each of the three basic needs (autonomy, competence, and relatedness) and recall. As expected, the extent to which children's basic psychological needs were supported correlated with the number of facts children recalled (autonomy $r(27)$ = 0.75, competence $r(27)$ = 0.70, and relatedness $r(27)$ = 0.47; all ps < 0.05). In addition, we again found no significant relation between the quality of the facts recalled (i.e., proportion accurate) and support across any of the three basic psychological needs.

Finally, one of our assumptions with this project was that supporting children's basic psychological needs would lead to stronger motivation to participate in the interview process. We propose that one aspect of this motivation is a willingness to stay engaged in the interview. In support of this prediction, we found a significant correlation between the level of autonomy support and the length of time children were willing to spend in the substantive portion of the interview, $r(27) = 0.45$, $p < 0.05$. We did not find a significant relation between autonomy support and time spent in rapport development, $r(27) = 0.01$, $p > 0.05$.

Discussion

Our goal in this chapter was to initiate a conversation on the value of considering SDT when assessing the efficacy of the CI. The preliminary findings reported here suggest that, within a CI, the extent to which child witnesses perceive their individual psychological needs to be met (versus thwarted) influences the amount of information they recall from an experienced event. Therefore, to the degree we are confident the scales developed for this study are actually measuring autonomy, competence, and relatedness, we can reasonably expect that interviewers' psychological need support plays a role in enhancing children's recall performance. Although the accuracy (or quality) of the information retrieved did not differ as a function of psychological need support within the interview, we are content insofar as we are always pleased to have a greater number of details about the target event at the same accuracy rate.

We also found that there was a relation between children's psychological need fulfillment, particularly autonomy support, and a willingness to stay focused on the interview task. That is to say, when the interviewer/child dynamic was one that independent raters deemed autonomy-supportive for the child, the substantive part of the interview lasted longer. Given, (a) the CI is likely to take more cognitive effort on the child's part, and (b) the length of the interview was determined by the child, this is noteworthy. Future researchers may want to explore this connection in greater detail to determine how this time is used. For example, does extra time spent in the interview generate more retrieval attempts or the use of additional retrieval mnemonics? Perhaps this will depend on the extent to which a particular need is more or less supported?

Future researchers may also explore how the degree to which a child's needs are met generally (i.e., outside the target setting) influences his or her motivation for the interview. Perhaps, having a reserve of autonomy, competence, and relatedness support from home may affect a child's interaction with the interviewer. Boland, Haden, and Ornstein (2003) demonstrated that a mother's reminiscing style affects her child's tendency for elaboration in recall. This supports the possibility that the need-supportiveness of a child's general environment (i.e., the family) may affect his or her feelings of need satisfaction in general. For example, a child whose mother uses a more elaborative style in reminiscing may feel more competent in general when faced with a situation in which he or she must respond to open-ended questions (which are meant to inspire more elaborate responses). Perhaps children who feel more competent in the interview setting, due to their mothers' reminiscing styles, elicit more psychological need-supportive behaviors from interviewers. Conversely, a child whose basic psychological needs are thwarted may be more dependent on the need support provided by the interviewer.

We also want to highlight the finding that paired child–interviewer scores for need fulfillment were strongly correlated. This finding is consistent with those of Jang et al. (2010), who found a significant relation between teachers' need-supportive behaviors and children's behavioral demonstration of engagement as well as students' self-reported feelings of autonomy. However, this does not rule out the possibility of a cyclical relationship between the interviewer's behaviors and the child's apparent feelings of autonomy, competence, and relatedness. These two aspects, studied here through independent observers' assessments, likely influence one another in dynamic ways throughout the interview. Future researchers may want to assess how such need support, as well as rapport, shifts even within discrete sections of an interview protocol. Several studies reviewed here suggest that a child's positive engagement with the task may serve to elicit increased need-supportive behavior from an adult (e.g., Furrer & Skinner, 2003; Jang et al., 2010). It is likely that need support leads to engagement, which may elicit yet additional need-supportive behavior from the adult, and so on. However, we also expect that there will be times in the interview when the interviewer stumbles. Therefore, another question that remains unanswered is whether the child always responds negatively to a controlling action from the interviewer. This may depend on how much social capital the interviewer has amassed prior to engaging in the controlling action (which could be as subtle as asking a direct question). Again, this could be assessed with detailed coding that assesses need fulfillment and the timing of recall across the interview.

We also note that interviewer–child interactions generally remained at the same level of need-supportiveness throughout the interview, or at least between the two time points selected for use in this study. We suggest future researchers measure support at additional points across the interview setting to assess whether this is truly fixed or varies throughout the interview. Furthermore, we want to highlight our position that psychological need support is not dictated by interview type. In other words, the quality of an adult–child interview (when quality is defined in terms of psychological need support) may vary considerably even when cutting across interview type.

We also are mindful of the fact that, in general, our observers rated the different aspects of psychological need support to be quite high. This was not a particular surprise, given the CI protocol requires that the interviewer spend time building rapport, explicitly instructing the child as to the purpose and procedure of the interview, transferring control to the interviewee, and using open-ended requests for information (McCauley & Fisher, 1995). All of these, as described in this chapter, support basic psychological needs. However, it is unclear whether need support in the interview may actually be more important than the type of protocol. Perhaps a standard interview format that explicitly supports a child witness's basic psychological needs would, on average, facilitate recall as well as a CI. We hope that future researchers will evaluate the efficacy of both interview protocol and psychological need support on children's recall.

We were particularly interested in the findings that when observers were asked to take the child's perspective in determining how need-supportive the interaction was (cf. assessing the interviewer's behaviors), their ratings were more valuable in terms of predicting total facts recalled. This is consistent with SDT, which states that it is not merely the presence of social-contextual factors that support one's needs, but one's perception of having needs met that predicts positive engagement, performance, and well-being outcomes (Deci & Ryan, 2000). Assuming the scales developed here adequately measure the need-supportiveness of the interviewer's interaction style, this finding raises some interesting questions for forensic interview research, which has focused primarily on memory retrieval techniques and the communication techniques of the *interviewer*. If what the interviewer does is not at least equally important in determining children's autobiographical recall performance as children's subjective experience of the interview, what does that mean for future forensic interview research? Additionally, if the need-supportiveness of the interviewer's personal communication style is important, how do we teach those skills to adults who interview children?

Finally, we are curious about the extent to which the CI serves to support *interviewers'* psychological needs. We suspect that the structure of the CI, along with the extensive training required to successfully use it, serves to support interviewers' sense of autonomy and competence. The quality of rapport with the child may affect relatedness of the interviewer. This then could facilitate interviewers' motivation to attend to and engage with witnesses. It is clear from prior research that there are significant differences in individual interviewers' success within a given protocol such that even "good" interviewers using "good" protocols demonstrate variability in witness performance. While some, or even much, of this may have to do with the specific witness, perhaps some of this variability can be explained by interviewers' need fulfillment in the particular interview?

In closing, we suggest it is valuable to consider SDT in understanding the mechanisms that underlie the effective communication techniques in the CI and other interview settings. Our view is that the CI is an incredibly valuable toolbox and that one underlying reason for this success may be that, by design, the CI supports witnesses' autonomy, competence, and relatedness. By taking a step back from the protocol to understand how we might increase witnesses' motivations to engage with the mnemonics, we believe we may facilitate even stronger recall performance in the future.

Note

1 The scale was developed and tested for reliability on a completely independent set of interviews prior to being tested here.

References

Ahern, E. C., Hershkowitz, I., Lamb, M. E., Blasbalg, U., & Winstanley, A. (2014). Support and reluctance in the pre-substantive phase of alleged child abuse victim investigative interviews: Revised versus standard NICHD protocols. *Behavioral Sciences & the Law, 32,* 762–774.

Akehurst, L., Milne, R., & Köhnken, G. (2003). The effects of children's age and delay on recall in a cognitive or structured interview. *Psychology, Crime & Law, 9,* 97–107.

Almerigogna, J., Ost, J., Akehurst, L., & Fluck, M. (2008). How interviewers' nonverbal behaviors can affect children's perceptions and suggestibility. *Journal of Experimental Child Psychology, 100,* 17–39.

Boland, A., Haden, C., & Ornstein, P. (2003). Boosting children's memory by training mothers in the use of an elaborative conversational style as an event unfolds. *Journal of Cognition and Development, 4,* 39–65.

Cleveland, E., & Reese, E. (2005). Maternal structure and autonomy support in conversations about the past: Contributions to children's autobiographical memory. *Developmental Psychology, 41,* 376–388.

Chapman, A. J., & Perry, D. J. (1995). Applying the cognitive interview procedure to child and adult eyewitnesses of road accidents. *Applied Psychology: An International Review, 44,* 283–294.

Darner, R. (2009). Self-determination theory as a guide to fostering environmental motivation. *Journal of Environmental Education, 40,* 39–49.

Davis, S., & Bottoms, B. (2002). Effects of social support on children's eyewitness reports: A test of the underlying mechanism. *Law and Human Behavior, 26,* 185–215.

Deci, E. L., & Ryan, R. M. (1985). *Intrinsic motivation and self-determination in human behavior.* New York: Plenum.

Deci, E. L., & Ryan, R. (2000). The "what" and "why" of goal pursuits: Human needs and the self-determination of behavior. *Psychological Inquiry, 11,* 227–268.

Deci, E. L., & Ryan, R. M. (2008). Self-determination theory: A macrotheory of human motivation, development, and health. *Canadian Psychology, 49,* 182–185.

Deci, E. L., Schwartz, A., Sheinman, L., & Ryan, R. (1981). An instrument to assess adults' orientations toward control versus autonomy with children: Reflections on intrinsic motivation and perceived competence. *Journal of Educational Psychology, 73,* 642–650.

Fisher, R. P., & Geiselman, R. E. (1992). *Memory enhancing techniques for investigative interviewing: The cognitive interview.* Springfield, IL: Charles C. Thomas.

Furrer, C., & Skinner, E. (2003). Sense of relatedness as a factor in children's academic engagement and performance. *Journal of Educational Psychology, 95,* 148–162.

Geiselman, R. E., Fisher, R. P., MacKinnon, D. P., & Holland, H. L. (1986). Enhancement of eyewitness memory with the cognitive interview. *American Journal of Psychology, 99,* 385–401.

Hayes, B. K., & Delamothe, K. (1997). Cognitive interviewing procedures and suggestibility in children's recall. *Journal of Applied Psychology, 82,* 562–577.

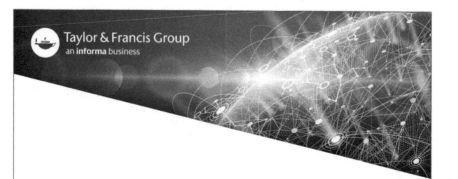

Lightning Source UK Ltd.
Milton Keynes UK
UKHW022026301222
414663UK00012B/95